Brother Charles

Exploring Methodism

Brother Charles

Barrie W. Tabraham

EPWORTH PRESS

Copyright © Barrie W. Tabraham 2003

British Library Cataloguing in Publication data

A catalogue record for this book is available
from the British Library

0 7162 0570 X

First published in 2003
by Epworth Press
4 John Wesley Road
Werrington
Peterborough PE4 6ZP

Typeset by Rowland Phototypesetting Limited,
Bury St Edmunds, Suffolk
Printed and bound in Great Britain by
Biddles Ltd, www.biddles.co.uk

Ad vulpem seniorem ab urso vetustiore

Contents

Foreword

On my first reading of *Brother Charles* I found myself reflecting on what a significant book it is. It is an important story, well told and in a very readable style. Like its predecessor in the series *The Making of Methodism* it fulfils the author's promise to make recent research available in a generally accessible form. So many areas of Charles Wesley's life have been illuminated by recent research, and here is an author able to convey the main scholarly findings in a judicious blend of clear explanation and relevant quotation from the main sources. In this way we are able to follow Charles Wesley's distinctive process of self-examination, self-discovery and personal renewal. We are, moreover, encouraged to engage creatively with that story, as a search for faith and for an awareness of faith, and so to seek its significance for today's world and today's church.

What emerges so movingly is an attractive and engaging picture: Charles' humanity and openness, warmth and humility, the extraordinary depths and heights he experienced and his ability to develop his own pattern of testimony and mission, and even to take his elder brother John to task when need be. The directness and honesty of Charles' writings, we discover, affords a securer access to Charles' person than John's voluminous works, which by contrast leave us with a puzzling and somewhat ambiguous portrait of their author. Charles' openness did not of course mean that he was equally at ease with everyone. His message was for everyone and concerned a salvation for everyone. But he found himself less at home in the kind of wealthy circles in which his sons Charles and Samuel moved than with the rejected and the poor whom he recognized as, and spoke of as, 'family'. As far as the Epworth family is concerned – his father, mother, brothers and sisters – those relationships and their ups and downs are recorded here as integral to the portrait of Charles. His frankness, forthrightness and compassion are evident in that context too.

The world in which the Methodist movement emerged is caught here in a host of miniatures. They place Charles Wesley's testimony in its historical setting and show his words and life as a witness to God's new creation in a troubled world.

There are areas of Charles' life which monographs can fail to compass. These are covered in *Brother Charles* with a perceptive selectivity. The author has a grasp of the material which helps him to concentrate on the important issues. That is particularly true of the area which does involve a voluminous literature:

Charles' poetic output and his brilliance as a lyrical writer. To summarize Charles' expertise and achievements in that area is no easy matter and it is excellently performed here.

Occasions such as the Tercentenary of John Wesley's birth quite properly draw attention to the elder brother's many achievements and John's particular gifts of clarity of thought, organization and indefatigable leadership. *Brother Charles* however succeeds in making a claim for John's younger brother which deserves to be heard, and which tells the story of a pilgrimage which stands at the heart of the origins of Methodism.

Brother Charles is a significant and timely book on which anyone could reflect with profit.

Ivor H. Jones

Preface

This is the sixth book in the series and, as such, is complete in itself. Whilst it is not strictly necessary for the reader to have looked at the opening volume, *The Making of Methodism*, this will help to understand more fully the religious and historical context in which Charles lived and the wider issues with which he was concerned. The format of *Brother Charles* follows its predecessor in the inclusion of extracts from original source material. These are placed in boxes throughout the text and are meant to be read alongside the main narrative. Certainly, one can read the book without recourse to the documents themselves but their purpose is to bring the characters and the period to life in a way that plain text can never do.

As with *The Making of Methodism*, I have included a Glossary, which partly overlaps the original but which naturally concentrates on the context in which Charles Wesley lived. Once more, there are questions for discussion at the end of each chapter, as it is anticipated that groups may wish to use *Brother Charles* as a study book. The Suggestions for Further Reading are more specialized as befits the subject matter. I have, therefore, included more details of original sources than in *The Making of Methodism*, as well as a selection of other, more general, works.

Brother Charles is not meant to be a 'standard biography'; nor does it pretend to be a work of great originality. I make no apology for this and I owe a great debt of gratitude to those whose recent scholarship has made so much material available. Rather, my intention has been to make sources which have hitherto been less readily obtainable accessible to the general reader, in order that Charles Wesley might be known as a person and not simply as the 'bard of early Methodism'.

Finally, I wish to pay tribute to those who have helped in so many ways with the writing of this book. Gerald Burt has been of great assistance with his advice and encouragement and I have valued the comments of the editorial panel of the Epworth Press. My thanks also go to Dr Ivor Jones for kindly agreeing to write the Foreword, and to Gaynor Stocker for proofreading the text. I am hugely indebted to my old friend Stuart Davis, who painstakingly studied the entire manuscript and made many helpful suggestions. However, my greatest debt is to my wife Joan, for her unfailing support and encouragement.

Introduction

O for a thousand tongues to sing
My great Redeemer's praise,
The glories of my God and King,
The triumphs of his grace!

My gracious Master and my God
Assist me to proclaim,
To spread through all the earth abroad
The honours of thy name.[1]

Charles Wesley has not received the attention from Methodists that he deserves. Ask any group of Christians to name three famous hymn-writers and the chances are that among such names as Isaac Watts, Graham Kendrick or Fred Pratt Green, their short-list will include the name of Charles Wesley. Ask them to name three or four of his hymns and they will probably do so quite easily. However, if you were to ask them to tell you something about Charles Wesley's character or life, then you would almost certainly be greeted by a quite different response. Charles Wesley is not well known and biographies of him are few and far between. There have been numerous studies of his hymns, but apart from John Vickers' short introduction[2] and Arnold Dallimore's recent work,[3] little has appeared for the general reader who wishes to know more about Charles as a person.

There are a number of reasons for this.

First, the immense stature of John Wesley has inevitably led historians to concentrate on him and neglect Charles. In the eyes of the general public,

John has been seen as the founder and driving force behind Methodism, with Charles simply as his 'assistant' and as a hymn-writer par excellence. Moreover, because their early careers for the most part followed parallel courses, Charles tended to be overshadowed by his elder brother John. They both went to Oxford University, both were involved in the group of undergraduates who comprised the 'Holy Club' and Charles accompanied John to Georgia in 1735 – even though he returned to England earlier. Their 'conversion' experiences in May 1738 also bear superficial similarities and in the years immediately after 1738 Charles followed his brother's lead in travelling around the country preaching, often in the open air. Indeed, whilst Charles led a more settled life in Bristol and London from about 1756 onwards, throughout their lives the two Wesleys enjoyed a natural partnership based on mutual affection and loyalty and, for the most part, the sharing of a common purpose.

Secondly, because John stands out as the key figure, his younger brother (so often referred to in parenthesis) has consequently been, to some extent, overlooked. This is a pity and does Charles great disservice, since his own story is important in its own right and makes for fascinating study.

The discrepancy between what has been written about John and Charles is reflected in the amount of material available to us from the brothers' own hands. John's writings run into millions of words and his letters, sermons, treatises, journal and diary provide enormous scope for both the serious student and the general reader. Condensed editions of his journal, sermons and the Explanatory Notes on the New Testament are readily accessible in paperback as popular editions. Charles, by contrast, has left us little. Apart from the huge number of his hymns, of course, we have a limited quantity of letters and just part of a journal which covers the years 1736 to 1756. Even this is an incomplete record.[4] Furthermore, it is only recently that Charles' sermons have appeared as a published collection.[5] It is not surprising, therefore, that Charles has received relatively little attention compared with John.

Why do we have so little of Charles' own writings?

One reason has to be the secondary place assigned to him by his contemporaries and immediate successors, who did not seem to think his writings of sufficient importance or interest to be preserved, still less published in any quantity. One early biographer suggested that the family papers were kept from public view because, in view of Charles' well known opposition to any move towards separation from the Church of England, 'many of the Methodists would cherish towards him an unfriendly feeling'.[6] Thus, for example, the public had to wait until 1849 before they could read Thomas Jackson's edition of his journal, which included 106 of his letters, and until 1948 before Frank Baker's *Charles Wesley as Revealed by His Letters* appeared in print, which uses over two hundred extracts from Charles' correspondence. The journal, which Charles initially wrote down on loose sheets of paper, was actually lost for a time and only discovered by chance when it was found lying amongst some straw on the floor of a warehouse where his son had stored some musical instruments!

The other reason lies with Charles himself. His own inclination towards self-effacement meant that, just as he allowed John to occupy most of the limelight, so he did not consider his writings worth publishing. Shortly after Charles' death in 1788, John wrote in a letter to his niece, Sally Wesley, that he regretted that his brother had stopped writing his journal so many years before. He put the cause down to the 'wrong humility'.[7] Charles had little

inkling that future generations might be interested in *him*!

Charles was also far less meticulous than his brother. Often his correspondence lacked either date or signature. Sometimes, when writing to family or close friends, his letters omitted both details. Furthermore, his handwriting in both journal and letters is not particularly easy to read, and the letters, which often contain shorthand, are interspersed with phrases in Latin and Greek.[8] These factors have tended to deter the casual reader and have been a cause of frustration to those wishing to study his life in depth.

Charles deserves to be better known, and not merely by his fellow Methodists.

It is true that he was overshadowed by his elder brother and 'had a lifetime habit of giving place to John'.[9] However, Charles was quite capable of independent thought and action. It was he, not John, who was first nicknamed 'Methodist' and his own quest for spiritual peace of mind took a distinctive road between 1736 and 1738. In addition to this, the brothers did not always see eye to eye. They disagreed – at times quite sharply – over family relationships, perhaps the most poignant example being the very different ways in which they treated their sister, Hetty. In the years after 1756, Charles fought a losing battle with John over the question of separation from the Church of England. He is said to have commented on one occasion:

all the difference between my brother and me was that my brother's first object was the Methodists and then the Church: mine was first the Church and then the Methodists. Our different judgement of persons was owing to our different tempers, his all hopes and mine all fears.[10]

Whilst having a broadly chronological framework, *Brother Charles* follows a more thematic approach and its purpose is not to be an exhaustive biography. Rather, it is intended to paint a brief picture of Charles *as a person*, for he was a man of great depth and humanity. As we shall see, Charles was in some ways a more attractive personality than John. John – a strong, dynamic personality who at times could display a ruthlessness and a severity that intimidated his colleagues – had the natural gifts of leadership for which Methodists will always be grateful. Charles, by contrast, was a kindly, sociable and altogether more gentle character. He was, in a sense, a 'Barnabas' to John's 'Paul'.[11]

It is as the 'sweet singer' of Methodism that Charles is chiefly remembered, and a later chapter examines his unique contribution to the universal Church in this respect. It is worth noting, however, that when John presented at the Conference of 1788 a short tribute to the recently departed Charles, he commented that 'his least praise was his talent for poetry'. This was a genuine tribute, born of a keen perception of Charles' inner qualities and a lifetime's understanding of his brother's character. It is important, therefore, that whilst giving due weight to Charles' gifts as a hymn-writer, we try to identify those characteristics for which he merited John's praise. That is the prime intention of this book.

I

The Early Years

Father, in whom we live,
  In whom we are, and move,
Glory and power and praise receive
  Of thy creating love.
Let all the angel throng
  Give thanks to God on high;
While earth repeats the joyful song,
  And echoes to the sky.

Charles Wesley was born at Epworth in Lincolnshire on 18 December 1707, the eighteenth child of Samuel and Susanna Wesley. The exact date of his birth was something of a mystery for a long time and Charles himself was never quite certain as to when precisely it was.[1] As with many children born into large families of modest means in the eighteenth century, Charles' early infancy was somewhat precarious – only ten of his brothers and sisters survived to reach adulthood. He was a premature baby and was kept wrapped in wool until the date he had originally been expected when, it is said, he at last opened his eyes and cried. In fact, Charles never enjoyed the robust health of his brother John, and his whole life was dogged with ailments of various kinds. While not exactly being a hypochondriac, Charles seemed, nonetheless, to be forever preoccupied with his own state of health and took great pains to document his numerous periods of illness!

Charles Wesley's Family Background

Before proceeding with Charles' boyhood, however, we need to say something about his family background. Eighteenth-century families tended to be much closer-knit than they are today and the influence of parents and immediate kin on the individual was correspondingly greater. Samuel and Susanna, in particular, deserve more than a passing mention as they had a profound effect on his early development.

Charles came from a family of strong religious convictions. His great-grandfather was the Revd Bartholomew Wesley,[2] who studied medicine and became the vicar of Charmouth in Dorset. Bartholomew's equally gifted son, John, proved a very able scholar at Oxford but opted for the priesthood instead of an academic career and was appointed to the Dorset living of Winterbourne, Whitchurch, in 1658. Four years later in 1662 (the year in which Samuel, Charles' father, was born) both Bartholomew and John were ejected from their livings under the Act of Uniformity,[3] because they refused to accept the new Book of Common Prayer.

Looking back from the present, when – in Britain at least – religious toleration is taken for granted, it is sometimes difficult for us to imagine the far-reaching effect these Uniformity Acts had upon both local congregations and their clergy. After 1662 John Wesley was condemned to both an unhappy and a precarious life. He was imprisoned on a number of occasions for preaching within five miles of his former church[4] and, probably as a consequence of his ill-treatment, died at a relatively young age in 1666.

Not surprisingly, Samuel Wesley, Charles' father, experienced a very unsettled childhood. As a result of his family's clashes with the established church, he was educated at a Dissenting academy rather than a church school. This was quite remarkable, considering his widowed mother's poverty. Despite the award of a modest grant, the four years' education Samuel received there must have put a heavy strain on the limited family budget. In later years Samuel and his brother Matthew were able to return her kindness and extraordinary self-sacrifice with financial help – despite Samuel's own inability to manage money. Thereafter, Samuel's gratitude extended to little more than a grudging acceptance of Dissenters in general and it was not long before he decided to 'return to the fold'. Having thus become a member of the established church, he was able to enter Exeter College, Oxford, and obtain a University degree.

After being ordained priest in 1689, Samuel held a naval chaplaincy briefly, then a curacy in London – where he met Susanna Annesley, who was to become his wife. From 1691 until 1697 they lived in South Ormsby in Lincolnshire, moving from there to the watery parish of Epworth in the same county, where Samuel was the rector until his death in 1735. A Tory and a high-churchman, he was a man of great faith and principle, but Samuel's strengths were also his weaknesses. His courage and tenacity often took the form of obstinacy and rigidity of thinking, factors which may have prevented his elevation to higher office.[5] His ministry was, therefore, confined to what was undoubtedly an 'unfashionable' living and he doggedly carried out his clerical duties to the best of his ability. Samuel also devoted considerable energy to writing, but his literary endeavours were not widely appreciated, least of all by his congregation. In truth, his attempts at poetry, history and devotional works were not of great merit and his life's work – a studious commentary on the Book of Job – was exceedingly dull. For their part, his parishioners felt that Samuel was out of touch with them and their relationship was never an easy one. Perhaps the lowest point was reached in 1709 when the Epworth rectory was completely destroyed by fire – an event to which we shall return.

Samuel's struggle to relate to his parishioners was not made any easier by his financial problems. Despite occasional help from various benefactors – including his brother Matthew, the Countess of Northampton and even the Archbishop of York – Samuel's life was dogged by shortage of money. It was not that he was particularly extravagant, nor was he lazy, it was simply that he had no head for business.[6] At one stage the situation deteriorated to such an extent that Samuel spent three months in Lincolnshire Castle prison for debt, though he bore this additional hardship with typical fortitude, as the accompanying extract from his letter on September 1705 to the Archbishop of York shows. [1] In the event, his release was secured by the kind efforts of Archbishop Sharpe who ensured that the £300 debt was paid in full.

Troubled by incessant financial worries and confronted by a difficult parish in which he had numerous enemies, Samuel, nonetheless, had many admirable qualities. A fiery, implacable and obstinate nature was redeemed by courage, stoicism and a high sense of duty arising from a resolute faith. Above all, he had a deep love for his family, though

---

1. A jail is a paradise in comparison of the life I led before I came hither. No man has worked truer for bread than I have done, and few have lived harder or their families either. I am grown weary of vindicating myself: not, I thank God, that my spirits sink, or that I have not right on my side, but because I have almost a whole world against me, and shall in the main leave my cause to the righteous Judge . . .

Most of my friends advise me to leave Epworth, e'er I should get from hence. I confess I am not of that mind, because I may yet do good there and 'tis like a coward to desert my post because the enemy fire thick upon me. They have only wounded me yet, and, I believe, *can't* kill me.

Source: Maldwyn Edwards, *Family Circle*, Epworth Press 1949, p. 20.

2. You have every reason to envy us, who could attend him in the last stage of his illness. The few words he could utter I saved, and hope never to forget ... The fear of death he had entirely conquered, and at last gave up his latest human desires of finishing Job, paying his debts, and seeing you. He often laid his hand upon my head, and said 'Be steady. The Christian faith will surely survive in this kingdom; you shall see it, though I shall not.'

Source: Frank Baker, *Charles Wesley as Revealed by His Letters*, Epworth Press 1948, p. 19.

he did not always understand them. An idea of Samuel's character may be gained from the following excerpt from a letter which Charles wrote to his elder brother, Samuel, shortly after his father's death. [2] Even from such a short passage, it is clear that Charles looked upon his father with great respect and affection.

It is worth comparing Charles' comments with similar reflections made by his brother John, though the latter were penned some years later. Apart from what they tell us of John's and Charles' reactions to their father's death, they provide an interesting comparison of styles, as well as revealing the rather more formal nature of John's relationship with Samuel. As we shall see, Charles tended to write in a more simple style than his elder brother and his journal and correspondence bear witness to his greater readiness to lay his heart open to his readers. In this extract, taken from a letter written to a friend in 1748, John pays tribute to his father's faith and courage. [3] The 'first Reformers' is a reference to the great European figures of the Reformation period, such as Luther and Calvin, and to the architects of the Reformation in England, such as Archbishop Cranmer, who was burned at the stake during the reign of Mary Tudor. 'The inward witness' describes a believer's personal experience of the presence of God.

We turn now to Charles' mother, Susanna, who was, in many ways, an even more remarkable person than Samuel.

Susanna was born in 1669, the twenty-second child of the Revd Dr Samuel and Susanna Annesley.[7] Dr Annesley was a noble, highly gifted character, of whom Dr Maldwyn Edwards writes: 'In him great learning, preaching ability, and moral courage were combined.'[8] Along with Bartholomew and John Wesley, and probably two thousand other clergymen, Dr Annesley was forced to quit his living in 1662 under the Act of Uniformity. Unlike the unfortunate Wesleys, however, he settled peacefully in Bishopsgate (where Susanna was born) and became the unofficial focus of London nonconformists for the last quarter of the seventeenth century. It was there – probably at his daughter Elizabeth's wedding in 1682 – that Susanna met the young curate, Samuel Wesley, whom she married on 12 November 1688.

It was undoubtedly a love match, and there is no reason to suppose that their marriage was an unhappy one. Yet Samuel and Susanna were so different. From her parents Susanna inherited a keen intellect, an independent spirit and a great deal of

3. My father did not die unacquainted with the faith of the gospel, or of the primitive Christians, or of our first Reformers; the same which, by the grace of God, I preach, and which is just as new as Christianity. What he experienced before, I know not; but I know that during his last illness, which continued eight months, he enjoyed a clear sense of his acceptance with God. I heard him express it more than once, although at that time I understood him not. 'The inward witness, son, the inward witness,' said he to me, 'that is the proof, the strongest proof, of Christianity.' And when I asked him (the time of his change drawing nigh), 'Sir, are you in much pain?' he answered aloud, with a smile, 'God does chasten me with pain – yea, all my bones with strong pain; but I thank Him for all, I bless Him for all, I love Him for all!' I think the last words he spoke, when I had just commended his soul to God, were, 'Now you have done all.' And, with the same serene, cheerful countenance, he fell asleep, without one struggle or sigh or groan. I cannot therefore doubt but the Spirit of God bore an inward witness with his spirit that he was a child of God.

Source: John Wesley, *Letters*, Vol. II, pp. 134–5.

common sense, which was matched by kindliness, charm and grace. She is also said to have been very pretty! The couple shared a devout faith and a strong commitment to the established church, to which Susanna had returned as Samuel had done – itself a remarkable example both of her precocity and of the methodical way in which she thought through the matter and came to this decision. Both were extremely determined characters with a high sense of duty but, in contrast to her husband's volatile temperament, Susanna was 'competent, businesslike and possessed of a cool, rational mentality'.[9] Early on in their married life Susanna remarked that she wondered if there was anything over which they did not disagree! To his credit, Samuel was always willing to acknowledge his wife's qualities, as an excerpt [4] shows. It is part of a letter written by Samuel to Archbishop Sharpe during his imprisonment in Lincoln.

---

4. I thank God, my wife was pretty well recovered and was churched[10] some days before I was taken from her; and I hope she will be able to look after my family, if they do not turn them out of doors as they have often threatened to do. One of my biggest concerns was my being forced to have my poor lambs in the midst of so many wolves. But the great Shepherd is able to provide for them and to preserve them. My wife bears it with that courage which becomes her, and which I expected from her.

Source: Maldwyn Edwards, *Family Circle*, Epworth Press 1949, p. 49.

Indeed, over the years Samuel and Susanna's relationship was often stormy. Perhaps the greatest disagreement between them came in 1701. Samuel had always been a staunch Tory and strongly supported William of Orange who became William III following the 'Glorious Revolution' of 1688. For her part, Susanna remained loyal to the exiled King James, even refusing to say 'Amen' at the close of evening prayers for King William. On this particular occasion, Samuel truculently announced, 'You and

I must part; for if we have two Kings, we must have two beds.' Thankfully, the accession of Queen Anne in 1702 ended the couple's political squabbles!

Interestingly, Susanna's writings have only become available in a single published volume comparatively recently.[11] Her letters, journals and essays make fascinating reading and reveal a woman attempting to define herself, over and against the established powers, as a 'competent, practical theologian-educator'[12] in her exploration of such issues as holiness, Christian perfection and the place of reason in faith. As such she deserves more than the popular epithet of 'John and Charles Wesley's mother'. Her keen intellect, spiritual insight and independence of thought made her a serious practical theologian in her own right and give her an important place in the history of female empowerment in general.

The Early Years at Epworth

> *Who live O God in thee,*
> *Entirely thine should be;*
> *Thine we are, a heaven-born race,*
> *Only to thy glory move,*
> *Thee with all our powers we praise,*
> *Thee with all our being love.*

Susanna kept an orderly household. With ten children to bring up,[13] often by herself when Samuel was away or otherwise engaged, she was compelled to be both well-organized and strict, even by the standards of the day. This was no mean task. In 1709 the Epworth rectory was completely demolished by a fire. There had been a previous alert in 1702 which Susanna felt had been divine retribution for Samuel's political views. The exact cause of the second fire is uncertain and it has been suggested that it was started by disaffected parishioners. The rescue of John ('Jacky') from an upstairs bedroom is well known. Charles, being an infant at the time, had no memory of the event, but in more than one hymn referred obliquely to it.[14] The seventeen-month-old child was rescued by a plucky maidservant. In a letter written in

February 1709 to Samuel Jr, who was at Westminster School at the time, Susanna described the fire in quite vivid terms. [5]

While the rectory was being rebuilt, the children

---

5. Dear Sammy!

When I received your letter wherein you complain of want of shirts, I little thought that in so short a space we should all be reduced to the same, and indeed a worse condition. I suppose you have already heard of the firing of our house by what accident we cannot imagine, but the fire broke out about eleven or twelve o'clock at night, we being all in bed; nor did we perceive it till the roof of the corn chamber was burnt through and the fire fell upon your sister Hetty's bed, which stood in the little room joining upon it. She waked and immediately run to call your father, who lay in the red chamber, for I being ill, he was forced to lie from me. He says he heard some crying fire in the street before, but did not apprehend where 'twas till he opened his door. He called at our chamber and bid us all shift for life, for the roof was falling fast and nothing but the thin wall kept the fire from the staircase.

We had no time to take our clothes, but ran all naked . . . We got the street door open, but the wind drove the flame with such violence that none could stand against it. I tried thrice to break through, but was driven back. I made another attempt and waded through the fire, which did me no other hurt than to scorch my legs and face . . . Your father carried sister Emly, Suky and Patty into the garden; then, missing Jacky, he ran back into the house to see if he could save him. He heard him miserably crying out in the nursery and attempted several times to get upstairs, but was beaten back by the flame; then he thought him lost and commended his soul to God and went back to look after the rest. The child climbed up to the window and called out to them in the yard; they got up to the casement and pulled him out just as the roof fell into the chamber . . . and so by God's great mercy we all escaped.

Source: Charles Wallace Jnr (ed.), *Susanna Wesley: The Complete Writings*, Oxford University Press 1997, pp. 65–6.

---

stayed with neighbouring families. On their return, Susanna made special efforts to bring them back to a 'proper mode of living'. During Samuel's absence in 1712, for instance, she set up a house meeting in the rectory kitchen to cover for the lack of an afternoon service. This was initially for the family, but before long the sessions attracted servants, parishioners and neighbours, until the gatherings numbered two hundred, and all this despite the opposition of the curate and Samuel's own annoyance. She was, indeed, a remarkable woman!

Susanna made such an impact upon her children that John often asked her to set out in detail the methods she had adopted. In a letter to John, written in July 1732, she finally acceded to his request. The extract from it [6] is brief, but is sufficient to give us a flavour of the Wesley household.

Into such a family was Charles born.

From Samuel, Charles inherited his high-churchmanship, strict doctrinal orthodoxy and a deep reverence for the sacraments – all of which he retained throughout his life. He also shared his father's volatile, emotional nature, whereas his brother John is seen to have been very much more his 'mother's son'. However, if Charles lacked that driving energy which made his brother such a natural leader, he had many other qualities. His capacity for contentment was greater than John's, so too was his sensitive understanding of human nature. It was true that at times he could be as obstinate and as wrong-headed as his father, yet he surpassed both his brothers Samuel and John in sociability, warmth and compassion.

Westminster School

> Then infuse the teaching grace,
> Spirit of truth and righteousness;
> Knowledge, love divine, impart,
> Life eternal, to my heart.

Until he was eight years of age, Charles lived at Epworth, where his education consisted of firm, but

6. The children were always put into a regular method of living, in such things as they were capable of ... When turned a year old (and some before), they were taught to fear the rod, and to cry softly, by which means they escaped abundance of correction which they might otherwise have had ...

As soon as they were grown pretty strong, they were confined to three meals a day. At dinner their little tables and chairs were set out by ours, where they could be overlooked; and they were suffered to eat and drink (small beer) as much as they would; but not to call for anything. If they wanted aught, they used to whisper to the maid which attended them, who came and spake to me ... Eating and drinking between meals was never allowed, unless in cases of sickness, which seldom happened ...

In order to form the minds of children, the first thing to be done is to conquer their will, and bring them to an obedient temper. To inform the understanding is a work of time, and must with children proceed by slow degrees, as they are able to bear it; but the subjecting of the will is a thing which must be done at once; and the sooner the better ... They pass for kind and indulgent, whom I call cruel parents, who permit their children to get habits which they know must be afterwards broken ...

I insist upon conquering the will of children betimes, because this is the only strong and rational foundation of a religious education; without which both precept and example will be ineffectual. But when this is thoroughly done, then a child is capable of being governed by the reason and piety of its parents, till its own understanding comes to maturity, and the principles of religion have taken root in the mind.

Source: Maldwyn Edwards, *Family Circle*, Epworth Press 1949, p. 58.[15]

loving instruction at the hands of his mother. The 'regular method of living' into which Susanna inducted him began on Charles' fifth birthday with the alphabet, then continued with reading the first chapter of Genesis – the very next day!

In 1716[16] he was sent to Westminster School in London, where he spent the next ten years, the first five under the watchful eye of his eldest brother, with whom he shared lodging. It is a pity that no documents have survived this period of Charles' life, though in old age he did put down on paper a summary of his early years. The accompanying extract is part of this long letter[17] which Charles wrote in April 1785 to Dr Thomas Bradbury Chandler, an Anglican minister, who was about to continue his ministry in America. [7] Charles gives only the barest details of his youth in this retrospective document, but the mention of his brother Samuel is quite significant.

Samuel was seventeen years older than Charles and by now was ordained. In 1713 he returned from Christ Church, Oxford, to become an assistant teacher and, eventually, senior Usher at Westminster, where he actually tutored Charles for a time. In his capacity as a junior member of staff, Samuel was in a position to help his youngest brother in all kinds of ways, not least in the matter of Charles' school fees, and it was almost certainly through his influence that Charles developed his high-churchmanship and love of the sacraments. There is every reason to think that Charles was happy at Westminster School – despite the relatively Spartan routine which entailed the boys rising at 5.15 a.m. and studying Latin and Greek grammar until breakfast at eight – and he appeared in the annual Latin play. Westminster's reputation for being a place of learning and strict discipline owed itself to a series of able headmasters, the most famous being Dr Busby who ran the school

7. As you are setting out for America, & I for a more distant Country, I think it needful to leave with you some account of myself & my companion through life. At eight years old in 1715, I was sent by my father, Rector of Epworth, to Westminster School, & placed under the care of my eldest brother Samuel, a strict churchman who brought me up in his own principles. In 1727 I was elected student of Christ Church. My brother John was then Fellow of Lincoln.

Source: Rupert Davies, A. Raymond George and Gordon Rupp (eds), *A History of the Methodist Church in Great Britain*, Vol. 4, Epworth Press 1988, p. 204.

for fifty-seven years until his death in 1695. When asked how he had managed to be so successful over such a long and tempestuous period of English history, he is said to have replied, 'The *fathers* govern the nation; the *mothers* govern the fathers; but the *boys* govern the mothers; and *I* govern the boys!'[18]

Whilst not being quite so academically inclined as either of his two brothers, Charles, nevertheless, was not afraid of hard work. He applied himself conscientiously to his studies and, like them, proved to be an able scholar, particularly of the classics.[19] In 1725 he received the honour of being made Captain of the School. An early example of the loyalty with which Charles stood by his friends is to be found in his defence, with his fists, of a new pupil who had been subject to bullying, probably because of his broad Scottish accent. The lad in question, James Murray, was to become Lord Mansfield and attain the position of Lord Chief Justice of England. He and Charles remained lifelong friends.

Another incident during Charles' Westminster days is worthy of mention, for it throws additional light upon his character. His father was approached by a distant relative, a wealthy Irish landowner named Garret Wesley, with a view to adopting Charles, since he himself was without an heir. Garret Wesley helped out with Charles' school fees, met the lad and the two became friends. Samuel and Susanna, in a gesture of both wisdom and unselfishness, permitted Charles to make the decision. Charles declined, thereby showing that he placed family loyalty above wealth. It is interesting to note that the eventual heir (Richard Colley) became the grandfather of the Duke of Wellington, following a change of the family's name from Wesley to Wellesley.[20] One could idly speculate as to the possible result of the

Battle of Waterloo had it been fought by a grandson of Charles! John, rather laconically, later referred to his brother's decision as a 'fair escape'.

In 1726 Charles was awarded a studentship at Christ Church, Oxford – gaining first place out of the candidates from Westminster School – and in the next chapter we shall examine the significance of the formative years he spent there.

Chronology

Note. Where no name is given in this and subsequent time lines, the details refer to Charles Wesley.

1662		Birth of Samuel Wesley
1669		Birth of Susanna Annesley Wesley
1703	28 June	Birth of John Wesley
1707	18 December	Charles Wesley born
1709		Fire at the Epworth rectory
1716	April	Entered Westminster School
1726	13 June	Elected to Christ Church College, Oxford
	October	Begins his university career

For Discussion

1. Who of Charles' immediate family had most influence upon him – and how?

2. How important were Charles' schooldays in his own personal growth?

3. What were the most significant factors which affected your own early development?

2

The Oxford Methodist

Lord, my time is in thy hand,
   My soul to thee convert;
Thou canst make me understand,
   Though I am slow of heart;
Thine in whom I live and move,
   Thine the work, the praise is thine;
Thou art wisdom, power, and love,
   And all thou art is mine.

Charles' years at Oxford were important for a number of reasons. Apart from his intellectual development, they marked notable strides in Charles' spiritual pilgrimage. Although for the latter part of this period his life was very closely linked with his brother's, his early steps of Christian commitment were made quite independently of John. They were years too that saw him grow from a teenager, with all the limitations and dependence of one who had been brought up within a strict family, to a young man who was self-aware of both his gifts and his weaknesses, and to one who had begun the quest for self-discovery – even if he was still unsure where the journey would take him.

Charles at Christ Church

In studying at Christ Church, Charles emulated his two elder brothers, but the choice of the college was made not just for family reasons. Among the Oxford colleges Christ Church was noted for its academic excellence, although its standards were certainly less demanding than nowadays. Charles entered university in high spirits and from time to time his father exhorted him to observe good habits. [8] The choice of the nautical metaphor in this excerpt was, perhaps, ironic in view of Charles' poor sea-faring record in the future!

In his biography of John Wesley, Stanley Ayling writes that 'until he was past twenty Charles Wesley, though he paid conventional allegiance to Christian beliefs and observances, showed no pronounced evidence of piety'.[1] While this judgement is rather harsh, there is little doubt that Charles enjoyed the university's social life and participated fully in its extra-curricular activities – particularly in his first year. In the summer of 1728 John visited Oxford, probably at the same time as his ordination as a priest. However, his father urged him to check on his younger brother's progress whilst he was there. John found that Charles 'pursued his studies diligently, and led a regular, harmless life; but if I spoke to him about religion he would warmly (i.e. 'heatedly' –

---

8. You must find time every day for walking . . . a little more exercise now and then will do you no harm. You are now launched fairly, Charles. Hold up your head, and swim like a man . . . But always keep your eye fixed above the pole star; and so God send you a good voyage through the troublesome seas of life, which is the hearty prayer of your loving father . . . Bear no more sail than is necessary, but steer steady.

Source: F. C. Gill, *Charles Wesley, the First Methodist*, Lutterworth Press 1964, p. 36.

Ed.) answer, "What! would you have me be a saint all at once?" and would hear no more.'[2] It was not his intention as an undergraduate to succumb completely to 'the gloomy and mechanical piety' of Oxford, as he playfully remarked to John, and he wrote later that 'my first year at College I lost in diversions'.[3]

Charles looked forward to taking his degree at Oxford but his studentship at Christ Church, which was worth about £100 a year, did not mean that he was free from financial worries. He found himself frequently short of money – as an extract from his letter to John in January 1728 shows. [9] This is the earliest letter of Charles' that we have, and apart from his impecunity ('twas ever thus, for students) it certainly reveals his cheerfulness in adversity. Even after he had graduated and had begun tutoring students in his own right, lack of funds continued to be a problem. In July 1734 he wrote to his brother Samuel, apologizing for not visiting him 'for want of time and money', and in the winter of that year was actually considering parting with some of his study furnishings in order to buy clothes. By the spring of 1735 he was down to a single shirt.[4]

The 'Moll' and 'Pat' referred to in the extract were, of course, Charles' sisters, Mary and Martha. The terms 'grizzle' and 'grumbletonial' were, of course, used playfully. Charles had a very deep affection for his sisters, and the same letter contains a poignant paragraph concerning Hetty (Mehetabel), probably the most gifted of all the girls, who shortly before had entered into a very unhappy marriage with a travelling plumber named William Wright.[5] Brother John, who had been ordained deacon in 1725 and become a Fellow of Lincoln College the next year, had responded to his father's appeal for help and left in 1727 to act in a part-time capacity as Samuel's curate at Wroot, rejoining Charles at Oxford in September 1729.

Until now it had been his brother Samuel who had had the greatest influence upon the young Charles, and it is worth digressing briefly to comment on this remarkable man.[7] Samuel's love for and loyalty to his family was not confined solely to Charles. It was

> 9. 'Twill most certainly have one of two widely-different effects upon me: make me a very hard student, or none at all; an excellent economist, or a poor desperate scoundrel; a Patient Grizzle like Moll, or a Grumbletonial[6] like Pat. 'Tis in the power of a few Epworth or Wroot guineas and clothes to give things the favourable turn, and make a gentleman of me. Come Money then, and quickly, to rescue me from my melancholy maxim, ex nihilo nihil fit – I can possibly save nothing, where there's nothing to be saved.
>
> *Source*: Frank Baker, *Charles Wesley as Revealed by His Letters*, Epworth Press 1948, p. 9.

largely through Samuel's support that John was elected Fellow of Lincoln College in 1726. He also helped John and his sisters financially, and throughout his relatively short working life was at pains to give assistance to his parents: a fact which Samuel Sr was only too ready to acknowledge.[8] This generosity continued after his father's death and, typically, Samuel forbade anyone to speak of it whilst he himself was alive. After serving for nearly twenty years as Usher at Westminster School, Samuel became headmaster of Blundell's School at Tiverton in Devon in 1732, where he quickly won a reputation for combining high standards with a deep pastoral care for the children. Ordained priest in the Church of England, Samuel was a gifted poet who perhaps channelled too little of his energy into hymn-writing, in which he excelled. Towards the end of his life he attempted (at a distance) to exercise a moderating influence on John and Charles in the early years of the Methodist revival. Had he lived beyond 1739, Methodism could well have assumed a slightly different character, as Samuel was one of the few people – much more so than Charles – who could offer sensitive, but frank criticism to John and be sure that his words were heard.

Charles and his eldest brother remained on close terms until Samuel's early death in 1739 – though Charles could not easily relate to Samuel's rather temperamental wife Ursula (known in family circles as 'Nutty'!)[9] – but from this point it seems that John took over as his mentor. It is possible that the meeting of the two brothers on the occasion of John's visit in 1728 had a sobering effect on Charles, so that the latter began to think in more serious terms about his spiritual condition. On 22 January 1729 he wrote a letter to John in terms which reveal something of this changed attitude. [10]

It may well be that a brief infatuation with an older woman (an actress named Molly Buchanan) helped the young Charles to be 'less addicted to gallantry', as he himself put it. Certainly, once the initial trauma of first love had passed, he treated this episode without undue seriousness, and resolved to concentrate his attention upon his studies. Conscientious he might be, but Charles found academic work less easy than John. A letter to John on 5 May 1729 shows both his good intentions and the difficulties which he encountered. [11] Undoubtedly Charles was being over-modest, for there was no doubting his keen mind and aptitude for study. Rather, such examples of his writing show his lack of pretension and his readiness to unburden his soul to those he trusted.

Incidentally, Charles did not only write to his immediate family. In 1725 his brother John had met

---

10. God has thought fit (it may be to increase my wariness)[10] to deny me at present your company and assistance. 'Tis through Him strengthening me I trust to maintain my ground till we meet, and neither before or after that time shall I, I hope, relapse into my former state of insensibility. 'Tis through your means, I firmly believe, God will establish what He has begun in me, and there is no one person I would so willingly have to be the instrument of good to me as you.

I verily think, dear brother, I shall never quarrel with *you* again till I do with my religion, and that I may never do *that* I am not ashamed to desire your prayers. 'Tis owing in great measure to somebody's (my mother's most likely) that I am come to think as I do, for I can't tell myself how or when I first awoke out of my lethargy – only that 'twas not long after you went away.

Source: Frank Baker, *Charles Wesley as Revealed by His Letters*, Epworth Press 1948, pp. 10–11.

---

11. In my pursuit of knowledge I own I have this advantage of you in some things. My brothers were born before me; I start at twenty. But then I'm sure I'm less indebted to nature than you. I'm very *desirous* of knowledge, but can't *bear* the drudgery of coming at it near so well as you could. In reading anything difficult, I'm bewildered in a much shorter time than I believe you used to be at your first setting out. My head will by no means keep pace with my heart, and I'm afraid I shan't reconcile it in haste to the extraordinary business of thinking.

Source: Frank Baker, *Charles Wesley as Revealed by His Letters*, Epworth Press 1948, p. 12.

Sally Kirkham, the daughter of the rector of Stanton in Gloucestershire, with whom he struck up a deep friendship. Together with two other women, Mary and Anne Granville, John exchanged regular correspondence. It was common in the eighteenth century for writers to adopt rather fanciful pen-names: John was 'Cyrus'; Sally Kirkham, 'Varanese' and Mary (later Mary Pendarves) and Anne Granville, 'Aspasia' and 'Selima' respectively. While he was at Oxford, Charles joined the letter-writing circle as 'Araspes'. Whilst not having quite the impact that Sally's friendship had upon John, the experience of exchanging intimate thoughts with this group served to broaden Charles' outlook and understanding of human nature. Indeed, when homesick in Georgia some years later, he continued to confide in Sally Kirkham, rather than his mother or Samuel.[11]

The 'Holy Club'

Meet it is, and just, and right,
   That we should be wholly thine,
In thine only will delight,
   In thy blessed service join:
O that every work and word
   Might proclaim how good thou art,
Holiness unto the Lord
   Still be written on our heart!

As we have seen, Charles was developing a more serious attitude both to his studies and to his own sense of Christian discipleship. The determination not to 'relapse into my former state of insensibility' which he announced in his letter to John[12] quickly took practical shape. In later years he described it in beautifully succinct terms. [12] This passage is part of the letter which Charles wrote in April 1785 to Dr Chandler, which was cited in the previous chapter. We shall return to this important document again, since it not only gives details of Charles' experiences in Georgia but also reveals a great deal about the way he viewed relations between Methodism and the Church of England.

It may come as something of a surprise to the reader to discover that Charles laid claim to being the first 'Methodist'. However, whether the group of undergraduates whom Charles gathered around him (which quickly became known in student circles as the 'Holy Club') would have developed in the way it did without John's active involvement, is very much open to question. Charles certainly claimed that it was *he* who had founded it, but it is clear that within a very short space of time his brother became its leader and directing force.

Dr Richard Heitzenrater, who justly gained fame for being the first to access John's diary by 'cracking the code', as it were,[13] has shown that the popular

picture of the 'Holy Club' does not tally with reality. The well-known painting by Marshall Claxton of John addressing the members who are depicted gathered together around a table and listening intently, gives an impression that is, in Heitzenrater's words, 'most unfortunate'.[14] The group, who are perhaps better described as the 'Oxford Methodists', was far from being a 'club' as such and was a much looser group than has been previously thought. In 1729 at least, their gatherings were neither regular nor attended by the same undergraduates on each occasion, nor was there a particular set routine. All this grew over a period of time.

The epithet 'Holy Club' was probably intended as an unkind jest,[15] and it is true that Charles' pre-occupation with his own spiritual state at this time was, in the main, the underlying reason why he sought the company of other like-minded young men. Writing to John at Wroot on 5 May 1729, he laid his soul bare – as he was to do so often in the future. [13]

Incidentally, an interesting feature of this particular letter is that Charles started to use abbreviations (like John) when he wrote personal correspondence. When he began to keep a diary in 1729, he asked John,

---

13. What you say about coldness has put me upon considering whence mine can proceed, and how it may [be remedied?] I think I may truly esteem it the nature and just consequence of my past life. One who . . . has for almost thirteen years been utterly inattentive at public prayers can't expect to find there the warmth he has never known at his first seeking: he must knock oftener than once before 'tis opened to him . . .

Be that how it will . . . I won't give myself *leisure* to relapse, for I'm assured, if I have no business of my own, the Devil will soon find me some. You may show this if you think proper to my mother, for I would gladly have a letter from her upon this subject.

Source: Frank Baker, *Charles Wesley as Revealed by His Letters*, Epworth Press 1948, p. 13.

---

12. My first year at college I lost in diversions. The next I set myself to study. Diligence led me into serious thinking. I went to the weekly Sacrament, and persuaded two or three young scholars to accompany me, and to observe the method of study prescribed by the Statutes of the University. This gained me the harmless nickname of 'Methodist'. In half a year my brother left his curacy at Epworth, and came to our assistance. We then proceeded regularly in our studies, and in doing what good we could to the bodies and souls of men.

Source: Rupert Davies, A. Raymond George and Gordon Rupp (eds), *A History of the Methodist Church in Great Britain*, Vol. 4, Epworth Press 1988, p. 204.

What particulars am I to take notice of? Am I to give my thoughts and words as well as deeds a place in it? I'm to mark all the good and ill I do; and what besides? What cipher can I make use of? If you would direct me to the same or a like method with your own, I would gladly follow it for I'm fully convinced of the usefulness of such an undertaking. I shall be at a stand till I hear from you.[16]

He was to develop this as time went on and eventually used a form of shorthand devised by John Byrom[17] – which he was to persuade John to adopt. As we shall see, both brothers were often to slip into Latin and Greek when they wished to hide parts of their letters from unwanted eyes.

In retrospect we can see that the pattern of devotion, study and fellowship that Charles had experienced at his home in Epworth was simply being repeated in Oxford. This was understandable, given the strong impact which both Samuel and Susanna had had upon him. Thus the methodical way in which he had been taught to read the divines (by his mother) and classical authors (by his father) was mirrored in the kinds of study in which Charles and his friends engaged. Such works as Thomas à Kempis' fifteenth-century classics, *The Imitation of Christ* and *Christian Pattern* were read and discussed along with more recent writings which included William Law's *Perfection* and *A Serious Call to a Devout and Holy Life*, and Bishop Jeremy Taylor's *Rules and Exercises of Holy Living and Dying* – all of which had helped John Wesley in his own spiritual journey. To these were added the writings of the Church Fathers, whose example did much to inspire this group of young students to pursue their devotions methodically.

Regular patterns of prayer (which included periods of fasting), sessions of mutual self-examination and frequent communion clearly met a deep inward need on Charles' part. Charles did not find this new 'seriousness' easy, as he confessed to John in another part of his letter of 5 May 1729. [14] This document is a reminder of the great importance which Charles

14. Last Saturday . . . I could not come home till eight at night: I then found myself utterly averse to prayer, and spent half an hour in vain striving to recollect my dissipated thoughts. Upon this I gave out, and passed the whole night in the utmost trouble and discomposure of mind. I rose in the morning two hours later than usual, in utter despair of receiving the Sacrament that day, or of recovering myself in less than two or three. In this condition I went immediately to church. On my way a thought came across me that it might be less sin to receive even without the least immediate preparation . . .

I accordingly resolved if I found myself anything affected with the prayers, to stay and communicate. I *did* find myself affected, and stayed. I not only received the Sacrament at that time with greater warmth than usual, but afterwards found my resolutions of pursuing considerably strengthened.

Source: Frank Baker, *Charles Wesley as Revealed by His Letters*, Epworth Press 1948, p. 14.

placed upon the sacrament of Holy Communion, as his hymns would testify in later years.

Charles' natural gregariousness kept him from being completely preoccupied with the state of his own soul, even though the primary aim of the 'Holy Club' was to save it. His innate charm and ability to form relationships easily was shown in the way he befriended George Whitefield, who attributed his conversion to Charles' kind attention. Whitefield was to record, 'I never knew what true religion was till God sent me that excellent treatise [Charles had lent him books – Ed.] by the hands of my never-to-be-forgotten friend.'[18] Charles also met a young man named William Morgan, who clearly had been going through a difficult time at Oxford. In the same letter to John, Charles described how their friendship began. [15] Other members of the 'Holy Club' – apart from John, Charles, the Morgans (William and his younger brother Richard) and George Whitefield – were Thomas Broughton from Exeter, John Clayton from Brasenose and James Harvey from Lincoln Colleges. Some of the above would feature prominently in Charles' life in the coming years. It is interesting to note here, that Benjamin Ingham, who was at Queen's College at the time, was *not* a member of the 'Holy Club' and did not attend its meetings. In fact, he himself initiated several groups which he organized along similar lines but which were quite separate.[19]

The members of the 'Holy Club' did not, however, confine themselves to the practice of spiritual self-edification, despite attracting further nicknames from their fellow undergraduates, such as 'Bible Moths', 'The Godly Club', 'Sacramentarians' and 'Enthusiasts'.[20] The term 'enthusiast' was particularly damning and one that was to be frequently levelled at Methodists in the years to come since it was, at the time, used to denote any kind of religious extremism. An important by-product of their reading was to lead Charles and his companions to look outwards. Heitzenrater writes that 'theology was not unimportant in this whole enterprise, but theology was the handmaid of holy living, a practical theology devoted to Christian living'.[21] The young men began their social outreach by giving alms to the poor and visiting prisoners, most notably at Newgate Gaol.

Some years later, in October 1732, John wrote a

15. Providence has at present put it in my power to do some good. I have a modest, humble, well-disposed youth lives next me, and have been (I thank God!) somewhat instrumental in keeping him so. He was got into vile hands, and is now broke loose. I assisted in setting him free, and will do my utmost to hinder his getting in with them again . . . He was of opinion that passive goodness was sufficient, and would fain have kept in with his acquaintance and God at the same time. He durst not receive the Sacrament but at the usual times for fear of being laughed at . . . By convincing him of the duty of frequent communication I have prevailed on both of us to receive once a week.

Source: Frank Baker, *Charles Wesley as Revealed by His Letters*, Epworth Press 1948, p. 15.

16. In November 1729, at which time I came to reside at Oxford, your son, my brother and myself, and one more agreed to spend three or four evenings in a week together. Our design was to read over the classics, which before we had read in private, on common nights, and on Sunday some book on divinity. In the summer following, Mr. Morgan told me he had called at the jail, to see a man that was condemned for killing his wife; and that, from the talk he had with one of the debtors, he verily believed that it would do much good if any one would be at pains now and then of speaking with them. This he so frequently repeated, that on the 24th of August, 1730, my brother and I walked down with him to the castle. We were so well satisfied with our conversation there, that we agreed to go thither once or twice a week; which we had not done long, before he desired me, August 31, to go with him to seek a poor woman in the town who was sick. In this employment too, when we came to reflect upon it, we believed that it would be worth while to spend an hour or two in a week; provided the minister of the parish in which any such person was were not against it.

Source: John Wesley, *Letters*, Vol. I, pp. 124–5.

long letter to William Morgan's father, Richard, on the occasion of the premature death of William, in the course of which he described some of the main emphases of the 'Holy Club'. [16] It makes interesting reading for a number of reasons. First, it is obvious that John considered the beginning of the 'Holy Club' as dating from November 1729 when *he* joined and not earlier, according to Charles' claim. Secondly, the extract makes it clear that new ventures, such as prison visitation (it was William Morgan who first suggested that John and the others begin this), did not come solely from either John or Charles. John was honest enough to admit *that*!

Of course, the young men saw this social work as a natural development of their devotional lives, but the truth is probably the reverse, in that the main purpose of these 'good works' was to contribute to their own moral and spiritual advancement.[22] Nonetheless, Charles' horizons were being gradually widened.

A Change of Direction

That I thy mercy may proclaim,
That all mankind thy truth shall see,
Hallow thy great and glorious name,
And perfect holiness in me.

Charles' fortunes were now inextricably linked with John's, and the Wesley brothers were to be the closest of colleagues for the next twenty years. As a young man, Charles readily followed his brother's lead and at times was willing to be overruled by him. John Gambold, who was a good friend of the Wesleys at Christ Church, wrote of Charles that he had 'never observed any person have a more real deference for another, than he constantly had for his brother ... He followed his brother entirely'.[23] The time would come when Charles and John would plough their own separate furrows and disagree sharply over a range of issues. That time, however, lay in the future.

It may have seemed natural for Charles to have followed his brothers in taking Holy Orders. Nevertheless, despite his growth in maturity, spiritual awareness and increased willingness to engage in 'serious thinking', such a momentous step did not figure in his thinking at this stage. Of much more immediate importance was the failing health of his father. In March 1735 he wrote a sad letter to his brother Samuel, part of which is reproduced here. [17] Whether Charles was closer to his father than John or Samuel because he shared more of his father's personal characteristics, is debatable. What is clear is that family relationships were to be of the utmost importance throughout his life.

Samuel had hoped that one of his sons would succeed him at Epworth. He had written to his eldest son in 1732, without success, and two years later approached John with the same request. The latter refused in a letter which did him little credit.[25] On a happier note, Samuel finally managed to complete his great life's work, his commentary on the Book of Job, even though it was not published until after his death. In fulfilment of the promise he made to his father, John presented the book to Queen Anne two days before he left for Georgia. The commentary, however, was too indigestible for the average reader and never achieved a wide circulation. After Samuel's death Susanna stayed briefly with her daughter Emily, at that time teaching at a school in Gainsborough, then with Samuel at Tiverton until 1737. From here she spent some years with Martha and finally came to reside with John at the Foundery in London, not far from where she had been born. Charles was particularly solicitous, and the close bond between him and his mother can be seen in the letters they exchanged in the late 1730s, to which we shall refer in a later chapter.

Charles was at a turning-point. The Wesley family were now scattered and his own future was cloudy. We have little evidence of the kind of issues that occupied his thinking in the months following his father's death, but an indication that all was not well with his spirit is to be found in letters he wrote to a young acquaintance named James Hutton, whose house was next door to Samuel's when the latter had been Usher at Westminster. In one of them he admitted, 'I feel the weight and misery of my nature, and long to be freed from this body of corruption'.[26] In spite of all that he had experienced in Oxford, Charles clearly felt that he lacked personal holiness. The fact that he *did* become a clergyman was more as a result of his brother's pressure than from a desire to follow any deep-seated inclination of his own – as he made clear in his 'retrospective' to Dr

17. This spring we hope to have followed our inclinations to Tiverton, but are more loudly called another way. My father declines so fast, that before next year he will in all probability be at his journey's end;[24] so that I must see him now, or never more with my bodily eyes. My mother seems more cast down at the apprehension of his death than I thought she could have been; and what is still worse, he seems so too.

Source: Frank Baker, *Charles Wesley as Revealed by His Letters*, Epworth Press 1948, p. 19.

Chandler in 1785. [18] We may smile a little at Charles' phrase 'exceedingly dreaded'; this was a direction he would probably follow at some stage in his life. At the time, however, he felt that ordination was rather premature, and there can be no doubt that his ordination as priest just a week after that of deacon – for his elder brother John the interval had been nearly three years – was a matter of expediency.

---

18. I took my degree, & only thought of spending all my days at Oxford; but my brother, who always had the ascendant over me, persuaded me to accompany him & Mr. Oglethorpe to Georgia.

I exceedingly dreaded entering into Holy Orders, but he over-ruled me here also; & I was ordained Deacon by the Bishop of Oxford one Sunday, & the next Priest by the Bishop of London.

Our only design was to do all the good we could as ministers of the Church of England, to which we were firmly attached both by education and principle. My brother still acknowledges her the best national Church in the world.

Source: Rupert Davies, A. Raymond George and Gordon Rupp (eds), *A History of the Methodist Church in Great Britain*, Vol. 4, Epworth Press 1988, p. 204.

Charles was now a young man who was determined to devote his life to God. He was rigorous in his personal devotions and showed a loving concern for the spiritual welfare of those around him. He had begun to evangelize (with mixed success) and, as we have seen, had acquired the beginnings of a social conscience. However, one has to conclude that for Charles, ordination was, in effect, a tool. It would facilitate the work he would shortly be undertaking in America, and perhaps enable him to achieve the spiritual peace of mind for which he so much longed. His brief stay in Georgia was, sadly, to prove otherwise.

Chronology

1726	13 June	Elected to Christ Church College, Oxford
	12 October	Birth of Sarah Gwynne (Mrs Charles Wesley)
	October	Charles begins his university career
1728		John ordained as priest
1729	January	Began to keep a diary
	March[27]	Initiated the 'Holy Club'
	November	John returns to Oxford and takes over the leadership of the 'Holy Club'
1730		Graduated and became a tutor at Oxford
1732		Introduced George Whitefield to the 'Holy Club'
1733	12 March	Received his Master's degree
1735	25 April	Death of Samuel Wesley Sr
	21 September	Ordained deacon by the Bishop of Oxford
	24 September	Appointed Secretary for Indian Affairs, Georgia
	29 September	Ordained priest by the Bishop of London
	14 October	Set sail for Georgia

For Discussion

1. The sacrament of Holy Communion was clearly very important for Charles. How important is it for you? How frequently do think it should be celebrated?

2. Do you get the impression that the 'Holy Club' was 'wholly club', or was it truly inclusive?

3. The 'Holy Club' was established in great part to provide a framework for regular, disciplined

study and devotion for its members. Are there sufficient opportunities for these in the life of your own church, and if not, do you feel they would be of value? How might they be developed?

4. 'The main purpose of these "good works" was to contribute to their own [i.e. the members of the 'Holy Club'] moral and spiritual advancement' (p. 17). Which should come first for the Christian, a commitment to social justice, or personal holiness?

3

Georgia

O let us still proceed
  In Jesu's work below;
And following our triumphant head,
  To further conquests go.

The vineyard of their Lord
  Before his labourers lies;
And lo! We see a vast reward
  Which waits us in the skies.

In the early part of 1735, Charles and John Wesley were settled in Oxford, both with every intention of continuing their academic careers at the University. Within a year the two brothers were engaged in an ill-fated venture in a place where we would have least expected to find them – the American colony of Georgia. How Charles and John came to be there and what impact the experience had upon Charles is the subject of this chapter. This phase in Charles' life is also interesting because it marks the point at which the surviving part of his journal begins,[1] which means that we have much more ready access to his thoughts and feelings from day to day. He also kept a diary during the outward voyage, but sadly, this has been lost or destroyed along with other papers.

The Background to the Venture

Popular legend has portrayed Georgia as a 'haven for debtors', but this does not quite match the real history of the colony. The driving force behind its development was a General James Oglethorpe, a remarkable individual who managed to combine a career in the army with a strong commitment to philanthropy. Having served with distinction with Prince Eugène of Savoy, he sat in Parliament as an MP from 1722 to 1754 and in 1728 was largely instrumental in setting up a committee of inquiry to look at the state of English gaols. Oglethorpe's vision of a place where criminals could be rehabilitated was shared with a group of London businessmen, who – for motives ranging from the altruistic to purely financial – formed a trusteeship for a piece of land in America given by King George II. Parliament, no doubt moved by the clear need to develop overseas trade and strengthen Britain's interests in the Carolinas in the face of French and Spanish encroachment, added a grant of £10,000. In 1732 Oglethorpe went out with a small group and founded Savannah, the future capital, returning two years later to seek additional support and to recruit more volunteers.

Oglethorpe was already known to the Wesley family. He had helped Samuel Sr when the latter was in financial difficulties and had taken a kindly interest in the eldest of the Wesley brothers.[2] In July 1735 John Wesley had chanced to meet a theologian named John Burton, who was one of the trustees of the colony and who provided John with the initial spark of enthusiasm. The trustees had recently published a pamphlet entitled *Reasons for establishing the Colony of Georgia*, part of which is reproduced here [19], in which they appealed to their readers' minds as well as to their hearts.

> 19. If one half of these [i.e. debtors], or only five hun-
> dred of them, were to be sent every year into Georgia,
> to be incorporated with those foreign Protestants who
> are expelled [from] their own countries for religion,
> what great improvements might not be expected in our
> trade, when these, as well as the foreigners, would be so
> many new subjects gained for England! for, while they
> are in prison, they are absolutely lost. The public loses
> their labour and their knowledge . . .
>
> The colony of Georgia will be a proper asylum for these
> . . . Are these people, with their liberty, to lose our
> compassion? Are they to be shut up from our eyes, and
> excluded from our hearts?
>
> *Source*: T. Jackson (ed.), *The Journal of The Rev.
> Charles Wesley, M.A.*, London, John Mason 1849,
> Vol. I, p. xvii.

The 'foreign Protestants' is a reference to religious communities such as the Moravians,[3] who were to have such an impact upon the Wesley brothers. We do not know whether John or Charles Wesley read the pamphlet, though it is quite likely that they did. However, following a series of rapid consultations with family and friends, it took very little time for John to make up his (and his brother's) mind. Any worries that Charles might have had concerning his newly widowed mother had been allayed by Susanna's encouragement and by the practical steps taken by Samuel and his sisters to take care of their mother. Emily and Patty were now married and so Charles, like John, was free to embark upon this adventure. He little dreamed that he would be returning to England within just twelve months.

The Wesleys' Departure

> *Thou, only Thou, the kind and good
> And sheep-redeeming Shepherd art:
> Collect Thy flock, and give them food,
> And pastors after Thine own heart.*

The plan, as eventually formulated, was for Charles to act as General Oglethorpe's secretary (under the title 'Secretary for Indian Affairs') as well as being the minister of Frederica – a small garrison on St Simon's Island, just off the coast – whilst John took on the role of pastor to the main settlement at Savannah and missionary to the Indians. For John, the prospect of preaching the pure gospel to the native inhabitants – a 'Paul to the gentiles' – was subordinate to his admitted aim of satisfying his own spiritual needs and saving his own soul.[4] Charles, for his part, did not exactly leave England as an eager missionary about to launch upon an exciting venture. As we have seen, he would have preferred to have spent the remainder of his days at Oxford. Also, neither he nor John had ever been to sea! Nonetheless, he determined to face his new calling with the same resolution that had characterized his years at the University.

The venture did not begin auspiciously. When the arrangements were being made in the late summer of 1735, Charles and John were fully expecting to travel with Westley Hall and Matthew Salmon. The former – a student of John's – had just married the brothers' sister, Patty Wesley, having managed to extricate himself from a simultaneous affair with youngest sister Kezzy. Hall's affairs became numerous, the marriage was unhappy and one can judge the degree of his reliability from the fact that, for reasons best known to himself, he withdrew from the mission at the very last minute. Salmon, who had studied at Brasenose College at Oxford and who was another friend of John's, also changed his mind and decided to stay in England. The Wesleys were accompanied, therefore, by Benjamin Ingham and Charles Delamotte, who stepped in at the eleventh hour. When Ingham reached Georgia he wrote a letter to his mother and in it described Delamotte as the 'son of a merchant in London, who had a mind to give himself up entirely to God and leave the world'.[5] Ingham himself had similarly lofty motives for going, naively thinking that there would be fewer opportunities for 'temptations to sensuality and indulgence among the Indians as in England'.[6] He was a very close friend of

Charles, who had taught him to keep a diary and who had become, in effect, his spiritual advisor.

It was originally intended that Charles should officiate in a temporary capacity at Frederica until a more permanent appointment could be made. Now that Westley Hall had declined to go, Charles was the only realistic replacement. Moreover, the Georgia trustees had already burned their boats by ensuring that the existing minister's authority there was revoked. The whole enterprise seemed laden with doom from the very outset, and the fact that Charles and his friends had little idea of what was in store for them in Georgia did not help.

The little group boarded the ship *Simmonds* and set sail from Gravesend on 22 October 1735, being held up at Cowes for a number of weeks before finally embarking on the hazardous voyage across the Atlantic. When they were 'in transit', as it were, on the Isle of Wight, the four friends signed a declaration [20], which bears all the hallmarks of John's influence. It was certainly 'methodistical', but its naivety and somewhat pretentious wording boded ill for the immediate future.

---

20. In the name of God, Amen. We, whose names are underwritten, being fully conscious that it is impossible, either to promote the work of God among the heathen, without an entire union among ourselves, or that such a union should subsist, unless each one will give up his single judgment to that of the majority, do agree, by the help of God:– first, that none of us will undertake anything of importance without first proposing it to the other three:– secondly, that whenever our judgments differ, any one shall give up his single judgment or inclination to the others:– thirdly, that in case of an equality, after begging God's direction, the matter shall be decided by lot.

John Wesley
Charles Wesley
Benjamin Ingham
Charles Delamotte

Source: Cited in F. C. Gill, *Charles Wesley, the First Methodist*, Lutterworth Press 1964, pp. 49–50.

There were 257 passengers and crew on the *Simmonds*,[7] among them twenty-six Moravian Christians. The Moravians were a Protestant evangelical community originating in Bohemia, where they had broken away from the Roman Catholic Church in 1467. In 1715, having suffered a history of persecution, they experienced a revival centred at Herrnhut in Saxony under a new leader, Count Nicolas Zinzendorf, and in 1727 they officially became a group within the Lutheran Church. One of the leading Moravians, August Gottlieb Spangenburg, the son of a Lutheran clergyman and a professor at Halle University, obtained Oglethorpe's permission to take a group of twenty-seven Moravians from Saxony to Georgia. They established a community at Savannah, on the lines of the one in Germany at Herrnhut ('The Lord's Watch'), and preached to the Creek Indians – with such success that a second group joined them, sailing on the same boat as the Wesleys and the other German emigrants from Salzburg.

The Moravians placed great emphasis upon the authority of the Bible and the need for personal salvation, their theology focusing on the death of Christ on the cross and, in particular, on the sacrificial element of the atonement.[8] They were concerned to revive the customs and faith of the early church, and their lifestyle was characterized by both deep inward devotion and a determination to preach the gospel to all who would listen.

The voyage across the Atlantic was not without incident. Understandably, given the time of the year, the *Simmonds* hit bad weather and at one point encountered such a severe storm that the ship was in danger of sinking. The calm behaviour of the Moravian passengers during this crisis made a deep impression on John Wesley, who in contrast was consumed by the fear of losing his life. This incident is well known and has been described elsewhere,[9] but we do not know what Charles' feelings were at the time. Almost certainly he was in his cabin being sea-sick! While his brother and the other two occupied themselves in the kind of activities in which they had been engaged in the 'Holy Club' (John even disciplining himself to learn German), Charles spent most of the two-month passage being ill. However, when his health allowed him, he joined the others in worship, prayer and study. He also wrote some sermons and began a long letter to Sally and Anne Kirkham. [21][10]

---

21.   On board the Simmonds off the
                         Island of Tibey in Georgia. Feb. 5. 1736

God has brought an unhappy, unthankful wretch hither, through a thousand dangers, to renew his complaints, and loathe the life which has been preserved by a series of miracles. I take the moment of my arrival to inform you of it, because I know you will thank Him, though I cannot. I cannot, for I yet feel myself. In vain have I fled from myself to America; I still groan under the intolerable weight of inherent misery! If I have never yet repented of my undertaking, it is because I could hope for nothing better in England – or Paradise. Go where I will, I carry my Hell about me. Nor have I the least ease in anything, unless in thinking of S[elima][11] and you.

Source: Frank Baker, *Charles Wesley as Revealed by His Letters*, Epworth Press 1948, p. 22.

This letter, the extract of which is the opening paragraph, shows just how depressed Charles had become. The months of relative inactivity, cooped up in confined quarters with a motley group of crew and passengers on board the *Simmonds*, together with his almost constant sea-sickness, all combined to lower his spirits. He poured out his heart to his two friends back in England, apart from whom, he commented rather inaccurately, he had 'no relations, no friends in England' to whom he could write or in whom he could confide. However, he knew that his arduous journey was almost at an end, and the sight of land revived him somewhat. Continuing the letter a week later, he turned his thoughts to more positive aspects of his mission. [22] Although he suffered from a desperate lack of confidence and a deep sense of unworthiness at the prospect of taking up

his duties in Frederica, he was determined to be a 'prisoner of hope' rather than despair.

---

22.   Feb. 14. off Peeper's Island

My friends will rejoice with me in the interval of ease I at present enjoy. I look with horror back on the desperate spirit that dictated the words above, but shall let them stand, as the naked picture of a soul which can never know reserve toward you. I will still call myself a *Prisoner of Hope*. God is able to save, to the uttermost, to break my bonds in sunder, and bring deliverance to the captive! 'To what am I reserved?' is a question I am continually asking myself – though God alone can answer it. This, I am persuaded, will now soon be determined, for I am come to a crisis. The work I see immediately before me is the care of fifty poor families (alas for them that they should be so cared for!), some few of whom are not far from the Kingdom of God. Among these I shall either be converted or LOST. I need not ask your prayers; you both make mention of me in them continually. Obstinate pride, invincible sensuality, stand betwixt God and me. The whole bent of my soul is to be altered. My office calls for an ardent love of souls, a desire to spend and to be spent for them, and eagerness to lay down my life for the brethren. May the Spirit that maketh intercession for us, direct you how to intercede for me.

Source: Frank Baker, *Charles Wesley as Revealed by His Letters*, Epworth Press 1948, p. 23.

The Arrival in Georgia

> *Christ, whose glory fills the skies,*
> *Christ, the true, the only Light,*
> *Sun of Righteousness, arise,*
> *Triumph o'er the shades of night;*
> *Day-spring from on high, be near;*
> *Day-star, in my heart appear.*

Anyone who has travelled abroad for the first time as an adult will testify to the sense of excitement and anticipation on first setting foot on foreign soil. This was true for Charles, and the first words that he penned in his journal are evidence of the extent to which he now felt revived. [23] Unworthy he might consider himself to be, but there was no denying his sincerity or determination.

Within a very short space of time, Charles set about his ministerial duties and – initially at least – had little opportunity to miss the company of John, who was a hundred or so miles south in Savannah, where his duties mainly kept him. He records that on the day after the party had landed, he led prayers 'to a few at the fire, before Mr. Oglethorpe's tent, in a hard shower of rain',[12] and engaged in a fruitless piece of counselling with one of the female colonists. A conversation that evening with another family concerning their child's baptism was followed by more pastoral work, in this case with the object of reconciling two colonists who had quarrelled.

Charles felt able to record much more than a series of observations on this colonial outpost in his journal. He was now writing as priest-in-charge of his own parish. The pages of his journal reveal his innermost thoughts and feelings, and show the heights

and depths – and 'depths' tended to figure prominently in his writings – of emotion that his soul could reach. Whilst historians have judged that there is less merit in Charles' writing than in his brother's much more extensive journal, it is a far more human document, in which we are allowed to glimpse Charles' real, raw self. Indeed, the fact that Charles never intended his journal to be published (and never imagined that eventually it would be) helps to account for the fact that he was less guarded in writing down his thoughts than John. This, of course, was to the ultimate benefit of future historians, for it is, above all, a very honest document.

All too soon, Charles came into conflict with Oglethorpe himself. The occasion concerned a request from Charles for some money for a 'poor woman'. The General seemed loathe to assist, and when Charles approached him the following day, he was 'surprised by a rougher answer' and what he perceived to be his 'increasing coldness'.[13] This was to be the first of a number of clashes between Charles and Oglethorpe, but we can sympathize with the General, who was burdened by the weight of his great responsibilities. In addition to the need to be constantly vigilant in the face of the ever-present threat of Spanish pirates and raids from native Americans, he was the governor of a heterogeneous assortment of undisciplined and quarrelsome civilians who were the source of perpetual problems. It was understandable if, at times, his temper became a little short!

Any thoughts Charles might have entertained of slipping into a comfortable regime as a preacher and pastor were quickly dispelled. Even worship could have its dramatic moments – but not quite in the way he ever had imagined. His first two Sunday services, whilst not being typical, were nonetheless far from being unusual for Frederica. [24]

Incidentally, when Charles preached he would often use his brother's sermons, there being nothing unusual about this practice in the eighteenth century. So, for example, when Charles refers to his sermon of 14 March as concerning 'singleness of intention', we find that it was actually penned by John and copied by Charles whilst on board the *Simmonds*.

---

23. TUESDAY, March 9th 1736, about three in the afternoon, I first set foot on St. Simon's island, and immediately my spirit revived. No sooner did I enter upon my ministry, than God gave me, like Saul, another heart. So true is that [remark] of Bishop Hall: 'The calling of God never leaves a man unchanged; neither did God ever employ any one in His service, whom He did not enable to the work He set him;' . . . The people, with Mr. Oglethorpe, were all arrived the day before . . .

I spent the afternoon in conference with my parishioners. (With what trembling ought I to call them mine!) At seven we had evening prayers, in the open air, at which Mr. Oglethorpe was present. The lesson gave me the fullest direction, and greatest encouragement.

Source: T. Jackson (ed.), *The Journal of The Rev. Charles Wesley, M.A.*, London, John Mason 1849, Vol. I, p. 4.

24. Sun., March 14. We had prayers under a great tree … I preached with boldness, on singleness of intention, to about twenty people, among whom was Mr. Oglethorpe. Soon after, as he was in Mrs. Hawkin's hut, a bullet (through the carelessness of one of the people who were exercising to-day) flew through the wall, close by him …

Sun., March 21st. Mr. Oglethorpe had ordered, oftener than once, that no man should shoot on a Sunday. Germain had been committed to the guard-room for it in the morning, but was, upon his submission, released. In the midst of the sermon a gun was fired. Davison, the constable, ran out, and found it was the Doctor; told him it was contrary to orders, and was obliged to desire him to come to the officer. Upon this the Doctor flew into a great passion, and said, 'What, do not you know I am not to be looked upon as a common fellow?' Not knowing what to do, the constable went, and returned, after consulting with Hermsdorf, with two centinels, and brought him to the guard-room. Hereupon Mrs. Hawkins charged and fired a gun; and then ran thither, like a mad woman, crying she had shot, and would be confined too. The constable and Hermsdorf persuaded her to go away. She cursed and swore in the utmost transport of passion, threatening to kill the first man that should come near her. Alas, my brother! what has become of thy hopeful convert?

Source: T. Jackson (ed.), *The Journal of The Rev. Charles Wesley, M.A.*, London, John Mason 1849, Vol. I, pp. 3–5.

Richard Heitzenrater, whose research has done so much to uncover such personal details as these (particularly in relation to John's diaries, as we have already seen), points out that 'John had written this sermon specifically for his brother.'[14] Indeed, it is likely that half the sermons Charles preached in Georgia were his brother's, and John provided him with a supply to take back to England and use there which, in fact, he did. Charles acknowledged his brother's authorship in his journal,[15] although we have no way of knowing if he admitted as much to his listeners! It provides an interesting comment, not only on Charles' dependence upon John in his early years as a preacher (after all, John had been preaching for ten years), but also because it shows that his basic theological approach was remarkably in tune with that of his brother at this stage of his life.

John, for his part, seemed to have settled in well at Savannah, and on 18 March told his mother in a letter that 'the place is pleasant beyond imagination'.[16] Unlike Charles, his health was robust and he added, rather smugly, 'I have not had a moment's illness of any kind since I set foot upon the continent.'[17] A few days later he wrote to Charles, whom he knew was undergoing a less fortunate introduction to colonial life. [25] It was a typical elder brother's letter, noteworthy for his use of Greek to conceal passages from unwelcome eyes (their letters were almost certainly opened and read before being delivered[18]), as well as for his prediction of troubled times ahead.

25.   Savannah, March 22, 1736.

DEAR BROTHER, – How different are the ways wherein we are led! Yet, I hope, towards the same end. I have hitherto no opposition at all. All is smooth and fair and promising. Many seem to be awakened. All are full of respect and commendation. We can't see any cloud gathering. But this calm cannot last; storms must come hither too: and let them come, when we are ready to meet them …

You are not, I think, at στρεφεσθαι εις τα εθνη, εως οι συμφυλεται σον απωθονσι σε.[1] If that period comes soon, so much the better. Only in the meanwhile reprove and exhort with all authority, even though all men should despise thee, Αποβησεται σοι εις μαρτυριον.[2]

[1] 'To turn to the Gentiles till your own countrymen shall cast you out.'
[2] 'It shall turn to thee for a testimony' : see Luke xxi. 13.

Source: John Wesley, *Letters*, Vol. I, pp. 198–9.

Turbulent Days

Surrounded by a host of foes,
Stormed by a host of foes within,
Nor swift to flee, nor strong to oppose,
Single, against hell, earth, and sin,
Single, yet undismayed, I am:
I dare believe in Jesu's name.

Charles' brief period of elation upon landing in Georgia quickly came to an end. He found living in a tent and sleeping on the ground irksome,[19] although it was better than being on board ship. His health, which was not good at the best of times, deteriorated in the rough conditions, and the entries in his journal are full of references to extreme fatigue, fever and 'distemper'.[20] His duties as a secretary were not particularly burdensome, but the plain fact of the matter was that Charles was neither a good secretary nor a willing one. As early as 16 March, as we have seen above, he confessed, 'I was wholly spent in writing letters for Mr. Oglethorpe. I would not spend six days more in the same manner for all Georgia.'[21]

More serious was the breakdown in Charles' relationship with the colonists. Why this should have happened so swiftly is not difficult to see. In his biography of Charles, Thomas Jackson pointed to 'the defectiveness of his theological views, and consequently of his own piety' as the main cause.[22] In his view, Charles (John, too) failed to give a balanced picture of the process of salvation, in that he concentrated upon 'reproving the vices and sins of the people with unsparing severity', whilst offering little more than 'the standard of practical holiness' as a solution. The result, according to Jackson, was that the colonists were 'strangers to [God's] forgiving mercy, and laboured under a just apprehension of his wrath'.[23] However, this suggests a one-dimensional approach to Charles' theology that was not entirely true. For example, Charles' sermon on 'The One Thing Needful', based on Luke 10.42, which he preached twice in September 1736, hardly fits Jackson's pattern,[24] even though it was actually

written for him by John. Furthermore, his inaugural sermon at Frederica, 'A Single Intention' (also his brother's), whilst stressing the need for holiness, also dwells on the importance of the work – and the fruits – of the Holy Spirit in a very positive and reassuring way.

Of more immediate significance in the alienation of the colonists was Charles' rigid churchmanship and insistence upon applying Oxford standards to Georgia. The emigrants were simply not prepared to put up with the kind of discipline Charles attempted to impose. His insistence upon employing high church methods – in the sacrament of baptism, for example – at first puzzled, then angered many of the colonists. Attendance at his services dwindled and gestures of ill-will multiplied rapidly. For example, on 30 March he noted in his journal, 'Having laid hitherto on the ground, in a corner of Mr Reed's hut, and hearing some boards were to be disposed of, I attempted in vain to get some of them to lie upon.'[25] When he did manage to acquire 'an old bedstead to lie on', it was removed after three days and not replaced.[26]

Early biographers of Charles have suggested that the colonists' hatred reached murderous proportions, and cite Charles' walk in the woods on 18 March when he recorded that 'a gun was fired from the other side of the bushes . . . Providence had at that moment turned me from that end of the walk, which the shot flew through; but I heard them pass close by me.'[27] However, this seems to have been the result of target practice rather than any serious attempt on Charles' life!

After less than three weeks from the beginning of his ministry at Frederica, relationships seem to have deteriorated completely, as Charles' entry in his journal for 31 March shows. [26] Added to this was Charles' difficulty in handling awkward people. His naivety and tendency towards stubbornness meant that personal conflicts were always likely to occur, especially with women, with whom he was inexperienced. Two in particular, Mrs Hawkins and Mrs Welch, were both scheming and vindictive, and contrived to set Charles and General Oglethorpe at

26. Wed., March 31st. I begin now to be abused and slighted into an opinion of my own considerableness. I could not be more trampled upon, was I a fallen Minister of state ... My few well-wishers are afraid to speak to me. Some have turned out of the way to avoid me. Others have desired I would not take it ill, if they seemed not to know me when we should meet. The servant that used to wash my linen sent it back unwashed ...

Source: T. Jackson (ed.), *The Journal of The Rev. Charles Wesley, M.A.*, London, John Mason 1849, Vol. I, p. 15.

loggerheads with each other. These women had begun to spin their web even whilst on board the *Simmonds*. First they told John Wesley that they had had affairs with General Oglethorpe, then they announced to Oglethorpe that Charles was spreading malicious gossip about his (supposed) illicit relationship with them. Neither story, of course, was true, but in such a claustrophobic community, gossip – especially when it concerned alleged adultery – tended to be readily believed and quickly repeated.

Charles' relationship with Oglethorpe constantly fluctuated. On 24 March, when praying for his enemies, he referred to the General as 'the chief of them'.[28] The following day, an unpleasant interview with Oglethorpe took place, in which Charles was called upon to defend himself against (false) charges that he had been urging the colonists to leave the settlement. Part of the conversation is recorded here. [27] Oglethorpe seemed to relent, but the machinations of Mrs Hawkins and Mrs Welch – the former, because she believed Charles had been responsible for her husband's arrest for shooting on a Sunday – resulted in further confrontations with the unhappy minister.

John wrote to Charles, encouraging him as best he could. He could hardly have been expected to offer his younger brother the kind of advice that would have made his life easier, since his own ministry was characterized by the same high-minded, rigid principles. The two brothers kept up a regular

correspondence, and the next extract [28] demonstrates that Charles, for his part, was quite prepared to pass on advice to John himself. The letter is also significant in that it reveals something of Charles' own journey of faith, for amidst the general air of despondency there are some faint glimmers of hope. It is also interesting that the brothers had such strikingly similar difficulties while they were in Georgia.

On hearing of his brother's distress, John visited Charles in April, and on his return to Savannah remarked in a letter to Oglethorpe, 'I found so little either of the form or power of religion at Frederica, that I am sincerely glad I am removed from it.'[29] Well he might be. Charles' determination to 'keep innocency'[30] in the midst of all his troubles failed miserably. Summoned again on 24 April by Oglethorpe, Charles was relieved to find that the General had not believed reports of his alleged sexual indiscretions, and the meeting ended with the two men reconciled.

27. Thur., March 25th. At half-hour past seven Mr. Oglethorpe called me out of my hut. I looked up to God, and went. He charged me with mutiny and sedition; with stirring up the people to desert the colony. Accordingly he said they had had a meeting last night, and sent a message to him this morning, desiring leave to go; that their speaker had informed against them, and me the spring of it all; that the men were such as constantly came to prayers, therefore I must have instigated them; that he should not scruple shooting half a dozen of them at once; but that he had, out of kindness, *first* spoke to me.

My answer was, 'I desire, Sir, you would have no regard to my brothers, my friends, or the love you had for me, if anything of this is made out against me. I know nothing of their meetings or designs. Of those you have mentioned, not one comes constantly to prayers, or sacrament. I never incited any one to leave the colony. I desire to answer my accuser face to face.'

Source: T. Jackson (ed.), *The Journal of The Rev. Charles Wesley, M.A.*, London, John Mason 1849, Vol. I, p. 8.

28.   Frederica, March 27th.

DEAR BROTHER,

I received your letter and box. My last to you was opened, the contents being publicly proclaimed by those who were so ungenerous as to intercept it. I have not yet complained to Mr. Oglethorpe . . .

Mr. Oglethorpe gave me an exceeding necessary piece of advice for you – 'Beware of hypocrites, in particular of *log-house* converts.' They consider you as favoured by Mr. Oglethorpe, and will therefore put on the form of religion, to please – not God, but you. To this I shall only add, Give no temporal encouragement whatsoever to any seeming converts, else they will follow you for the sake of the loaves. Convince them thus, that it can never be worth their while to be hypocrites . . .

God, you believe, has much work to do in America. I believe so too, and begin to enter into the designs which He has over *me*. I see why He has brought me hither, and hope ere long to say with Ignatius, 'It is now that I *begin* to be a disciple of Christ.' God direct you to pray for me. Adieu.

Source: Frank Baker, *Charles Wesley as Revealed by His Letters*, Epworth Press 1948, p. 24.

It was all too late, however. Charles' health had been thoroughly undermined and, despite the promise of a house, his will to continue was now at an end. A reference to dysentery in his journal on 1 April as 'a friendly fever' was a clear indication of his depressed state.[31] On 25 July he wrote laconically in his journal, 'I resigned my Secretary's place, in a letter to Mr. Oglethorpe,' and the following day, on his departure, 'When the boat put off I was surprised that I felt no more joy in leaving such a scene of sorrows.[32] His stay in Georgia had lasted less than five months.

Charles' Return from Georgia

See the Lord, thy keeper, stand,
  Omnipotently near!
Lo! He holds thee by thy hand,
  And banishes thy fear;
Shadows with his wings thy head;
  Guards from all impending harms:
Round thee and beneath are spread
  The everlasting arms.

Charles' homeward journey was at least as eventful as his outward trip. From Frederica he sailed to Charleston further up the coast, where he met his brother. John took up Charles' duties as Secretary to General Oglethorpe and attempted – with little apparent success – to create a society in Frederica along the lines of the one he had founded in Savannah. Like Charles, John found that his style of ministry was not widely welcomed and he, too, became prey to gossip and accusations.[33] Forced to abandon 'the great experiment', as he called it, John finally left the colony in December 1737.

The brief stop-over at Charleston gave Charles the opportunity to observe other aspects of colonial life. He found slavery extremely distasteful, as his journal entry for 2 August shows. [29] At least this short interlude took his attention away from his own problems, but the cruelty he witnessed made a deep impression upon him.

While he had been at Frederica, Charles had met up with a young Dutchman named Thomas Appee, who preyed upon Charles' good nature under the pretence of religious sincerity and, among other things, borrowed money from him which was never returned. This devious character followed Charles to Charleston and from there to Boston where they both embarked for England at the end of October. On the voyage home he proved a thorough nuisance, cheated the captain of his fare, and was finally arrested and gaoled.[34]

During his brief stay in Massachusetts – which he loved, but could not really savour due to continued

29. Mon., August 2nd. I had observed much, and heard more, of the cruelty of masters towards their negroes; but now I received an authentic account of some horrid instances thereof. The giving a child a slave of its own age to tyrannize over, to beat and abuse out of sport, was, I myself saw, a common practice. Nor is it strange, being thus trained up in cruelty, they should afterwards arrive at so great a perfection in it; that Mr. Star, a gentleman I often met at Mr. Lasserre's, should, as he himself informed L., first nail up a negro by the ears, then order him to be whipped in the severest manner, and then to have scalding water thrown over him, so that the poor creature could not stir for four months after. Another much-applauded punishment is, drawing their slaves' teeth . . .

I shall only mention one more . . . of a Mr. Hill, a dancing-master in Charleston. He whipped a she-slave so long, that she fell down at his feet for dead . . . Her crime was over-filling a tea-cup.

Source: T. Jackson (ed.), *The Journal of The Rev. Charles Wesley, M.A.*, London, John Mason 1849, Vol I, pp. 36–7.

ill-health – Charles had the time to reflect upon the past months. In a letter to John [30] he confessed to his failure in Georgia but still entertained hopes of pursuing a useful ministry. 'I cannot help exclaiming', he wrote rather ruefully (referring to New England), 'O happy country, that cherishes neither *flies*, nor *crocodiles*, nor *informers*.'[35] A week later he was consumed by morbid thoughts of death, and concluded by saying, 'I am just now much worse than ever; but nothing less than death shall hinder me from embarking.'[36] Despite pleas to wait until he felt stronger, Charles boarded the *Hannah* for England.

The voyage home proved as hazardous as the outward trip. Predictably, the ship hit a heavy storm two days out from Boston, so severe that the *Hannah* was in grave danger of foundering. In an interesting contrast to his brother's experience on the west-bound journey, Charles found the strength and spiritual resources to comfort and reassure his fellow

passengers. His journal entry for 28 October is a remarkably honest piece of writing, as he described in vivid terms the dire predicament they were in. [31] Charles' comments say a great deal about his own spiritual progress, as well as his courage in adversity. He had not yet found that sense of assurance for which he craved, but he had reached the stage of possessing a genuine sense of hope. It was an important step forward.

At last, on 3 December 1736, the travellers reached land, Charles being 'thankful for the divine mercies'. Stepping on to dry land, he offered a prayer of gratitude and 'blessed the Hand that had conducted me through such inextricable mazes'.[37] He was a sadder, wiser man than the one who had left England fourteen months before, but he had learned as much about himself as he had about the world.

30. Boston, Oct. 6.

DEAR BROTHER,

If you are as desirous as I am of a correspondence, you must set upon Byrom's shorthand immediately . . .[38]

I take [advantage?] of the deepest seriousness and best temper I have known since the fatal hour I left Oxford, to lay open my very heart, as I call God to witness that what I now write comes from it. You know what has passed in Georgia . . . The snare is broken, and I am delivered by the only expedient that could have saved me . . . I sometimes think how to dispose of the remainder of a [mad?] life. I can either live at Oxford or with my brother, who before I left England had provided for me without my asking. He will labour all he can to settle me. But I trust God will not suffer me to set up my rest there . . .

But Georgia alone can give me the solitude I seek after. I cannot look for a long life there, but neither do I count that a blessing

Source: Frank Baker, *Charles Wesley as Revealed by His Letters*, Epworth Press 1948, pp. 26–7.

31. Thurs., October 28th. The Captain warned me of a storm approaching. In the evening, at eight, it came, and rose higher and higher, after I thought it must have come to its strength; for I did not lose a moment of it, being obliged by the return of my flux to rise continually. At last the long-wished-for morning came, and brought no abatement of the storm. There was so prodigious a sea that it quickly washed away our sheep, and half our hogs, and drowned most of our fowl . . .

I rose and lay down by turns, but could remain in no posture long; strove vehemently to pray, but in vain; persisted in striving, yet still without effect. I prayed for power to pray, for faith in Jesus Christ, continually repeating His name, till I felt the virtue of it at last, and knew that I abode under the shadow of the Almighty.

It was now about three in the afternoon, and the storm at the height. I endeavoured to encourage poor Mr. Brig and Cutler,[39] who were in the utmost agony of fear. I prayed with them, till four; at which time the ship made so much water, that the Captain, finding it otherwise impossible to save her from sinking, cut down the mizen mast. In this dreadful moment, I bless God, I found the comfort of hope; and such joy in finding I could hope, as the world can neither give nor take away. I had that conviction of the power of God present with me, overruling my strongest passion, fear, and raising me above what I am by nature, as surpassed all rational evidence, and gave me a taste of the divine goodness.

Source: T. Jackson (ed.), *The Journal of The Rev. Charles Wesley, M.A.*, London, John Mason 1849, Vol. I, p. 49.

Chronology

1735		Settlement founded at Savannah, Georgia
1735	25 April	Death of Samuel Wesley

	21 September	Ordained deacon by the Bishop of Oxford
	24 September	Appointed Secretary for Indian Affairs in Georgia to General Oglethorpe
	29 September	Ordained priest by Dr Edmund Gibson, Bishop of London
	22 October	Set sail for Georgia
1736	9 March	Arrives at St Simon's Island
	25 March	Charles accused of sedition
	24 April	Charles and Oglethorpe reconciled
	25 July	Resigns as Secretary
	26 July	Leaves Georgia
	31 July	In Charleston
	24 September	Arrives in Boston
	26 October	Leaves for England
	3 December	Lands at Deal

For Discussion

1. Even in the twenty-first century, the pamphlet produced by the Georgia trustees (see Extract 19) may strike you as being a radical approach to the issue of imprisonment. Do you think that today, 'the public loses their [prisoners'] knowledge and their labour'?

2. Charles suffered considerable physical and mental hardship while in Georgia. To what extent did this affect his spiritual development?

3. The last sentence of the chapter says that Charles Wesley had 'learned as much about himself as he had about the world'. Imagine you are an elderly Charles reflecting back on his time in Frederica. If you had the time over again, how would you approach things differently? What lessons did you learn about yourself?

4

'Wrestling Jacob'[1]

Where shall my wondering soul begin?
How shall I all to heaven aspire?
A slave redeemed from death and sin,
A brand plucked from eternal fire,[2]
How shall I equal triumphs raise,
Or sing my great Deliverer's praise?

Charles was now just short of his twenty-ninth birthday.[3] The next eighteen months were to see the fruits of his recent experiences coalesce in a process of self-examination and renewal that would set the tone for the rest of his life.

Charles Back in England

Charles' first few weeks back in England were relatively happy ones. Despite his continued frailty, he was welcomed by friends, some of whom, he said, had 'given me over for dead',[4] since it had been reported that the *Hannah* had been lost in mid-Atlantic. On his arrival his first undertaking was to fulfil the tasks given to him by Oglethorpe before he left Georgia. In an act of kindness the General had smoothed over Charles' obvious failure by providing him with letters and documents for delivery to the trustees. He had been hoping that Charles would reconsider his resignation and return to Georgia and that this face-saving gesture might persuade him to change his mind. When Charles reported to the Georgia trustees and the Board of Trade – he was frequently asked to give an assessment of the situation there – he said nothing of his own troubles, but spoke positively about the colony's successes, which says a great deal about his loyalty to Oglethorpe.

When the General himself arrived in England in January,[5] he expressed a certain amount of displeasure at what Charles had written in his journal, saying that it 'was writ with a deal of spirit'. Charles defended himself by replying that it 'was writ with a great deal of truth'.[6] However, despite speaking of 'the mischief of private journals' in a later meeting,[7] Oglethorpe tried hard to persuade the younger Wesley to return to Georgia.

At this stage Charles gives the impression of being pulled in different directions. The prospect of returning to Georgia was still in his mind and at times he entertained hopes of going back there in some capacity. On 15 February he wrote, 'I told Mr. Oglethorpe of my desire of returning with him to Georgia, if I could be of any use there as a Clergyman; but as to my Secretary's place, I begged him to tell me where, when, and how, I should resign it.'[8] Once bitten, twice shy!

There were family matters to attend to as well, of course. In March 1737, Charles travelled to Tiverton where his mother was staying with Samuel. It may well be true that Susanna took a special interest in John following his narrow escape from the rectory fire and vowed at the time to be 'more particularly careful of the soul of this child'.[9] Nonetheless, she exercised an interest and concern for *all* her children's welfare. An example of her care for Charles can be found in a letter she wrote to him in 1735,

32. . . . that as pleases God, but if while I have life and any remains of health, it may be useful or pleasing to you, that we hold a correspondence together by letters, I shall gladly do it. But then, dear Charles, let us not spend our time in trifling, in talking of impertinent matters that will turn to no account . . .

This consideration will readily suggest to your good sense that we ought carefully to improve our time. And in order to do it effectually, I must earnestly conjure you to set apart two hours every day for private devotion; one in the morning, the other in the evening . . . It is not for me to fix the particular hours; those must be determined by yourself, who best know the method of your studies and what time you are least engaged. But then having once made your choice, you must peremptorily adhere to it, nor suffer company, pleasure, or any business that is not truly unavoidable to break in upon you, and cause you to neglect your retirement. For what is once devoted to God, ought never to be alienated from him. 'Tis probable you will find some difficulty in this practice at first, and when it is observed, perhaps you may sometimes lie under the imputation of singularity, moroseness, or ill breeding – but let not such things trouble you, for they are not worth regarding.

Source: Charles Wallace (ed.), *Susanna Wesley: The Complete Writings*, Oxford University Press 1997, pp. 167–8.

shortly before his departure for Georgia, which amply illustrates both her watchful concern and her understanding. [32]

In June, Charles went to see his uncle Matthew Wesley, who had been taken gravely ill, and when this kindly man – who had come to the family's assistance on more than one occasion – died shortly after his visit, attended his funeral. Visits to his former colleagues in Oxford, whom he exhorted 'to resume all their rules of holy living',[10] interviews with the Bishops of London and Oxford, reunions with the Granvilles and the Kirkhams – all these filled the early months of 1737.

Spiritual Struggles, 1737–1738

Fainting soul, be bold, be strong,
Wait the leisure of thy Lord;
Though it seem to tarry long,
True and faithful is his word:
On his word my soul I cast –
He cannot himself deny;
Surely it shall speak at last;
It shall speak, and shall not lie.

During this 'post-Georgia' period, Charles was continually aware that his spiritual life was lacking something. His journal entry on his twenty-ninth birthday found him 'in a murmuring, discontented spirit',[11] and when he was with Mrs Pendarves ('Aspasia') in January, his reaction to her reading a letter saying that he had drowned, was to exclaim rather morbidly, 'Happy for me, had the news been true! What a world of misery would it save me!'[12] Yet he described receiving 'comfort with the sacrament' on his first Sunday back in England. It was probably at this time that Charles wrote 'Hymn for Midnight', part of which is reproduced here. [33] It is interesting that Charles put his finger on one of the real problems with which he was struggling, when he referred to woe being 'solid' whereas joy merely appeared to be 'shadowy'. When his brother John read the hymn he changed the word 'death' in the last line of the third verse to 'faith', which altered the sense somewhat, but perhaps not quite in the dramatic way that Charles' first biographer suggested.[13] Rather, it shifted the focus from 'death' to 'faith' by preserving the sense of hope which the hymn already contained.

A significant meeting took place in late August with William Law, whose writings – particularly his *On Christian Perfection* and *A Serious Call to a Devout and Holy Life* – had made a considerable impression upon both Charles and John. Law was one of the 'non-jurors' who had lost their livings on the accession of George I in 1714. 'Non-jurors' were members of the Church of England who refused to

33.   While midnight shades the earth o'erspread,
          And veil the bosom of the deep,
      Nature reclines her weary head,
          And Care respires and Sorrows sleep:
      My soul still aims at nobler rest,
      Aspiring to her Saviour's breast.

      Aid me, ye hovering spirits near,
          Angels, and ministers of grace;
      Who ever, while you guard us here,
          Behold your heavenly Father's face!
      Gently my raptured soul convey
      To regions of eternal day.

      Fain would I leave this earth below,
          Of pain and sin the dark abode;
      Where shadowy joy, or solid woe,
          Allures or tears me from my God;
      Doubtful and insecure of bliss,
      Since Death alone confirms me his.

      Till then, to sorrow born, I sigh,
          And gasp and languish after home;
      Upward I send my streaming eye,
          Expecting till the Bridegroom come:
      Come quickly, Lord! thy own receive,
      Now let me see thy face, and live!

Source: Reproduced from Thomas Jackson, *The Life of
the Rev. Charles Wesley, M.A.*, London 1841, p. 108.

mind. Charles accepted the importance which Law
laid upon 'internal religion' but his meetings with
him in the summer of 1737 do not appear to have
resolved all his questions. Perhaps he found this wiry,
rather forbidding ascetic a little intimidating. The
next extract from Charles' journal gives a flavour of
their conversations, and also points to the increasing
interest he was taking in the subject of spiritual
renewal. [34]

A glance through Charles' journal entries from
April 1737 onwards reveals that he had become
increasingly preoccupied with the subject of conversion and spiritual renewal. Technically, he was
still Oglethorpe's secretary and, as such, received
a modest salary which enabled him to travel and
preach, now that his business with the Georgia
trustees was finished. At Hatfield on 25 August we
find him discussing 'the new birth' with a Mr
Chadwick and on 12 September he spent an hour
with his sister Hetty, 'in discoursing on the inward
change'.[15] Three days later he noted in his journal,
'I rose with earnest desires of resigning myself

take the oaths of allegiance and supremacy to
William and Mary on the grounds that they would be
perjuring themselves, in that they still regarded their
previous oaths to James II as being valid. Between
1727 and 1737 Law was a tutor at the home of the
Gibbon family (their son was Edward Gibbon, the
historian) and later founded a small religious community at Kings Cliffe, spending the remainder of his
days writing, engaging in philanthropic work and
living in great simplicity. Law's mysticism[14] was to be
rejected by both the Wesleys, as we shall see in a later
chapter, but his vigorous, straightforward style of
teaching and counselling provided a useful sounding-
board for Charles in his quest for spiritual peace of

34.   Wed., August 31st. I talked at large upon my state
with Mr. Law, at Putney. The sum of his advice was,
'Renounce yourself; and be not impatient.'

Fri., September 9th. I consulted Mr. Law a second time,
and asked him several questions: 'With what comment
shall I read the Scriptures?' 'None.' 'What do you think
of one who dies unrenewed, while endeavouring after
it?' 'It concerns you neither to ask, nor me to answer.'
'Shall I write once more to such a person?' 'No.' 'But I
am persuaded it will do him good.' 'Sir, I have told you
my opinion.' 'Shall I write to you?' 'Nothing I can
either speak or write, will do you any good.'

Sat., September 10th. Calling at Mr. Delamotte's I
found Miss Hetty[16] there, and gave her her brother's
letter. We soon fell into talk about the new birth . . .

Source: T. Jackson (ed.), *The Journal of The Rev.
Charles Wesley, M.A.*, London, John Mason 1849,
Vol. I, p. 74.

up entirely to God.'[17] On 16 September he called 'accidentally' on another of his sisters – Kezziah – who was in considerable spiritual turmoil, and wrote, 'she anticipated me, by saying she had felt here what she had never felt before, and believed now there was such a thing as the new creature'.[18] These instances give the impression that Charles was an agonized observer, who understood in part what his friends were experiencing, but who clearly did not feel able to share in them fully. He was, however, 'still growing in humility and love'[19] and on 16 October, when with the Delamottes, 'prayed with them for conversion'.[20]

Charles also met George Whitefield, with whom he had been close friends at Oxford. Whitefield was now making something of a name for himself as a preacher in London and his sermon, 'Ye must be born again' had been printed and was being widely read. On 5 November Charles heard him preach, 'not with the persuasive words of man's wisdom, but with the demonstration of the Spirit and with power'. He added in his journal that 'the churches will not contain the multitudes that throng to hear him'.[21]

The overall impression we gain from reading Charles' own account of these months is of an unhappy soul, striving for something that seemed just out of his reach. Despite his strenuous attempts to find what he was looking for in prayer, worship, daily devotions[22] and an earnest attempt to do good works and to live unselfishly, the periods of relative peace of mind were interlaced with longer ones of deep dejection. John was likewise occupied in a spiritual conflict of his own, but although their aim was the same – and they reached their goal at approximately the same time – the experience of the two brothers was quite different. John, with his more reasoned and logical approach, engaged in 'the intellectual struggles of a man who will not make his judgement blind'.[23] Charles, on the other hand, was in many ways more receptive and his quest for peace of mind a much more emotional one.

Charles was not only influenced by his friends and people such as Law and Whitefield. Help also came from another significant source. Until his return from Georgia we do not find much mention of the Moravians in his journal or letters, though he had encountered them on board the *Simmonds* and had met August Spangenberg. His brother had also come into contact with the Moravian leader, who had put John on the defensive with some searching questions about his relationship with God through Christ.[24] It was now Charles' turn! By coincidence, Count Zinzendorf himself was in London in early 1737 and Charles met him on a number of occasions. When in the company of the Count and his wife – 'a woman of great seriousness and sweetness' – he thought himself 'in a quire of angels'.[25] On 26 November Charles wrote to Zinzendorf, unburdening his soul. [35] The passage from his letter shows that, even at this stage, a return to Georgia was still a possibility.

However, it was another Moravian who was to have an even greater influence on Charles. The

---

35. LONDON, November 26, 1737.

TO THE REVEREND SUPERINTENDENT NICOLAUS VON ZINZENDORF.

UNENDING SALVATION (GREETING) IN CHRIST.

After wandering through all the miseries of passion, I would fain turn at last to thee, to myself, and to God. It would be superfluous to write of my affection. But I send a few words on the matter. While I hung back and struggled, the Lord snatched me away and tore me with violence from my idol. In grief and despair I flung away the yoke of Christ defiantly, and lay for a long time in sin, having no hope and without God. At last, with difficulty and hesitation, I seem to be rising again. I would once more play the warrior and force my way to freedom. May thy prayers and the prayers of the community at Herrnhut accompany me, and, I beg, may thy letters follow me, as I return to Georgia. Pray God on my behalf that I may be willing to be free, that I may thirst for Him alone, that I may fulfil my ministry . . .

Source: Quoted in John Wesley, *Letters*, Vol. I, pp. 227–8.

latter's journal for Monday 20 February 1738 contains the single entry, 'I began teaching Peter Böhler English.' This man was to make a dramatic impact upon both Charles and his brother John.

Peter Böhler was a 25-year-old Moravian pastor who had come to London on his way to Georgia. Thomas Jackson describes him as 'a young man of deep and enlightened piety, and of sound learning',[26] and both were certainly true. Interestingly, for one who had taught theology in the University of Jena, Böhler had the gift of being able to preach and teach in a simple and straightforward way. Like Spangenberg and Zinzendorf, he was not afraid to speak very directly, when the occasion demanded. Shortly after Böhler first met Charles, he paid a visit when Charles was ill. Whilst not quite being a hypochondriac in the modern sense of the word,[27] Charles – as we have seen – did not enjoy the best of health, and tended to feel rather sorry for himself when unwell. This time, however, it was pleurisy, and he was seriously ill.

---

36. Fri., February 24th. At six in the evening, an hour after I had taken my electuary, the toothache returned more violently than ever. I smoked tobacco; which set me a-vomiting, and took away my senses and pain altogether. At eleven I waked in extreme pain, which I thought would quickly separate soul and body. Soon after Peter Böhler came to my bedside. I asked him to pray for me. He seemed unwilling at first, but, beginning very faintly, he raised his voice by degrees, and prayed for my recovery with strange confidence. Then he took me by the hand, and calmly said, 'You will not die now.' I thought within myself, 'I cannot hold out in this pain until morning. If it abates before, I believe I may recover.' He asked me, 'Do you hope to be saved?' 'Yes.' 'For what reason do you hope it?' 'Because I have used my best endeavours to serve God.' He shook his head, and said no more. I thought him very uncharitable, saying in my heart, 'What, are not my endeavours a sufficient ground of hope? Would he rob me of my endeavours? I have nothing else to trust to.' . . .

Source: T. Jackson (ed.), *The Journal of The Rev. Charles Wesley, M.A.*, London, John Mason 1849, Vol. I, p. 82.

The extract is a record of their conversation, and makes interesting reading. [36]

The picture of this young Moravian questioning an ordained minister of the Church of England as to whether or not he believed himself to be saved, is one which might strike us as being rather incongruous. Yet Böhler clearly felt that Charles' greatest need at that moment was spiritual, despite (or, perhaps, resulting in) the severity of his sickness. The excerpt also throws further light on Charles' perception of the way to salvation. There is no reason to suppose that he was unaware of the simple requirement of faith: it was simply that he saw faith in terms of being *faithful*, in the sense of being his 'best endeavours to serve God'.

Charles' Pentecost – 21 May 1738

Long my imprisoned spirit lay
Fast bound in sin and nature's night;
Thine eye diffused a quickening ray –
I woke, the dungeon flamed with light;
My chains fell off, my heart was free,
I rose, went forth, and followed thee.

Charles' health gradually improved during the following weeks, but his illness made him realize the folly of returning to Georgia and on 3 April he wrote to General Oglethorpe confirming his decision to resign as Secretary. Towards the end of April Charles was at Blendon with the Delamottes, where they were joined by John. A heated discussion took place which showed that the two brothers could disagree quite sharply, even though John could usually hold sway in an argument! [37]

Later that month, while staying briefly with his old friend James Hutton, his fever returned. Again, Peter Böhler was at hand. Charles wrote afterwards in his journal:

I immediately thought it might be that I should again consider Böhler's doctrine of faith; examine myself whether I was in the faith; and if I was not,

> 37. Tues., April 25th. Soon after five, as we were met in our little chapel, Mrs. Delamotte came to us. We sang, and fell into a dispute whether conversion was gradual or instantaneous. My brother was very positive for the latter, and very shocking; mentioned some late instances of gross sinners believing in a moment. I was much offended at his worse than unedifying discourse. Mrs. Delamotte left us abruptly. I stayed, and insisted, a man need not know when first he had faith. His obstinacy in favouring the contrary opinion drove me at last out of the room . . .
>
> *Source*: T. Jackson (ed.), *The Journal of The Rev. Charles Wesley, M.A.,* London, John Mason 1849, Vol. I, p. 82.

never cease seeking and longing after it, till I attained it.[28]

As in the past, the sacrament of Holy Communion helped meet Charles' needs, and though he was convinced of his lack of faith and felt no assurance of pardon, was able to affirm 'a small anticipation of peace'.[29]

The actual circumstances surrounding Charles' 'conversion' are less well known than John's experience at Aldersgate, but make just as interesting a story. On 11 May, still far from well, he moved from James Hutton's home where he had been staying, to the home of a Mr Bray, above a shop in Little Britain. Charles was carried to his house in a chair; he found Bray's sister 'in earnest pursuit of Christ' and his wife 'well inclined to conversion'. Charles described Bray himself as 'a poor ignorant mechanic, who knows nothing but Christ; yet by knowing him, knows and discerns all things'.[30] It was this godly family who were, in Wesley's words, 'now to supply Böhler's place'.

The next week saw Charles continuing to fluctuate between moments of elation and even greater despondency. Examples from his journal graphically illustrate the painful nature of his search for assurance. On 12 May he found himself 'hungry and thirsty after God' and, on reading from Isaiah,

'encouraged to pursue the glorious prize held out to us by the evangelical Prophet'. The following day he 'waked without Christ; yet still desirous of finding him', and the next morning, 'very heavy, weary, and unable to pray'.[31]

Coincidentally, John and Charles found the writings of Martin Luther a source of inspiration. John was moved by the preface of Luther's commentary on Paul's Epistle to the Romans; Charles, by his preface to the Galatians, which he began reading on 17 May. [38] In this passage Luther drew a distinction between two kinds of righteousness: active and passive. He maintained that the former – which is associated with 'works' – is necessary, but must always be a *consequence* of the latter. 'Active righteousness', Luther asserted, is a divine gift, 'which we have not of ourselves, but receive it from heaven; which we work not, but which by grace is wrought in us, and apprehended by faith, whereby we mount up above all law and works'.[32] Luther went on to explain that the result of this is that for

> 38. Wed., May 17th. I experienced the power of Christ rescuing me in temptation. To-day I first saw Luther on the Galatians, which Mr Holland[33] had accidentally lit upon. We began, and found him nobly full of faith. My friend, in hearing him, was so affected, as to breathe out sighs and groans unutterable. I marvelled that we were so soon and so entirely removed from Him that called us into the grace of Christ, unto another Gospel. Who would believe our Church had been founded on this important article of justification by faith alone? I am astonished I should ever think this a new doctrine . . .
>
> From this time I endeavoured to ground as many of our friends as came in this fundamental truth, salvation by faith alone, not an idle, dead faith, but a faith which works by love, and is necessarily productive of all good works and all holiness.
>
> *Source*: T. Jackson (ed.), *The Journal of The Rev. Charles Wesley, M.A.,* London, John Mason 1849, Vol. I, p. 88.

the individual 'there can be no anguish of conscience, no fear, no heaviness'.[34] It is easy to understand why these words made such a deep impression upon Charles' troubled mind.

It may seem to us that Charles was making very heavy weather of his journey, since the words 'marvelled' and 'astonished' give the impression of spiritual naivety. The clue to his mental processes at this time, however, is to be found in his use of the phrase 'necessarily productive'. Charles knew in his mind that the faith he sought produced 'all good works and all holiness', but until now he had been caught in a trap of his own making, in that he had persisted in attempting to create faith *by* the character of his lifestyle.

His torment was soon to end. He had to endure a final trial – the return of his pleurisy on Thursday 18 May – and was, at this point, probably as low as he had ever been in his life. On the Friday he failed to gain comfort from the sacrament of Holy Communion, but was encouraged by Mrs Turner, a friend of the Brays who had come to visit, who told him that he should not rise from that bed until he believed. Hearing her testimony, Charles wrote later that he felt 'an anticipation of joy upon her account', but Saturday saw him again 'much disappointed' and 'in great dejection, which the sacrament did not in the least abate'; even Mr Bray 'seemed troubled at my not yet believing'.[35] Nonetheless, when his kindly friend read to him from Matthew's Gospel (the first eight verses from Chapter 9 – the story of Jesus healing a paralytic) the sight of Bray's tears of joy lifted Charles' spirits: 'and I saw herein, and firmly believed, that his faith would be available for the healing of me'.[36]

Final relief from misery, and the attainment of the peace for which he had so earnestly striven, came on Sunday 21 May 1738 – appropriately, the day of Pentecost. Let Charles tell how it happened in his own words. [39]

In fact, it was Mr Bray's sister, Mrs Turner, who spoke to Charles, having been convinced in a dream that Christ had appeared to her and ordered her to go to Wesley. Two days later he began to compose a

---

39.   THE DAY OF PENTECOST

Sun., May 21st, 1738. I waked in hope and expectation of His coming. At nine my brother and some friends came, and sang an hymn to the Holy Ghost. My comfort and hope were hereby increased. In about half-an-hour they went: I betook myself to prayer; the substance as follows:- 'O Jesus, thou hast said, "I will come unto you;" thou hast said, "I will send the Comforter unto you;" thou hast said, "My Father and I will come unto you, and make our abode with you." Thou art God who canst not lie; I wholly rely upon thy most true promise: accomplish it in thy time and manner.' Having said this, I was composing myself to sleep, in quietness and peace, when I heard one come in (Mrs. Musgrave,[37] I thought, by the voice) and say, 'In the name of Jesus of Nazareth, arise, and believe, and thou shalt be healed of all thy infirmities.' I wondered how it should enter into her head to speak in that manner. The words struck me to the heart. I sighed, and said within myself, '*Oh that Christ would but speak thus to me!*' ...

... I rose and looked into the Scripture. The words that first presented were, 'And now, Lord, what is my hope? Truly my hope is even in Thee.' I then cast down my eye, and met, 'He hath put a new song in my mouth, even a thanksgiving unto our God. Many shall see it, and fear, and shall put their trust in the Lord.' ...

... I now found myself at peace with God, and rejoiced in the hope of loving Christ. My temper for the rest of the day was, mistrust of my own great – but before unknown – weakness. I saw that by faith I stood; by the continual support of faith, which kept me from falling, though of myself I am ever sinking into sin. I went to bed still sensible of my own weakness (I humbly hope to be more and more so), yet confident of Christ's protection.

Source: T. Jackson (ed.), *The Journal of The Rev. Charles Wesley, M.A.*, London, John Mason 1849, Vol. I, pp. 90–2.

'hymn upon my conversion', though with a touch of the old despair added that he 'was persuaded to break off, for fear of pride'.[38] Dr Frank Baker writes that 'depression was still to dog his footsteps, for it was one of the predominant traits of his volatile temperament'.[39] The hymn was 'Where shall my wondering soul begin', though his later composition, 'Come O Thou Traveller unknown', is a far better description of the spiritual conflict through which he had passed.

When John heard 'the surprising news' that his brother 'had found rest to his soul',[40] he joined him in prayer, although John himself had 'continual sorrow and heaviness' in his heart.[41] He had not long to wait, and we turn now briefly to examine John's experience.

John Wesley's Experience at Aldersgate Street, 24 May 1738

> *My prayer hath power with God; the grace*
> *Unspeakable I now receive;*
> *Through faith I see thee face to face,*
> *I see thee face to face, and live!*
> *In vain I have not wept and strove:*
> *Thy nature and thy name is Love.*[42]

The story of John's spiritual progress in the months leading to May 1738 has been told in detail elsewhere,[43] and we need only note the brief details of the events here. Like Charles, he had learned a great deal from his experience in Georgia: the foundations of much of his later writing – the *Notes* on both Old and New Testaments, his sermons and the *Christian Library*, which he edited – were all developed in his Oxford and Georgia years. The rigours of colonial life and his own particular trials in Savannah had likewise forced him to modify his rigid outlook. He would always be methodical and disciplined, but future years would see him become more adaptable and perhaps more understanding of human nature – though never quite in the sense that Charles was. Above all, John 'had had some of his most deeply seated notions concerning the nature of faith and salvation challenged'.[44]

John, too, had renewed his acquaintance with the Moravians and was also greatly influenced by Peter Böhler, who urged him to commit himself to finding personal rather than philosophical solutions to his spiritual problems, in order to find the true peace of mind for which he longed. He also convinced John that instantaneous conversion was possible and, indeed, had plenty of biblical precedent. Despite John's reservations, Böhler encouraged him to continue preaching, saying to him in words that have since become immortalized, 'Preach faith till you have it; and then, because you have it, you will preach faith.'[45]

On Wednesday 24 May, John, still in a very low state, went to St Paul's but the anthem, 'Out of the deep have I called unto Thee, O Lord', failed to lift him. He found peace of mind that evening, however, when he visited a small group of Moravians who were holding a meeting in Aldersgate Street. John described his experience in words that have become familiar to Methodists throughout the world, and which have been inscribed on a bronze memorial in the shape of a flame which has been erected near the original site. [40]

Analysis

> *Lord, in the strength of grace,*
> *With a glad heart and free,*
> *Myself, my residue of days,*
> *I consecrate to thee.*
>
> *Thy ransomed servant, I*
> *Restore to thee thy own;*
> *And, from this moment, live or die*
> *To serve my God alone.*

The exact nature of what happened to Charles and John Wesley in May 1738 has been the subject of considerable debate over the years, and it is important to spend a moment reflecting on the nature of their 'conversion' experience. What did it mean for Charles?

The comments which Dr John Newton has made,

40. In the evening I went very unwillingly to a society in Aldersgate Street, where one was reading Luther's preface to the Epistle to the Romans.[46] About a quarter before nine, while he was describing the change which God works in the heart through faith in Christ, I felt my heart strangely warmed. I felt I did trust in Christ, Christ alone, for salvation; and an assurance was given me, that He had taken away my sins, even mine, and saved me from the law of sin and death.

I began to pray with all my might for those who had in a more especial manner despitefully used me and persecuted me. I then testified openly to all there, what I now first felt in my heart. But it was not long before the enemy suggested, 'This cannot be faith; for where is thy joy?' Then was I taught, that peace and victory over sin are essential to faith in the Captain of our salvation; but that, as to the transports of joy that usually attend the beginning of it, especially in those who have mourned deeply, God sometimes giveth, sometimes withholdeth them, according to the counsels of His own will.

After my return home, I was much buffeted with temptations; but cried out, and they fled away. They returned again and again. I as often lifted up my eyes, and He 'sent me help from His holy place.' And herein I found the difference between this and my former state chiefly consisted. I was striving, yea, fighting with all my might under the law, as well as under grace. But then I was sometimes, if not often, conquered; now I was always conqueror.

Source: John Wesley, *Journal*, Wednesday 24 May 1738.

quoted by the author in *The Making of Methodism* relating to John, can be applied almost equally to Charles:

Until now we have used the word 'conversion' in inverted commas to describe what happened to the Wesley brothers in May 1738. But what was he converted from, and what was he converted to? He certainly wasn't converted from a pagan to a Christian. Nor was he converted from a nominal, 'almost' Christian to a committed one. Even less

was he converted from an Anglican to a Methodist! We should remember that throughout his early years, John's will was entirely devoted to serving God in every part of his life.[47]

It is true that Charles uses the word 'conversion' without the modern tendency to employ inverted commas to indicate some degree of qualification. But since nowhere did he feel the need to record a detailed definition of the word, we may conclude that he assumed anyone reading his journal would understand what he meant. The references which he makes to 'faith', 'new birth', 'the inward change' and being made into 'a new creature' that have been noted earlier in this chapter, all suggest that he thought of conversion as something fairly radical. But if it was not from unbelief to belief, or from being a nominal Christian to a fully committed one, in what sense did he mean it?

Problems have sometimes arisen because Christians have tended to apply contemporary meanings to the word 'conversion' which simply did not exist in the eighteenth century. Readers will be aware that different branches of the Christian Church tend to see the word in different senses. Some will see the process in classic evangelical terms, i.e. as a relatively sharp transition from salvation by works to salvation by faith. Others, who hold what one might call a 'Catholic' view,[48] regard this definition as being too limited in scope.

Among the former, historians such as Arnold Dallimore have tended to use the term 'conversion' in a literal, unqualified sense which leaves many questions begging.[49] If Charles and John had something akin to a Pauline experience, then did this not devalue much of what had gone before? Canon Overton, studying the Wesleys from an Anglican perspective, wrote, 'if John Wesley was not a Christian in Georgia God help millions of those who profess and call themselves Christians'.[50] The problem with laying too sharp a distinction between Charles' spiritual state before and after 21 May 1738 – likewise with John – is that it gives the impression that both their 'conversions' were instantaneous, which ignores the testimony of the brothers themselves.

Even after 21 May, Charles' journal and surviving letters bear witness to continued doubt and periods of spiritual depression. Only three days later, he was writing, 'I was assaulted by the fear of my old accustomed deadness', though he added, 'but soon recovered my confidence in Christ'.[51] On Thursday 1 June his journal entry read, 'I was troubled to-day, that I could not pray, being utterly dead at the sacrament'; the next day, 'I was still unable to pray; still dead in communicating'; and on Saturday, 'I rose exceeding heavy and averse to prayer . . . and I could not help asking myself, "Where is the difference between what I am now, and what I was before believing?"'[52] It is clear that Charles was more susceptible than most to rapid mood-swings, though 'underlying the choppy surface of his Christian experience were the calm deeps of his new certainty of God's love for him'.[53] As late as 1760, however, when writing to his wife, a note of uncertainty still remained as to what had happened so many years before. [41]

---

41.   Whitsunday, 1760. Westminster.

MY DEAREST SALLY,
This I once called the anniversary of my conversion. Just twenty-two years ago I thought I received the first grain of faith. But what does that avail me, if I have not the Spirit now? I account that the longsuffering of the Lord is salvation; and would fain believe, He has reserved me so long for good, and not for evil.

Source: Frank Baker, *Charles Wesley as Revealed by His Letters*, Epworth Press 1948, p. 33.

The other main school of thought is represented by such scholars as Maximin Piette in his *John Wesley and the Evolution of Protestantism*, which appeared in 1937. It was he who first coined the phrase 'moral conversion' in applying it to John in 1725, and he went on to describe the latter's experience at Aldersgate Street in 1738 as nothing more than a sudden wave of emotion which set his life on a slightly different course. Unfortunately, in order to strengthen his argument, Piette tried to show that Aldersgate Street was about John Wesley simply being awakened from sin and becoming aware of the power of forgiveness, when all the evidence suggests the opposite, in that 'he had the makings of a first-class pharisee'.[54]

The discussion continues, and Methodists and non-Methodists alike will always share differing viewpoints as to the nature of conversion as a religious experience.

This is not to say that there were no debates in Charles' day. We recall that he and his brother were in sharp disagreement as to what precisely was meant by instantaneous conversion.[55] Even John, who made remarkably little reference to his Aldersgate experience in subsequent writings, seemed to feel that he had over-emphasized his lack of faith prior to that year. His journal entry for 29 January 1738 had contained the following comment:

> It is now two years and almost four months since I left my native country, in order to teach the Georgian Indians the nature of Christianity: but what have I learned myself in the meantime? Why (what I the least of all suspected), that I who went to America to convert others, was never myself converted to God . . .*
> * I am not sure of this.[56]

The footnote at the end of this extract looks curious but is highly significant. John Wesley added it later, no doubt feeling that this judgement of himself at the time had been somewhat exaggerated. Indeed, both John and Charles tended to write about their own spiritual state in extreme terms. Robert Tuttle, who wrote a very imaginative biography of John, speaks of the year 1725 – when he resolved to give his whole life to God and was ordained deacon – as marking his 'religious conversion', as opposed to his 'evangelical conversion' thirteen years later.

Over the years both brothers were to change their views on many issues regarding faith, and even though Charles could not totally free himself from doubt and introspection after 1738, he was in no doubt that what he had experienced at Bray's house was a deep and lasting experience – as so many hymns were to testify. *He* felt that he had been 'converted', though whether it was a theological or a psychological change is very much open to question!

It may be helpful here to consider some of the correspondence between Charles and his mother in the months following Pentecost 1738, because Susanna's comments shed some contemporary light on this subject. Susanna wrote to Charles in October of that year saying, ''Tis with much pleasure I find your mind is somewhat easier than formerly, and heartily thank God for it . . . blessed be God which gave you those convictions of the evil of sin as contrary to the purity of the divine nature and the most perfect goodness of His laws.'[57] However, no doubt sharing some of her eldest son Samuel's reservations about the Methodist Revival, she was at pains to point out to Charles that some of his language was excessive and misleading. 'I would gladly know what your notion is of justifying faith,' she asked, 'because you speak of it as a thing you have but lately obtained.'[58] She wrote to him again in December, this time focusing more sharply on the question of conversion. [42]

The argument Susanna used may help resolve some of the present-day differences of opinion which continue to exist. The point she was making to Charles was that, rather than being devoid of faith before 1738, his spiritual crisis in May had enabled him to appropriate the grace of God that was already present in his life. We would say today that, for Charles, the 'penny dropped'.

From henceforth, like his brother, he was able to combine personal holiness with personal faith, and no longer feel himself quite such a slave to duty. Perhaps the truth was that he was *being* converted, and that what happened on 21 May 1738 was that he was given an inward realization and an assurance that he was loved and accepted by God. He had surely been a Christian before 1738, but from now on, with peace and joy in his heart, he was a happier one.

---

42.   Dec: 6th 1738

Dear Charles,

I should write much oft'ner had I better health and should be very glad if you received as much benefit from my letters as I do comfort from yours.

My notion of justifying faith is the same with yours, for that trusting in Jesus Christ or the promises made in him is that special act of faith to which our justification or acceptance is so frequently ascribed in the gospel . . .

I do not judge it necessary for us to know the precise time of our conversion. 'Tis sufficient if we have a reasonable hope that we are passed from death to life by the fruits of the Holy Spirit wrought in our hearts. Such are repentance, faith, hope, love, etc. Our Lord acts in various ways and by various means on different tempers, nor is the work of regeneration begun and perfected at once . . .

I think you are fallen into an odd way of thinking. You say that till within a few months you had no spiritual life nor any justifying faith. Now this is as if a man should affirm he was not alive in his infancy, because, when an infant he did not know he was alive. A strange way of arguing, this! Do you not consider that there's some analogy in spiritual to natural life? A man must first be born and then pass through the several stages of infancy, childhood, and youth, before he attain to maturity . . . spiritual strength is the work of time, as well as of God's Holy Spirit. All then that I can gather from your letter is that till a little while ago you were not so well satisfied of your being a Christian as you are now. I heartily rejoice that you have now attained to a strong and lively hope in God's mercy through Christ. Not that I can think you were totally without saving faith before, but then 'tis one thing to have faith and another thing to be sensible we have it.

Source: Charles Wallace (ed.), *Susanna Wesley: The Complete Writings*, Oxford University Press 1997, pp. 175–7.

Chronology

1736	December	Charles Wesley back in England
1737	January	Meets with the Georgia trustees
	June	Death of Matthew Wesley
	August	Conversations with William Law
	October	Meets with George Whitefield
	December	John leaves Savannah
1738	February	John arrives back in England; he and Charles meet Peter Böhler
		Charles contracts pleurisy
	3 April	Resigns as Oglethorpe's secretary
	11 May	Lodges with the Brays
	21 May	Charles' 'conversion' experience
	24 May	John at Aldersgate Street

For Discussion

1. Is there any particular aspect of Charles' spiritual struggle with which you identify?

2. What has been your experience of 'conversion'?

3. Who have been the most significant people in helping you grow as a Christian?

5

Marriage and Family

Ev'n now we think and speak the same,
  And cordially agree;
Concentred all, through Jesu's name,
  In perfect harmony.

We all partake the joy of one,
  The common peace we feel,
A peace to sensual minds unknown,
  A joy unspeakable.

And if our fellowship below
  In Jesus be so sweet,
What heights of rapture shall we know
  When round his throne we meet!

Before moving on to examine Charles Wesley's contribution to the growth and development of Methodism, we turn to more domestic matters. This chapter continues the story of his relationship with the other members of the family and introduces Sarah Gwynne, whom he married in 1749.

We have seen in previous chapters that the Wesleys were a close-knit family. Charles had inherited much of his father's emotional makeup and there can be no doubting the esteem with which he regarded Samuel, whom he addressed as 'honoured sir' even when an adult. Samuel died when Charles was twenty-seven years old, and what can be said about Charles' relationship with his father can, in the main, only be inferred from the little evidence which remains.[1]

Susanna Wesley

Me, if thy grace vouchsafe to use,
  Meanest of all thy creatures, me:
The deed, the time, the manner choose,
  Let all my fruit be found of thee;
Let all my works in thee be wrought,
By thee to full salvation brought.

Rather more of the correspondence between Charles and his mother has survived, however. Although in many ways she was closer to her two elder sons, Susanna continued to take a lively interest in Charles' spiritual development.[2] This was particularly true of the period following Samuel Jr's death in 1739, as can be seen from the letter she wrote to Charles in December of that year. [43] Susanna realized that Charles and John could only visit her for relatively short periods but she kept in close contact with them both, needing their support and reassurance as much as – she believed – they needed hers.

By the end of 1739 she had moved to the Foundery at Moorfields, in London. This building, which had become derelict following an explosion in 1716, was bought by John for £115 and converted into a preaching house, with adjoining rooms fitted out for various other purposes, including a dispensary, a day school, an almshouse and accommodation for himself and visiting preachers.[3] There is every reason to suppose that Susanna's last years at the Foundery, where she lived in relative comfort, were happy ones, despite increasing frailty.

---

43. Thurs: Dec: 27, [1]739

My dear Charles,

You cannot more desire to see me than I do to see you. Indeed, your brother (whom henceforward I shall call Son Wesley; since my dear Sam is gone home) hath done more, I think, than could be expected to supply temporal wants . . . yet that was not the principal thing I desired. I am in a state of great temptation and want to talk with you about many things. I need your direction and instruction how to act in the present situation, particularly in relation to a very disagreeable companion . . . Other matters I would speak with you about concerning my worldly affairs, but these are of comparatively little moment . . . My dear Son Wesley hath just been with me and much revived my spirits . . . but his visits are seldom and short . . .

But, my dear Charles, still I want either him or you, for indeed in the most literal sense I am become a little child and want continual succour . . .

I hope we shall shortly speak face to face, and I shall then, if God permit, impart my thoughts more fully. But then, alas, when you come, your brother leaves me. Yet that is the will of God, in whose blessed service ye are engaged, who hath hitherto blessed your labours and preserved your persons. That he may continue so to prosper your work and protect ye both from evil – and give ye strength and courage to preach the true gospel in opposition to the united powers of evil men and angels, is the hearty prayer of,

my dear Charles,

thy loving mother, SW.

I wish you a happy year – and many, very many such.

Source: Charles Wallace (ed.), *Susanna Wesley: The Complete Writings*, Oxford University Press 1997, pp. 180–1.

We have seen in the previous chapter that the letters Susanna exchanged with Charles after May 1738 played an important part in the way his thinking on Christian perfection evolved. In October 1740 she gently chided him for letting his tendency towards self-effacement run away with him, [44] the extract from this letter showing that she believed it possible for a Christian to combine modesty with a genuine confidence in God's saving grace.

A further letter dated 28 April 1741, which has only recently been recovered and which is too long to reproduce here, also made a great impact upon Charles. We shall be returning to the development of Charles' theological views in a later chapter, suffice it to note at this point that Susanna expressed very strong opinions which clearly influenced Charles' thinking. In this particular letter she urged him to be aware of the dangers of the quietism[4] of the 'little Moravian foxes', who she felt encouraged people to neglect the importance of practical goodness in Christian living, and also of the teachings of George

---

44. Foundry, London, October 2nd, 1740

Dear Charles,

I do heartily join with you in giving God thanks for your recovery. He hath many wise reasons for every event of providence, far above our apprehension, and I doubt not but his having restored you to some measure of health again will answer many ends which as yet you are ignorant of . . .

You ask many questions which I care not to answer; but I refer you to our dear Lord, who will satisfy you in all things necessary for you to know. I cannot conceive why you affirm yourself to be not Christian; which is, in effect, to tell Christ to his face that you have nothing to thank him for, since you are not the better for anything he hath yet done or suffered for you. Oh, what a great dishonour, what wondrous ingratitude, is this to the ever-blessed Jesus! I think myself far from being so good a Christian as you are, or as I ought to be; but God forbid that I should renounce the little Christianity I have: nay, rather let me grow in grace and in the knowledge of our Lord and saviour Jesus Christ. Amen.

Source: Charles Wallace (ed.), *Susanna Wesley: The Complete Writings*, Oxford University Press 1997, pp. 185–6.

Whitefield, with whom both Charles and John were to part company. However, she concluded this, her last surviving letter to Charles, by saying,

'. . . but now I see the power of our Lord so plainly manifested in your brother and consider that his God and Saviour is yours also, my fears are at an end, and I need not desire you to join hand and heart with your brother in vindicating the glory and honour of our blessed Redeemer! Proclaim his universal love and free grace to all men . . . I send thee my love and blessing.'[5]

We can safely say, therefore, that Susanna's earlier doubts, concerning the path that Charles and John were now following, had been dissipated.

Susanna was not to survive her move to the Foundery for very long. Charles was out of London during her last illness and unfortunately there is a gap in his journal from 22 September 1741 to 2 January 1743, so we have no record of his reactions to her death in July 1742.[6] All her daughters were present when she died. Susanna was buried in Bunhill Fields Cemetery, opposite what is now Wesley's Chapel in City Road, and Charles composed some verses which were engraved upon her tombstone. They were, in truth, a poor reflection on his gifts as a poet. The second of the four verses is particularly puzzling:

> True daughter of affliction she,
> Enured to pain and misery,
> Mourn'd a long night of griefs and fears,
> A legal night of seventy years.

The last line has been variously interpreted, some writers having suggested that Charles' use of the word 'legal' was meant as a comment on her spiritual journey. This may well be another example of Charles' use of extreme language to which, as we have seen, he was prone. It is also possible that Charles was referring – albeit rather clumsily – to his mother's high sense of duty, rather than to her having a legalistic faith. On the other hand, it has also

been suggested that the term simply refers to the scriptural (thus 'legal') declaration of a human life being 'three score years and ten'. However, to say, as some have done, that until she was quite elderly she 'had remained in darkness' is an unfair judgement,[7] and a study of her writings gives quite a different picture. Fiercely independent she might be, with a strength of character that bordered upon inflexibility at times, but there can be no doubting the purity and depth of Susanna's faith and trust in the grace of God.

Samuel Wesley Jr

During his years at Westminster, Samuel Jr became a surrogate foster-father to Charles, and we have already noted how his influence remained strong until his sudden death in November 1739. Samuel, however, did not share his mother's growing approval of his brothers' activities. On 4 July 1738 Charles received a letter from Samuel 'full of heavy charges',[8] and in one of the last letters he wrote to his mother (in October 1739), Samuel gave vent to his feelings of dismay at the direction in which John and Charles were going. [45]

One cannot help but be sympathetic with Samuel's position. Living at a distance from London, much of the information concerning John and Charles came from letters penned by a friend of the two younger Wesleys – a Mrs Hutton, with whom they were lodging in the period immediately following their return from Georgia. Mrs Hutton was naturally disturbed by what she perceived as their lapse into 'enthusiasm', and wrote to that effect to their elder brother. Samuel could not be expected to have understood the new direction John's and Charles' lives had taken, and was highly critical of their response to his letters of warning and disapproval.

Had he lived, Samuel might have become completely alienated from John, though it has been suggested that in the final weeks of his life he had become a little more reconciled to what his two brothers were doing. One can only speculate as

45. John and Charles are now become so notorious the world will be curious to know when and how they were born, what schools bred at, what Colleges in Oxford and when matriculated; what degrees they took, and where and when and by whom ordained; what books they have written or published. I wish they may spare so much time as to vouchsafe a little of their story. For my own part I had much rather have them picking straw within the walls, than preaching in the area of Moorfields.

It was with exceeding concern and grief I heard you had countenanced a spreading delusion, so far as to be one of Jack's congregation. It is not enough that I am bereft of both my brothers, but must my mother follow too? I earnestly beseech the Almighty to preserve you from joining a schism at the close of your life, as you were unfortunately engaged in one at the beginning of it. It will cost you many a protest, should you retain your integrity, as I hope to God you will. They boast of you already as a disciple . . .

Source: Maldwyn Edwards, *Family Circle*, Epworth Press 1949, pp. 79–80.

to how his relationship with Charles would have developed, since Charles – as we shall see in later chapters – shared many of Samuel's misgivings about the position of Methodism with regard to the Church of England. It is interesting to note that, at this point in their careers, John and Charles were clearly bracketed together in their elder brother's opinion.

Charles' Sisters

O *what a blessed hope is ours,*
  While here on earth we stay,
We more than taste the heavenly powers,
  And antedate that day:
We feel the resurrection near,
  Our life in Christ concealed,
And with his glorious presence here
  Our earthen vessels filled.

Space precludes us from making more than a brief mention of Charles' sisters, whose story in most cases makes fascinating but tragic reading. The dates of their births and deaths can be found in the Appendix, but many of these are only approximations.

Emilia ('Emily'), the eldest of Samuel and Susanna's daughters, does not, as far as we can tell, receive any mention in Charles' writings. She became virtually a second mother to the children – especially John and Charles – but later on, mainly because of family finances, went to work as a teacher in a private boarding school, though she always remained very close to John. Emily's thrifty nature enabled her to open her own private school in Gainsborough, Lincolnshire, and thus to help the family out financially. She was over forty years of age when she finally married, but it was an unhappy match. Her husband, a local chemist in Epworth by the name of Robert Harper, spent all her capital and then disappeared to America, leaving Emily and their very sick baby Tetty behind. The baby died shortly afterwards and in 1740 Emily left Epworth to join John in his new headquarters in London, where she worked with him until she died at the age of 79.

Susanna (who was known affectionately as 'Sukey' by her family) was sent to London to stay with her uncle following the rectory fire and thereupon decided to follow an independent path, in spite of long, appealing letters from her mother. She married a wealthy farmer named Richard Ellison, whom her mother described as a 'coarse, vulgar, immoral man', and who had few redeeming features. After years of abuse, Sukey left him but never really recovered from her ill-treatment at his hands. Ellison actually seems to have repented in his final years, and took to attending services of worship at the Foundery. Charles Wesley conducted his funeral service and, in a letter to his (own) wife in April 1760, wrote movingly of the occasion. [46]

Mary ('Molly'), the third Wesley daughter to survive infancy, was a tragic child in many ways. She was born with a disability which impaired her walking, but developed into a delightful girl with a lovely, gentle personality aptly summed up by Charles'

46. Yesterday evening I buried my brother Ellison. S[ister] Macdonald, whom he was always very fond of, prayed by him, in his last moments. He told her he was not afraid to die, and believed God for Christ's sake had forgiven him. I felt a most solemn awe overwhelming me, while I committed his body to the earth. He is gone to increase my father's joy in paradise; who often said, every one of his children would be saved, for God had given them all to his prayer. God grant I may not be the single exception!

Source: T. Jackson (ed.), *The Journal of The Rev. Charles Wesley, M.A.,* London, John Mason 1849, Vol. II, pp. 232–3.

endearing reference to her as a 'Patient Grizzle'.[9] Her marriage to John Whitelamb, her father's curate, was blissfully happy, but after just one year of marriage, whilst giving birth to her first baby, Molly died at the age of 38 years.

Mehetabel ('Hetty') was perhaps the most gifted of all the Wesley children. A very attractive child, she was also very bright indeed, and by the time she was eight years old, could read the whole New Testament in Greek! In her late teens and early twenties, she was surrounded by young suitors, but her disapproving father acquired a job for her as a governess at Louth in Lincolnshire. While she was there, she met a young lawyer, named William Atkins. Atkins had a respectable family background and, after a whirlwind romance, asked Samuel for his daughter's hand in marriage. Samuel's point-blank refusal, despite Hetty's tears, led to an elopement, but Atkins abandoned her and the now pregnant (but unmarried) Hetty went back home to her parents. Her father was furious and unforgiving, and banned her from his sight and home, with the result that Hetty vowed to marry the next man she met, who happened to be the local plumber and glazier, William Wright. Then four months later she bore her first child which, sadly, died within a year. Wright proved to be a drunk and a lout and, like Sukey's husband, abused her physically. Nevertheless, she was determined to remain faithful and had three children by

him, all of whom died in early infancy and Hetty always maintained that this was caused by the lead fumes from her husband's workshop which was part of the house.

Samuel maintained his rejection of Hetty for the rest of his days, forbidding any of the family to have contact with her. She was completely crushed by this separation and by her tragic experiences and was to die at the age of fifty-three in 1750. Whereas John complied with his father's strictures concerning Hetty, Charles stood by her, as he was especially fond of his sister. Shortly after arriving at Oxford for his university studies, Charles wrote a long letter to his brother John, to which we have already referred in Chapter 1. In another part of this letter he mentioned Hetty, and there can be no doubting the bond which existed between them. [47]

Indeed, Charles makes numerous references in his journal to visits which he paid to Hetty and William, and his magnanimity is clearly shown by the attention he gave to William after Hetty's death. Evidence suggests that Hetty's melancholy did eventually ease slightly. Even though her health deteriorated in the last seven or eight years of her life, she found consolation both in her faith and in her growing allegiance to Methodism, being a regular worshipper

47. One sister I parted from with great regret . . . Poor Sister Hetty! It grieves me almost to think how exceedingly kindly she treated me, who am seldom so happy as to meet with bare humanity from others. 'Tis a shocking comparison! 'twas but a week before I left London that I knew she was at it. Little of that time, you may be sure, did I lose, being with her almost continually. I could almost envy myself the deal of pleasure I had crowded within that small space. In a little neat room she has hired did the good-natured, ingenious, contented wretch and I talk over a few short days which we both wished had been longer. As yet she lives pretty well, having but herself and honest Will [Wright] to keep, though I fancy there's another a-coming.

Source: Frank Baker, *Charles Wesley as Revealed by His Letters*, Epworth Press 1948, p. 8.

at the Foundery. In her final weeks Charles was often with this 'gracious, tender, trembling soul; a bruised reed, which the Lord will not break'.[10] On the day she died he wrote that he had had 'sweet fellowship with her', and on 26 March 'followed her to her quiet grave, and wept with them that wept'.[11] Only Charles, out of all her brothers and sisters, was present.

Anne, who was born in 1701 and known in the family as 'Nancy', married John Lambert, a land surveyor, and lived happily in Hatfield. Little evidence survives concerning them, though the couple were often visited by John and Charles during their travels. Charles took a particular interest in his brother-in-law, who at one stage took to drink under the influence of a friend. He noted in his journal in December 1738, 'this evening, my brothers Lambert and Wright visited me. The latter had corrupted the former, after all the pains I have taken with him, and brought him back to drinking'.[12] Whether Lambert ever changed his drinking habits is not known, but he and Nancy seem to have had a relatively happy life together, and Nancy – though never taking Charles' earnest attempts at counselling seriously – nevertheless paid several visits to the Foundery, notably in 1741 when John was ill, and she was there at her mother's bedside in the summer of the following year.

Martha, usually called 'Patty', was very like her elder brother John in both appearance and personality. Even her handwriting was almost identical to his, and she was closer to him than Charles, even though the latter was only a year younger. It is said that Patty had virtually no sense of humour, which helps to explain Charles' description of her as a 'Grumbletonial', even though she was barely twenty-one.[13] Despite this, Patty was never short of male friends (including Benjamin Ingham), but became secretly engaged to Westley Hall, whom John had taught at Oxford. Hall, however, was completely devoid of principle, and, whilst betrothed to Patty, made secret advances to her youngest sister Kezzy. He and Patty were married in 1735 and Patty had ten pregnancies, but only one child survived – a boy, who caught chickenpox when he was fourteen and died. Charles composed a number of verses on the tragic death of his nephew, of whom he was particularly fond, and the tenth stanza leaves no doubt as to Charles' feelings about the boy's father:

> Thy God forbade the son to bear
> The father's wickedness below;
> And, O! thou canst not suffer there
> His foul reproach, his guilty woe;
> His fearful doom thou canst not feel,
> Or fall, like him, from heaven to hell.[14]

Westley Hall continued his affairs and finally left Patty for another woman and departed for the West Indies. Patty was a proud and courageous woman and carried on, becoming a great friend of Sally, Charles Wesley's wife. She outlived all the family, dying just four months after her dear brother John, when she was eighty-five years old. She was buried with him in the same vault, behind what is now Wesley's Chapel in City Road, London.

Kezziah was the youngest of all the children, and was referred to generally as 'Kezzy'.[15] She was the only one never to marry, although she did become involved, as we have seen, with Westley Hall.[16] Kezzy's short life was dogged by ill-health, though she lived contentedly for a number of years at the home of the vicar of Bexley in Kent, dying at the relatively young age of thirty-two. A lively, independent soul, Kezzy became particularly devoted to her brother Charles, who was only just over a year older than her. When he was ill with pleurisy in February 1738, Charles expressed his gratitude for the ministrations of his sister, 'who has been with me from the beginning, and no small comfort to me'.[17] Of course, they did not always see eye to eye, and Charles strongly disapproved of her habit of taking snuff!

Kezzy seems to have gone through a crisis in her own journey of faith. Charles mentions in his journal that he gave her spiritual counsel on a number of occasions. In September 1737 – well before his own experience of May the following year – he called on

48. Calling accidentally in the evening at my sister Kezia's room, she fell upon my neck, and in a flood of tears begged me to pray for her. Seeing her so softened, I did not know but this might be her time, and sat down. She anticipated me, by saying she had felt here what she never felt before, and believed now there was such a thing as the new creature. She was full of earnest wishes for divine love; owned there was a depth in religion she had never fathomed; that she was not, but longed to be, converted; would give up all to obtain the love of God: renewed her request with great vehemence that I should pray for her; often repeating, 'I am weak, I am exceeding weak.' I prayed over her, and blessed God from my heart.

Source: T. Jackson (ed.), *The Journal of The Rev. Charles Wesley, M.A.*, London, John Mason 1849, Vol. I, p. 75.

her and found her very receptive to his guidance, as can be seen from the extract above. [48] On this particular occasion he read to her from William Law's works, and she asked him to write out Pascal's *Prayer for Conversion* which he prayed with her. A year and a half later, we find Charles still offering her spiritual advice and on 8 November 1738 he recorded that, at the end of their conversation, 'she burst into tears, fell on my neck, and melted me into fervent prayer for her'.[18]

John Wesley makes only one reference to Kezzy's death in his writings, mistakenly blaming her physical decline on Westley Hall. Charles' journal has a frustrating gap between December 1740 and April 1741, but it is likely that he was with her when she died (probably on 9 March), when 'she commended her spirit into the hands of Jesus and fell asleep'.[19]

Charles Wesley and Sally Gwynne

Two are better far than one,
For counsel or for fight!
How can one be warm alone
Or serve his God aright?

Join we then our hearts and hands;
Haste, my sister, dearest friend,
Run the way of His commands,
And keep them to the end![20]

Charles' courtship and marriage is altogether a more happy story. Whilst in Georgia, General Oglethorpe had recommended that Charles marry, suggesting that it would not only suit his temperament but actually enable him to find spiritual peace of mind more easily. Until 1747 he had not formed any significant relationships – the brief infatuation with Molly Buchanan as an undergraduate cannot be classed as such – and he was entirely innocent of any alleged impropriety whilst in America. There were certainly young women who were attracted to him in the same way that John attracted female suitors, but he was nearly forty years of age when he met and fell in love with the one who was to be his lifelong partner.

Sally Gwynne came from a wealthy family who lived near Builth Wells, in what was then known as Radnorshire. Her father Marmaduke was county sheriff and, like his wife Sarah, a devout Christian. Both the Gwynnes were very sympathetic to Methodism and opened their house (Garth Manor) to Methodist preachers. Charles' first meeting with Sally was probably on 28 August 1747, when she and her father came to see him at Builth Wells. He remarked in his journal, 'my soul seemed pleased to take acquaintance with them',[21] and in a later letter to Sally confided that it was from this first meeting that she began to grow in his affections.[22] In September 1747 Charles joined his brother in Ireland and from Dublin wrote (probably for the first time) to Sally, expressing 'sure and stedfast [*sic*] hope of meeting you'.[23] On his return from Ireland in the spring of the following year, worn out and ill, he stayed once more at Garth, this time to be nursed by Sally and her family.

Charles was falling rapidly and deeply in love. Sally was nearly nineteen years younger than Charles; she was a gifted and attractive young woman possessing great commonsense and wisdom, and reciprocated his feelings. Very quickly, Charles moved from addressing her in his letters as 'Miss Gwynne' or

'Miss Sally', to 'My Dearest Friend', and by the early part of 1748 there was no doubting his ultimate intentions.

Ever since John's return from Georgia, the two brothers had promised each to consult the other before marrying,[24] but Charles understandably wished to sound out opinion more widely. He seems to have been anxious about the reactions of his fellow Methodists, though he need not have worried. In April 1748 we find him making approaches to his 'wise and worthy friend'[25] the Revd Vincent Perronet, the vicar of Shoreham. [49] Both Charles and Sally had their admirers. For example, a young woman named Elizabeth Cart had become attracted to Charles following her baptism and he wrote of this to Sally, saying, '*My cheerfulness has murdered hers.*'[26] For her part, Sally had to contend with the persistent advances of Edward Phillips, the rector from nearby Maesmynis.

Despite the generally favourable reactions to the news, Charles had an important hurdle to overcome – Mrs Gwynne! It was not that Sally's mother had any objections to Charles personally. In December

---

49. Tues, April 19th. I had communicated my embryo intentions to my brother while in Ireland, which he neither opposed, nor much encouraged. It was then a distant first thought, not likely ever to come to a proposal; as I had not given the least hint, either to Miss Gwynne or the family. To-day I rode over to Shoreham, and told Mr. Perronet all my heart. I have always had a fear, but no *thought* of marrying, for many years past, even from my first preaching of the Gospel. But within this twelve month that thought has forced itself in, 'How know I, whether it be best for me to marry, or no?' Certainly better now than later: and if not now, what security that I shall not then? It should be now, or not at all.

Mr. Perronet encouraged me to pray, and wait for a providential opening. I expressed the various searchings of my heart in many hymns on the important occasion.

Source: T. Jackson (ed.), *The Journal of The Rev. Charles Wesley, M.A.*, London, John Mason 1849, Vol. II, p. 12.

50.

Dear Madam,

Till now I neither knew nor cared what my writings and my brother's were worth. But I ordered my printer at B[ristol] to make an exact estimate. His account of their value ... is £2500, exclusive of the book I am now publishing, which will bring in more than £200 clear, besides a new version of the Psalms worth as much or more, and my journals and sermons, which I am daily called upon to publish. What all these copies amount to I will have computed and sent to you, when you have the leisure to examine them.

I am ashamed to trouble you with this strange kind of writing, however necessary. Permit me only to add one thing more. If after the strictest scrutiny you are satisfied as to a provision, and Mr. Gwynne and you see cause to give your consent, I would desire Miss Sally might secure her fortune in case of her own mortality, that it may return to her own family. I seek not hers but her; and if the Lord should give and take away I shall want nothing upon earth. I abhor the thought of being a gainer by her in temporals, and could not rest unless secured from this danger. Your regard for me must not here interpose to hinder what would vindicate my character, and be most for the credit of the Gospel.

Source: Frank Baker, *Charles Wesley as Revealed by His Letters*, Epworth Press 1948, p. 63.

1748 when Charles spoke with Sally's sister Becky, the latter agreed to speak to Mrs Gwynne, whose reply was that 'she would rather give her child to Mr. Wesley than to any man in England'.[27] Her only misgivings concerned what she referred to as Charles' 'want of fortune'. Charles promised that he would provide £100 a year for Sally, which satisfied Mrs Gwynne, her husband being content to leave such matters to her. However, Charles realized that his own optimism needed to be placed on rather firmer footing and he quickly took stock of his potential sources of income, which would come mainly from his writings. He wrote to his future mother-in-law to this effect in January 1749. [50]

A letter from his brother John guaranteeing the £100 per annum did not appear to satisfy Mrs Gwynne. After all, Charles had neither land nor even a home which he could call his own. Nevertheless, Mrs Gwynne was reassured by another letter, this time from Vincent Perronet, who confirmed Charles' estimate of the value of the brothers' writings.[28] After further reassurances concerning Miss Cart and Edward Phillips, Charles could hardly contain his sense of relief when Mrs Gwynne finally gave her consent on 23 January. 'Hope and I had long since shook hands and parted', he admitted.[29] On 15 February he was again at Garth, and wrote that 'Mrs Gwynne was extremely open and affectionate; has fought my battles against her own relations, particularly her son, who has behaved very violently towards her.'[30]

The first week in March found Charles at Bristol, where he discussed his impending marriage with George Whitefield and a group of Methodists there. He wrote in his journal on 6 March, 'I mentioned it to the select band, desiring their prayers, *not their advice*.'[31] The last three words of his statement were significant. By now, Charles' doubts and fears as to whether his union with Sally would actually take place were almost at an end. The next few weeks were spent travelling and preaching in London (where he 'narrowly escaped being crushed to death by a dray on London bridge'[32]), Oxford, Cirencester and South Wales. On 7 April he arrived at Garth, and the following day was married to Sally in the small chapel at Llanlleonfel. Charles described the wedding in the next excerpt. [51] Charles' journal entries at this point give the impression of a man who, if not quite in a state of delayed shock, was overwhelmed by the solemnity of the occasion. 'We were cheerful without mirth, serious without sadness,' he wrote. 'A stranger . . . said, "It looked more like a funeral than a wedding." My brother seemed the happiest person among us.'[33] This was perhaps typical of Charles' tendency to exaggerate. He was undoubtedly a very happy man.

A honeymoon followed, though modern newly-weds would hardly credit it as such today. The

---

51.
Sat., April 8th.

> 'Sweet day! so cool, so calm, so bright,
> The bridal of the earth and sky.'

Not a cloud was to be seen from morning till night. I rose at four; spent three hours and a half in prayer, or singing, with my brother, with Sally, with Beck. At eight I led MY SALLY to church. Her father, sisters, Lady Rudd, Grace Bowen, Betty Williams, and, I think, Billy Tucker, and Mr. James, were all the persons present. At the church-door I thought of the prophecy of a jealous friend, 'that if we were even at the church-door to be married, she was sure, by revelation, that we could get no farther.' We both smiled at the remembrance. We got farther. Mr. Gwynne gave her to me (under God): my brother joined our hands. It was a most solemn season of love! Never had I more of the divine presence at the sacrament.

Source: T. Jackson (ed.), *The Journal of The Rev. Charles Wesley, M.A.,* London, John Mason 1849, Vol. II, p. 55.

---

couple spent a fortnight at Garth, but Charles preached every day! Then, determined that people should not think that marriage had lessened his work ethic, he left for Bristol. His sense of duty got the better of him, however, and he ruefully admitted 'we made so much haste, that I left all my strength behind me. I was glad to go to bed, as soon as I got in.'[34]

By September 1749 Charles and Sally had established themselves at No. 4 Charles Street, in Bristol, and though their peace was sharply interrupted by the Grace Murray affair – which is described in the final section of this chapter – they settled happily into their new home. At the age of nearly forty-two, Charles could say of his first night in Charles Street, 'I slept comfortably in my own house . . .'[35] As time went on, Charles' life became more and more settled and the role of loving father was added to that of devoted husband. Sally came with him on a number of his trips, but these gradually diminished as the family grew and as Charles' health deteriorated with advancing years. Even in old age he would still be away from her for weeks at a time, mainly in London, though these absences always grieved him. In 1757 he wrote to Sally (his 'dearest of dear ones'), 'you are never absent from my heart. I go on heavily without you . . .'[36]

Five of Charles and Sally's children died in infancy. The eldest, baptized John (naturally) after his uncle, was to survive just over a year, dying on 7 January 1753 from the same outbreak of smallpox that nearly cost Sally her life and which, sadly, left her facially scarred. There is another gap in Charles' journal at this time, though a recent discovery of a manuscript fragment covering the week 4–11 December 1753, mainly written in shorthand, bears witness to the agonies through which the family was going. Three girls and another boy all failed to live beyond early childhood,[37] which was a source of great sadness to Charles and Sally, and perhaps explains why many of Charles' later hymns are so concerned with death. However, the three children who survived – Charles (often referred to as 'Charley' in his parents' correspondence), Sarah ('Sally') and Samuel ('Sammy') – brought the Wesleys lasting joy.

Young Sally became a particularly devout Christ-

ian and grew very close to her aunt Patty, being with her when she died. Charles took a close fatherly interest in her development, even though he was past fifty when she was born and, therefore, a lot older than most of her peers' fathers. His letters of advice, encouragement and – inevitably, knowing Charles' disposition – anxiety, show him to be a strict, but loving parent, as can be seen by the extract from one that he wrote to her in 1777, when she was sixteen. [52]

Neither of the boys went to public schools, all three youngsters being educated by Charles, Sally and, from time to time, by private tutors. Charles and Samuel showed none of their father's Methodist passions and in this they were both something of a disappointment to him. Nonetheless, he was immensely proud of them both, particularly of their musical talents. When a friend expressed misgivings about young Charley playing in concerts, Charles sprang to his son's defence with a letter that would do credit to any parent. [53]

---

52. I think you may avail yourself of my small knowledge of books and poetry. I am not yet too old to assist you a little in your reading, and perhaps improve your taste in versifying. You need not dread my severity. I have a laudable partiality for my own children. Witness your brothers; whom I do not love a jot better than you. Only be you as ready to show me your verses, as they their music.

The evenings I have set aside for reading with you and them. We should begin with history. A plan or order of study is absolutely necessary. Without that, the more you read the more you are confused, and never rise [above] a smatterer in learning.

Source: Frank Baker, *Charles Wesley as Revealed by His Letters*, Epworth Press 1948, p. 115.

---

53. I always designed my son for a clergyman. Nature has marked him for a musician: which appeared from his earliest infancy. My friends advised me not to cross his inclination. Indeed I could not if I would. There is no way of hindering his being a musician but cutting off his fingers. As he is particularly fond of church music, I suppose if he lives he will be an organist.

Source: Frank Baker, *Charles Wesley as Revealed by His Letters*, Epworth Press 1948, p. 110.

Samuel, nine years younger than his brother, also showed early signs of being gifted musically. In the final extract in this section – a letter to Samuel when the latter was just seven years old – we can see that Charles struggled with a desire to encourage his son's interest in and aptitude for music, and with a desperate concern for Samuel's spiritual welfare. [54] In the event, whereas Charles Jr never became an ardent churchgoer, Samuel was eventually received into the Roman Catholic Church. His son, Samuel Sebastian Wesley, was even more gifted as an

> 54.   London, March 6, 1773
>
> Come now, my good friend Samuel, and let us reason together. God made you for Himself, that is to be for ever happy with Him. Ought you not therefore to serve and love Him?
>
> You should now begin to live by reason and religion. There should be sense even in your play and diversions. Therefore I have furnished you with maps and books and harpsichord. Every day get something by heart: whatever your mother recommends. Every day read one or more chapters in the Bible. I suppose your mother will take you now, in the place of your brother, to be her chaplain, to read the psalms and lessons when your sister does not . . .
>
> As for music, it is neither good nor bad in itself. You have a natural inclination to it: but God gave you that: therefore God only should be thanked and praised for it. Your brother has the same love of music much more than you, yet he is not proud or vain of it. Neither, I trust, will you be. You will send me a long letter of answer, and always look upon me both as
>   Your loving father and friend
>   C. Wesley
>
> *Source*: Frank Baker, *Charles Wesley as Revealed by His Letters*, Epworth Press 1948, p. 111.

organist and achieved national fame, being offered a knighthood by Queen Victoria in 1873.

John Wesley's Marriage

> *Didst thou not make us one,*
>   *That we might one remain,*
> *Together travel on,*
>   *And bear each other's pain;*
> *Till all thy utmost goodness prove,*
> *And rise renewed in perfect love?*

Before leaving Charles and Sally's domestic life, we should say something of John, particularly the events leading up to his marriage in February 1751, since Charles played no small part in an extraordinary episode which took place shortly after Charles' move to Bristol. John's relationships with women were far from being straightforward. Whether his childhood or his ideal of womanhood had been over-influenced by his mother, or whether he was simply a 'ditherer', it is impossible to say. A tendency towards diffidence with women of his own age and his unwillingness to be 'owned' by anyone, contributed to his lack of success in matters of the heart.

The affair which has been referred to above, and in which Charles became embroiled, concerned Grace Murray, John Wesley and John Bennet. Bennet, who was one of John's closest allies in the early years of the Methodist revival,[38] had fallen in love with Grace Murray. So too, had John. Grace Murray was an attractive widow who had become closely linked with John and Charles Wesley (mainly due to the latter's influence) and whose relationship with John had deepened when she had nursed him whilst he was ill in Newcastle. John, now in his late forties, may have envisaged Grace taking on the role of a housekeeper, but he was clearly in love with her. It has been mentioned already that the Wesley brothers had agreed that each should consult the other before marrying, but John chose not to do so on this occasion. Grace was clearly in a quandary, as she was attracted to both John Wesley and John Bennet, both of whom, moreover, were under the impression that they were engaged to her.

When Charles heard the news of his brother's designs, he was horrified. Not only was he anxious that John's marrying would jeopardize the future of Methodism, but also he feared the reaction of the Methodist societies. His own case was different of course, because *he* did not see himself as having quite the same pivotal role as John. In addition, Grace was of relatively humble origin, which may have made matters worse. In Charles' eyes, it had all the hallmarks of a scandal. He wrote to her immediately, letting her know exactly how he felt. [55]

With almost indecent haste, Charles rode to Newcastle to see Grace in person; from there to

55. Fain would I hope that you can say something in your defence (when I come to talk with you) which now I know not. But the case appears thus to me:

You promised J[ohn] B[ennet] to marry him – since which you engaged yourself to another.

How is this possible? And who is that other? One of such importance that his doing so dishonest an action would destroy both himself and me and the whole work of God. It was on the very brink of ruin; but the snare is broken, and we are delivered.

Source: Frank Baker, *Charles Wesley as Revealed by His Letters*, Epworth Press 1948, p. 72.

Whitehaven to see his brother, saying that 'all our preachers would leave us, all our societies would disperse';[39] then back to Grace. After bringing Grace and John Bennet together once more, Charles urged them to marry, which they did on 3 October 1749. John Wesley was devastated, but despite the (still) angry Charles berating him as he would 'a heathen man or a publican',[40] the two brothers were temporarily reconciled through the good offices of George Whitefield. In March 1750 Charles wrote to Bennet, saying that he and John had 'agreed to bury all in oblivion', though he admitted in another letter in December of the same year that 'only me he cannot love as before'.[41]

The damage had been done, and when John did marry, it was so speedily after the Grace Murray affair that one cannot help but conclude that it was 'on the rebound'. The woman was Molly Vazeille, the 41-year-old widow of a wealthy banker and, in Charles' opinion, an even less suitable choice. On his first meeting with her in the summer of 1749 he referred to her as 'a woman of a sorrowful spirit'.[42] John did at least inform Charles of his intentions on this occasion, but his younger brother was even more aghast, as his journal entries for February 1751 testify. [56]

Charles' worst fears were soon realized. He tried his best to be civil to Molly and even, a few months later, took her to his home and listened patiently to 'her complaints of my brother'.[43] Molly, however,

was a difficult woman and was soon jealous of the trust which existed between the two brothers. She also objected to John's financial guarantee to Charles, and before too long Charles and Sally did their best to keep out of her way. In future letters to his wife, Charles was to refer to her sarcastically as 'my best friend'.

John's marriage, unlike that of Charles, proved to be an unhappy one. By the 1770s they separated and John penned the oft-quoted words, 'Non eam reliqui; non dismissi; non revocabo.' (I did not leave her; I did not send her away; I will not recall her.)[44] When she died in October 1781, John did not attend her funeral. The story of their ill-fated relationship has been told elsewhere, suffice it to say that it did not detract from John's work with the Methodist movement as a happy marriage might have done. For this, Charles must have been profoundly grateful.

56.

Sat., February 2d.
My brother, returned from Oxford, sent for and told me *he was resolved to marry!* I was thunderstruck, and could only answer, he had given me the first blow, and his marriage would come like the *coup de grace.* Trusty Ned Perronet followed, and told me, the person was Mrs. Vazeille! one of whom I had never had the least suspicion. I refused his company to the chapel, and retired to mourn with my faithful Sally. I groaned all the day, and several following ones, under my own and the people's burden. I could eat no pleasant food, nor preach, nor rest, either by night or by day.

Sun., February 17th.
. . . At the Foundery I heard my brother's apology. Several days afterwards I was one of the last that heard of his unhappy marriage.

Source: T. Jackson (ed.), *The Journal of The Rev. Charles Wesley, M.A.*, London, John Mason 1849, Vol. II, pp. 78–9.

Chronology

1726		Birth of Sarah Gwynne
1735	25 April	Death of Samuel Wesley Sr
1739	November	Death of Samuel Wesley Jr
1742	30 July	Death of Susanna Wesley
1747	August	Charles meets Sally for the first time
1749	8 April	Charles and Sally's wedding day
	September	Charles and Sally move to Bristol
1749	3 October	Grace Murray marries John Bennet
1751	February	John Wesley marries Molly Vazeille

For Discussion

1. Having read about the Wesley family, with whom do you particularly identify, and why?

2. Has family life changed for better or for worse since Charles Wesley's time, and in what ways?

3. A present-day social worker might regard the Wesleys as a dysfunctional family. To what extent does family background help or hinder our development?

6

Preacher and Pastor

My talents, gifts and graces, Lord,
Into thy blessed hands receive;
And let me live to preach thy word,
And let me to thy glory live;
My every sacred moment spend
In publishing the sinners' friend.

We now widen the scope a little in order to explore the part that Charles Wesley played in the development of early Methodism. As a preacher-evangelist he tended to be overshadowed by John, partly because his itinerant ministry was much reduced after the 1750s and partly because he achieved so much success as a hymn-writer.

Nonetheless, Charles was an extremely able preacher. His sermon 'Awake Thou That Sleepest', which he preached at Oxford University in April 1742, was published as a pamphlet and became the best-selling piece of Methodist literature in his lifetime. Based on Ephesians 5.14, the following short extract from this sermon is sufficient to give an indication of Charles' style and illustrates his gift both for plain speaking and for making extensive use of scriptural allusions.[1] [57]

We have noted earlier that Charles used many of his brother's sermons, particularly at the outset of his preaching ministry, and that this practice was not frowned upon in the eighteenth century as it might, perhaps, be today.[2] On the first recorded occasion we have of Charles preaching, on 30 November 1735 on board the *Simmonds*, he used a sermon that he had probably written himself, but this was not to

be the general rule. At the first service he conducted at Frederica, Charles preached on 'A Single Eye' (Matthew 6.22–3), a sermon which almost certainly had been written specially for him by John.[3] John might have had high expectations of both himself and Charles, but even he realized that his newly ordained younger brother was being thrown in at the deep end, as it were, and deserved some assistance. Whilst in Georgia, at least half of the sermons Charles preached were supplied by his older brother, and John provided him with a stock of manuscripts when he left America, which he then transcribed and continued to use after his return to England.

Charles still used his brother's sermons from time

> 57. O may the Angel of the Lord come upon thee, and the light shine into thy prison! And mayest thou feel the stroke of an Almighty Hand, raising thee, with, 'Arise up quickly, gird thyself, and bind on thy sandals, cast thy garments about thee, and follow me.'
>
> Awake, thou everlasting spirit, out of thy dream of worldly happiness! Did not God create thee for himself? Thou canst not rest until thou restest in him. Return, thou wanderer! Fly back to thy ark. This is not thy home. Think not of building tabernacles here. Thou art but a stranger, a sojourner upon earth; a creature of a day, but just launching out into an unchangeable state. Make haste. Eternity is at hand. Eternity depends on this moment; an eternity of happiness or an eternity of misery!
>
> *Source: Sermons by the Late Rev. Charles Wesley, A.M.*, London, Baldwin 1816.

to time, his favourite seeming to be one 'On Faith', which we have a record of him preaching on at least four occasions in 1738.[4] These examples of borrowing material from John show, perhaps, that Charles' thinking paralleled that of his elder brother to a remarkable degree during these early years of the Methodist revival.

Charles' preaching underwent a subtle, but noticeable change after the events of May 1738. His journal entries show that he now had a far greater degree of eagerness for the task. His preaching also displayed a sense of urgency that had been absent until now. 'At this juncture', one of his biographers comments, 'he plunged headlong after every lost sheep and gave no rest to those whom he pursued.'[5]

If 'Awake Thou That Sleepest' was the most popular of Charles' sermons, 'The One Thing Needful' (based on Luke 10.42 and which he transcribed from John) is the one which perhaps most accurately summarizes the main emphasis of his early preaching. It encapsulates Charles' passionate concern for the salvation of every soul – and in this, like John, he never wavered from his Arminian[6] convictions in preaching that salvation was a free gift, available to all, by the grace of God. But this sermon also hinted at the way in which Charles would develop his ideas on sanctification and Christian perfection. The next extract contains some of its main points. [58]

Incidentally, 'The One Thing Needful' was written (by John in its original form) *before* May 1738 – probably in the spring of 1734 – and Charles preached it before and after his experience at Pentecost.[7] This may be food for thought for those who would wish to draw too sharp a distinction between Charles' spiritual condition before and after 21 May 1738, since the sermon sounds strange from one who had not yet been 'converted'.

Nonetheless, there was a 'fire in his belly' that Charles had not really felt before. In October 1738 he noted in his journal, 'I preached the one thing needful at Islington, and added much extempore ...'[8] The sermon possibly lent itself more readily than others to being preached extempore, but Charles had the gift

58. Now this great work, this one thing needful, is the renewal of our fallen nature. In the image of God was man created ... But sin has now effaced the image of God! ... From the glorious liberty in which he was created, he is fallen into the basest bondage.

Now the recovery of the image of God, of this glorious liberty, this perfect restoration, *is* the one thing needful upon earth, appears first from hence, that the enjoyment of them was the end of our creation; for man was created to love God, and to this end alone, even to love the Lord his God with all his heart, and soul and mind, and strength ... By love, man is not only rendered like him, but in some sense one with him ... Love is perfect freedom.

The same truth appears, secondly from its being the end of our redemption by Jesus Christ; of all that our blessed Lord died and suffered for us; of his incarnation, his life, his death, his resurrection, his ascension into heaven, and the descent of the Holy Spirit. All these miracles of love were wrought with no other view than to restore us to health and freedom, to happiness and immortality.

Thirdly, it is the one end of all the dispensations of Providence ... The will of God ... is solely for our sanctification; our recovery from the vile bondage ... all the dispensations of God, all the influences of his Holy Spirit, whether he gives us joy or sorrow of heart, whether he inspires us with vigour and cheerfulness, or permits us to sink into deadness of soul, into dejection and heaviness, it is the same view; namely, to restore us to health, to liberty, to holiness ...

Be we then continually watchful over our souls; that there be no duplicity in our intentions; be it our one view in all our thoughts and words, and actions, to be partakers of the divine nature, to regain the highest measure possible of faith which works by love, that faith which unites us to God!

Source: Sermons by the Late Rev. Charles Wesley, A.M., London, Baldwin 1816.

for adapting his material to his hearers. Unlike his elder brother, he never had his sermons printed as a collection.[9] There were probably a number of reasons for this: his modesty, his talent for spontaneity, and the fact that he simply never organized his paperwork in a way that would have made it easily possible. Often, when Charles began to prepare a sermon, he would open the Bible, read the first sentence his eye lighted upon, and work from there. This may seem a rather haphazard approach, but we should remember that Charles possessed an extensive knowledge of Scripture and that his use of the Bible was governed by a scholarly grasp of theology and a strict sense of discipline in the way he interpreted texts. Spontaneous he might have been – in the same way that he used Scripture for his personal devotions – but the process was far removed from being a lottery. Charles also used his gift for extemporizing when he led prayers in public, 'after God' as he put it, rather than confining himself solely to the Book of Common Prayer.[10]

Field-Preaching

Outcasts of men, to you I call,
Harlots, and publicans, and thieves!
He spreads his arms to embrace you all;
Sinners alone his grace receives:
No need of him the righteous have;
He came the lost to seek and save.

Charles had been quite ill in the spring of 1738 but now the recovery of his physical strength fuelled his renewed enthusiasm for preaching. Gradually his activities widened, but he was to find fewer and fewer places – both churches and other institutions, such as Oxford University – where he was welcome.

Then in early 1739 George Whitefield invited both John and Charles Wesley to join him in Bristol, where his open-air preaching was having a tremendous impact on the miners of Kingswood.[11] John had been reluctant to preach in the open air. He was a high-churchman with a built-in reverence for conse-

crated places of worship which, in his view, were the proper places to preach. It went against all his instincts as an Oxford don and a gentleman. The prospect of open-air preaching, though not without its precedents, seemed contrary to the established nature of the Church of England. This was particularly true when it was done without invitation or permission from other Anglican clergy, of whom some were sympathetic but many were not. John's comment in his journal for 2 April 1739 that he 'submitted to be more vile' was, therefore, understandable.[12]

Charles shared his brother's misgivings. He had had very mixed experiences in Georgia.[13] Moreover, he lacked both his brother's experience and his confidence. Charles was faced with a further dilemma. He could see a great need to preach the gospel to those whom the established church either could not or would not reach. On the other hand, his ecclesiastical superiors were far from enthusiastic. When he and John saw the Archbishop of Canterbury in February 1739, the interview, whilst being amicable, left the brothers in no doubt as to the Archbishop's reservations. 'He showed us great affection,' noted Charles in his journal, 'spoke mildly of Mr. Whitefield; cautioned us to give no more umbrage than was necessary for our own defence; to forbear exceptionable phrases; to keep to the doctrines of the Church.'[14] On the same day they were given much the same message by the Bishop of London.[15]

Charles could see the dangers of religious extremism, which many people perceived as the cause of so much bloodshed and civil unrest in the previous century. He was also aware of the fears which the Church had concerning the excesses of 'enthusiasm'. Nevertheless, he was saddened by the reaction of his fellow clergymen. In April 1739 he wrote of 'the growing spirit of delusion',[16] and later that month he was forbidden by the churchwardens at Islington to preach from the pulpit there. When invited by a Quaker to preach at Thackstead [sic] on 31 May 1739, therefore, Charles qualified his reservations. 'I scrupled preaching in another's parish,' he wrote, 'till I had been refused the church.'[17]

A further conversation with the Archbishop in June showed the degree to which the situation had deteriorated. This time Charles was accompanied by his friend, the Revd Henry Piers, the vicar of Bexley.[18] 'His Grace expressly forbad him to let any of us preach in his church: charged us with breach of the canon.'[19] The meeting ended with the Archbishop dismissing them, 'Piers with kind professions; me, with all the marks of his displeasure.'[20]

The end of this period of indecision came quickly. Despite the disapproval of the Anglican hierarchy and his own reluctance to preach in the open air, Charles succumbed to his own inner convictions and to George Whitefield's persuasion. Whitefield had for some time been urging Charles to give up the idea of resuming his former duties as General Oglethorpe's secretary, because in his opinion Charles' gifts were far better employed where they were most needed – in Britain. Charles had needed a great deal of convincing, and the accompanying extracts from his journal show how difficult the decision had been. [59]

In the journal entry for 24 June, Charles gives the

---

59. **Sat., June 23rd.** My inward conflict continued. I perceived it was the fear of man; and that, by preaching in the field next Sunday, as George Whitefield urges me, I shall break down the bridge, and become desperate. I retired, and prayed for particular direction; offering up my friends, my liberty, my life, for Christ's sake and the Gospel's . . .

Sun., June 24th. St. John the Baptist's day . . . I went forth, in the name of Jesus Christ. I found near ten thousand helpless sinners waiting for the word, in Moorfields. I invited them in my Master's words, as well as name: 'Come unto me, all ye that travail, and are heavy laden, and I will give you rest.' The Lord was with me, even me, his meanest messenger, according to his promise.

Source: T. Jackson (ed.), *The Journal of The Rev. Charles Wesley, M.A.,* London, John Mason 1849, Vol. I, p. 155.

---

60. **Fri., August 10th.** I gave George Whitefield some account both of my labours and my conflicts.

'Dear George, – I forgot to mention the most material occurrence at Plaistow; namely, that a Clergyman was there convinced of sin. He stood under me, and appeared, throughout my discourse, under the strongest perturbation of mind. In our return we were much delighted with an old spiritual Quaker, who is clear in justification by faith only. At Marylebone a footman was convinced of more than sin; and now waits with confidence for all the power of faith . . .

'I am continually tempted to leave off preaching, and hide myself like J. Hutchins. I should then be freer from temptation, and at leisure to attend my own improvement. God continues to work *by* me, but not *in* me, that I can perceive. Do not reckon upon me, my brother, in the work God is doing: for I cannot expect He should long employ one who is ever longing and murmuring to be discharged. I rejoice in your success, and pray for its increase a thousand fold.'

Source: T. Jackson (ed.), *The Journal of The Rev. Charles Wesley, M.A.,* London, John Mason 1849, Vol. I, pp. 158–9.

---

number of people present at Moorfields as 'near ten thousand'. Whether or not he exaggerated the size of his congregations (in the way that many preachers have done since time immemorial!) is not important. What *is* certain is that he frequently preached to huge crowds which few church buildings could accommodate. The more he, John, George Whitefield and others engaged in open-air preaching, the more opposition came from official quarters. The end of June found Charles at Oxford University again, where the Dean 'spoke with unusual severity against field-preaching',[21] and his sermon the next Sunday provoked a strong negative response. There were still doubts in his own mind, of course, and in August he wrote to Whitefield confessing his weaknesses. [60]

Nevertheless, Charles' resolve was growing week by week. In his journal he noted the occasions when, despite making polite enquiries beforehand, he was rebuffed by local vicars: at High Wycombe on 16 August and in Gloucester ten days later, where the local minister ('one of the better disposed') offered him a glass of wine, despite refusing to allow him the use of his pulpit.[22] However, these setbacks were more than outweighed by the fruits of his labours. The following day Charles preached to an enormous crowd of people, an account of which is reprinted here, and which is of particular interest as he mentions the fact that he sang during the service, a theme to which we shall return in a later chapter. [61]

There were many such instances where people welcomed him with great enthusiasm and responded eagerly to his message. On 3 September 1739, after lambasting a crowd of several thousand on the outskirts of Bristol for their sinful ways, he wrote, 'I marvelled at their taking it so patiently, when I showed them that they were all adulterers, thieves, idolaters, etc.'[23] There could be no doubting Charles' candour! The next day he was with the miners at Kingswood and 'triumphed in God's mercy to these poor outcasts', concluding, 'O how gladly do the poor receive the Gospel! We hardly knew how to part.'[24] A week later he preached to another enormous throng in Bristol: 'It rained hard, yet none stirred. I spoke with great freedom and power.'[25]

In October 1739 Charles was invited by Joseph Williams to speak at Kidderminster. Williams was a dissenter and Charles noted, 'Of what denomination he is, I know not; nor is it material: for he has the mind which was in Jesus.'[26] Charles left no account of his visit there, since a gap exists in his journal between November 1739 and March 1740. However, Joseph Williams was so taken with what he had heard that he made a special journey to Bristol to hear him. His description of Charles, in a letter he wrote soon afterwards, is interesting because it is one of the few contemporary pictures we have of the younger Wesley – albeit a biased one – and invites comparison with Charles' own accounts of his preaching. [62]

Charles' congregations became very emotional on occasions, but the same could be said of Charles himself. Often he became carried away, and phrases such as 'much melted' and 'tears of love' crop up frequently in his writings, particularly during his early years as a preacher. On horseback, he would frequently break into song as he rode along with his companions. On 8 June 1738, for example, whilst riding with Mr Bray,[27] 'I was full of delight, and seemed in new heavens and a new earth. We prayed and sang, and shouted all the way.'[28] Once, when travelling to London by coach, a fellow passenger was so annoyed by Charles' high spirits that she threatened to beat him! Charles noted in his journal, with a touch of humour, 'I declared, I deserved nothing but hell; so did she.'[29] Even when he was travelling by coach, Charles wasted no opportunity to share the good news, as can be seen from another extract from his journal. [63]

---

61. Runwick, August 26th.

In the afternoon I preached again to a Kennington congregation. The church was full as it could crowd. Thousands stood in the church-yard. It was the most beautiful sight I ever beheld. The people filled the gradually-rising area, which was shut up on three sides by a vast perpendicular hill. On the top and bottom of this hill was a circular row of trees. In this amphitheatre they stood, deeply attentive, while I called upon them in Christ's words, 'Come unto me, all that are weary.' The tears of many testified that they were ready to enter into that rest. God enabled me to lift up my voice like a trumpet; so that all distinctly heard me. I concluded with singing an invitation to sinners.

It was with difficulty we made our way through this most loving people, and returned amidst their prayers and blessings to Ely.

Source: T. Jackson (ed.), *The Journal of The Rev. Charles Wesley, M.A.*, London, John Mason 1849, Vol. I, p. 165.

62 Hearing that Mr. Charles Wesley would preach in the afternoon, just out of the city, I got a guide and went to hear him. I found him standing on a table, in an erect posture, with his hands and eyes lifted up to heaven in prayer, surrounded with, I guess, more than a thousand people; some few of them persons of fashion, both men and women, but most of them of the lower rank of mankind . . .

He then preached about an hour, from 2 Corin. V. 17–21, in such a manner as I have seldom, if ever, heard any Minister preach . . . [His] points he supported all along, as he went on, with many texts of Scripture, which he explained and illustrated . . . and used a great variety of the most moving arguments and expostulations, in order to persuade, allure, instigate, and, if possible, to compel all to come to Christ and believe in him for pardon and salvation. Nor did he fail to inform them thoroughly, how ineffectual their faith would be to justify them in the sight of God, unless it wrought by love, purified their hearts, and reformed their lives . . .

Afterwards I waited on Mr. Wesley, asked him many questions, and received much satisfaction from his answers.

Source: F. C. Gill, *Charles Wesley, the first Methodist*, Lutterworth Press 1964, pp. 97–8.

---

63. Wed., September 27th. In our way to Oxford, I talked closely with my fellow-traveller, Mr. Coombes. he expressed his desire of faith: I was moved to sing, 'Salvation by faith,' then 'Faith in Christ.' I told him, if the Spirit had convinced him of unbelief, he could of righteousness also, even before we reached Oxford. I stopped and prayed that he might believe. Immediately he told me, he was in such a blessed temper, as he never before experienced. We halted, and went to prayers. He testified the great delight he felt, saying, it was heaven, if it would but continue . . . We sang and shouted all the way to Oxford.

Source: T. Jackson (ed.), *The Journal of The Rev. Charles Wesley, M.A.*, London, John Mason 1849, Vol. I, p. 131.

The Prison Pastor

Plenteous He is in truth and grace;
He wills that all the fallen race
Should turn, repent, and live;
His pardoning grace for all is free;
Transgression, sin, iniquity,
He freely doth forgive.

During his 'Holy Club' days Charles had visited the inmates at the Castle Prison in Oxford, and whilst in Georgia he had preached to the prisoners in Skiddoway.[30] Perhaps in view of his father's brief incarceration in Lincolnshire Castle, Charles took a special interest in the spiritual welfare of prison inmates. He now turned his attention to the condemned prisoners at Newgate.

Britain's penal system in the eighteenth century was very different from that of today. The punishment for well over a hundred offences – including such relatively trivial crimes as stealing five shillings[31] from a shop and taking two pounds from a dwelling-house – was death by hanging. Prisons were squalid and overcrowded, places of unbelievable corruption and disease. Criminals, therefore, faced either with a slow death from illness and neglect in prison or a (relatively) quick death at the end of a rope, would just as soon commit even more serious offences to avoid capture. In July 1738 Charles wrote an account of his first visit to the prison and, as always, was honest in admitting his doubts as to whether 'death-bed repentance' was possible in such cases. [64] The Revd Sparks referred to in the extract was one of the Wesleys' earliest supporters.

Charles continued his visits during that summer, noting the reactions of the prisoners, who were often 'deeply affected' by his words. On one occasion he talked with a black slave who had robbed his master and had been condemned to death. 'He listened with all the signs of eager astonishment; the tears trickled down his cheeks while he cried, "What! was it for me? Did God suffer all this for so poor a creature as me?" I left him waiting for the salvation of God.'[32]

64. Mon., July 10th. At Mr. Sparks's request, I went with him, Mr. Bray, and Mr. Burnham, to Newgate; and preached to the ten malefactors, under sentence of death; but with a heavy heart. My old prejudices against the possibility of a death-bed repentance still hung upon me; and I could hardly hope there was mercy for those whose time was so short. But in the midst of my languid discourse, a sudden spirit of faith came upon me, and I promised them all pardon, in the name of Jesus Christ, if they would then, as at the last hour, repent, and believe the Gospel. Nay, I did believe they would accept of the proffered mercy, and could not help telling them, 'I had no doubt but God would give me every soul of them.'

Source: T. Jackson (ed.), *The Journal of The Rev. Charles Wesley, M.A.*, London, John Mason 1849, Vol. I, p. 117.

65. Some time after my arrival in London I witnessed . . . thirteen criminals all hanged at the same time. The day before the execution those who desire it may receive the sacrament, provided the chaplain thinks that they have sincerely repented and are worthy of it. On the day of the execution the condemned prisoners, wearing a sort of white linen shirt over their clothes and a cap on their heads, are tied two together and placed on carts with their backs to the horses' tails . . .

When all the prisoners arrive at their destination they are made to mount on a very wide cart made expressly for the purpose, a cord is passed round their necks and the end fastened to the gibbet, which is not very high. The chaplain who accompanies the condemned men is also on the cart; he makes them pray and sing a few verses of the Psalms. The relatives are permitted to mount the cart and take farewell. When the time is up, the chaplain and the relatives get off the cart, which slips from under the condemned men's feet. You often see friends and relations tugging at the hanging men's feet so that they should die quicker and not suffer.

Source: De Saussure, *A Foreign View of England in the Reigns of George I and George II*, Murray 1902.

66. Wed., July 19th. I rose very heavy, and backward to visit them for the last time. At six I prayed and sang with them all together . . . At half-hour past nine their irons were knocked off, and their hands tied . . . By half-hour past ten we came to Tyburn, waited till eleven: then were brought the children appointed to die. I got upon the cart with Sparks and Broughton: the Ordinary [the local chaplain – Ed.] endeavoured to follow, when the poor prisoners begged he might not come; and the mob kept him down . . .

None showed any natural terror of death: no fear, or crying, or tears. All expressed their desire of our following them to paradise. I never saw such calm triumph, such incredible indifference to dying. We sang several hymns; particularly,

'Behold the Saviour of mankind,
Nail'd to the shameful tree.'

We left them going to meet their Lord, ready for the Bridegroom. When the cart drew off, not one stirred, or struggled for life, but meekly gave up their spirits. Exactly at twelve they were turned off. I spoke a few suitable words to the crowd; and returned, full of peace and confidence in our friends' happiness. That hour under the gallows was the most blessed hour of my life.

Source: T. Jackson (ed.), *The Journal of The Rev. Charles Wesley, M.A.*, London, John Mason 1849, Vol. I, pp. 122–3.

In the eighteenth century executions had almost become a form of public entertainment and special stands were erected for spectators, some of whom included children. A French visitor who was in London at the time witnessed such an event at Tyburn and described what happened. [65]

Charles' journal entries of the times spent with prisoners at Newgate makes poignant reading, particularly the occasion on which he himself was present on 19 July 1738 at the execution of several of the men to whom he had been ministering. His own account of the occasion provides an interesting contrast to that of De Saussure's. [66]

Charles, not surprisingly, never found this aspect of his ministry easy. On 5 October 1738 he said that he was 'shamefully unwilling' to go to Newgate; in March the following year he went 'with my usual reluctance'. However, he continued to visit Newgate throughout his life, having free access to the prison. At the age of seventy-seven, he told John Fletcher, one of the most famous of the early Methodist preachers, 'A fortnight ago I preached the condemned sermon to about twenty criminals. Every one of them, I have good grounds to believe, died penitent. Twenty more must die next week.'[33]

The Perils of Itinerancy

And are we yet alive,
And see each other's face?
Glory and praise to Jesus give
For his redeeming grace!

What troubles have we seen,
What conflicts have we passed,
Fightings without, and fears within,
Since we assembled last!

The singing of that hymn of Charles Wesley's, written in the early 1740s, and of which the first and third verses appear above, became a tradition at the beginning of each Methodist Conference as the preachers assembled from distant parts of the country.[34] It conjures up a vivid picture of the difficulties encountered by the Wesleys and their companions in the early years of the Methodist revival. One can perhaps understand why Charles' renewed enthusiasm for proclaiming 'the one thing needful'[35] after May 1738 sometimes became too uncompromising, when we bear in mind that the reception he received at Newgate was in such stark contrast to the opposition he encountered elsewhere.

Opposition did not only come from groups within the Church of England. Not all those who gathered to hear John and Charles preach were favourably disposed towards the brothers and their fellow preachers. Ignorance and superstition, drunkenness and bigotry, all combined to create a volatile atmosphere in many places the early Methodist preachers visited, and Charles faced more than his share of threatening mobs. The following account of his visit to Sheffield in May 1743, when he had a fortunate escape, was by no means unusual. The 'floods' mentioned in the second paragraph is a poetical reference, typical of Charles' style of writing, to the mob which threatened him. [67]

There were many other such instances when Charles was threatened with physical injury. At Tavistock in June 1746 'a large herd of wild beasts were got together, and very noisy and tumultuous

---

67. Wednesday, May 25th.

In the afternoon I came to the flock in Sheffield, who are as sheep in the midst of wolves; the Ministers having so stirred up the people, that they are ready to tear them to pieces . . .

At six I went to the Society-house. As soon as I was in the desk, the floods began to lift up their voice. An officer (Ensign Garden) contradicted and blasphemed. I took no notice of him, and sung on. The stones flew thick, hitting the desk and people. To save them and the house, I gave notice I should preach out, and look the enemy in the face.

The whole army of the aliens followed me. The Captain laid hold on me, and began reviling . . . The stones often struck me in the face. After sermon I prayed for sinners, as servants of their master, the devil; upon which the Captain ran at me with great fury, threatening revenge for my abusing, as he called it . . . He forced his way through the brethren, drew his sword, and presented it to my breast. My breast was immediately steeled. I threw it open, and, fixing mine eye on his, smiled in his face, and calmly said, "I fear God, and honour the King." His countenance fell in a moment, he fetched a deep sigh, put up his sword, and quietly left the place.

Source: T. Jackson (ed.), *The Journal of The Rev. Charles Wesley, M.A.*, London, John Mason 1849, Vol. I, p. 309.

they were. At first I stood on a wall, but their violence forced me thence.'[36] Two days later, in Plymouth, when refused the use of the church by the vicar, Charles decided to preach in the main street, where he was confronted with 'an whole army of soldiers and sailors . . . shouting and blaspheming'.[37] The dangers he faced were very real – in April 1740 William Seward (one of the first Methodist lay preachers) was actually killed during a service – and Charles was realistic enough to accept the fact that he, too, might one day meet with the same fate.

Nonetheless, Charles' reaction to such violence was always to stand his ground and remain calm. Once, when faced with a man who, clearly mentally unbalanced, threatened to shoot him with a pistol, Charles recalled afterwards, 'I sat still, and felt the hand of God upon me; had not the least temptation to anger or fear; said with perfect calmness . . . "I have learned to turn the other cheek."'[38]

Apart from human opposition, travelling in eighteenth-century Britain was hazardous to say the least. The days when travelling by road became both speedy and safe lay in the distant future[39] and there would be no national railway network for over a century. The early Methodists made their way about the country on foot or by horse along roads which can only be appreciated by one who has visited an under-developed country today. Heavily-laden wagons resulted in the surfaces becoming deeply rutted, which in turn became ribbon dung-heaps in many places from the passage of livestock. The journey from London to Edinburgh could take over a fortnight, and even more modest trips, to places like Norwich or Bath, needed an overnight stop.

It is a wonder that Charles' none too robust health withstood the rigours of the routine he set himself, particularly in the early years of his itinerant ministry. He was often ill. 'I could scarce sit my horse,' he wrote on one occasion, 'the wind and rain were so troublesome. I got, almost senseless, to Bristol; and to the room, but could not stand; yet spoke, I know not how, for an hour, and hastened to my bed, utterly

---

> **68. Gloucester, August 25th.**
>
> By ten last night the Lord brought us hither through many dangers and difficulties. In mounting, I fell over my horse, and sprained my hand. Riding in the dark, I bruised my foot. We lost our way as often as we *could*. Two horses we had between three; for Robin bore us company. Here we were turned back from a friend's house, by his wife's sickness. Last night my voice and strength wholly failed me. To-day they are in some measure restored.
>
> *Source*: T. Jackson (ed.), *The Journal of The Rev. Charles Wesley, M.A.,* London, John Mason 1849, Vol. I, p. 163.

---

exhausted.'[40] On another, he remarked jocularly, 'we had only one shower – but it lasted from morning to night'.[41] This, and an extract from a letter he wrote from Gloucester on 25 August 1739, give a good impression of the problems Charles faced as a travelling preacher. [68]

Not only was the condition of the highways poor, often becoming impassable in bad weather, but other dangers awaited travellers, even on well-used roads. In the days before the existence of a police force, a journey – even in broad daylight – could be interrupted by robbers who had few scruples about attacking the unwary and unprotected. On one occasion Charles himself was accosted by a highwayman, and he took pains afterwards to describe the incident in some detail. [69]

There were few places where Charles did not find some opportunity of preaching. He proclaimed the gospel in the open fields and common land, churchyards, market places, bowling greens, inns, public buildings, quay-sides, domestic dwellings – anywhere in town or country where people would gather to listen to his message.

69. Tues., October 11th.

I set out for London. In a mile's riding my horse fell lame. I sung the 91st Psalm, and put myself under the divine protection. I had scarce ended, and turned the hut, on Shotover-Hill, when a man came up to me, and demanded my money, showing, but not presenting, a pistol. I gave him my purse. He asked me how much there was. 'About thirty shillings.' 'Have you no more?' 'I will see;' put my hand in my pocket, and gave him some halfpence. He repeated the question, 'Have you no more?' I had thirty pounds in a private pocket; bade him search himself; which he did not choose. He ordered me to dismount, which I did; but begged hard for my horse again, promising not to pursue him. He took my word, and restored him. I rode gently on, praising God. My bags, and watch, and gold, the robber was *forced* to leave me. By the evening I reached Westminster.

Source: T. Jackson (ed.), *The Journal of The Rev. Charles Wesley, M.A.*, London, John Mason 1849, Vol. I, pp. 77–8.

Charles in Ireland

To Thee let all the nations flow,
  Let all obey the gospel word;
Let all their suffering Saviour know,
  Filled with the glory of the Lord.

It is almost certain that Methodism came to Ireland by way of the army. Among the junior officers who were posted to regiments in Ireland were young men who either had heard John or Charles Wesley preach or had come under the influence of one of the early Methodist preachers. The first Methodist society (in Dublin) came into existence at some point in the mid-1740s, although the details are not clear.[42] In early 1747, one of the members of the Dublin group wrote to John Wesley, inviting him to come to Ireland, which he did in August of that year.

The following month Charles made the first of two visits to Ireland to support the work which his brother had just started. The early months were a struggle, since the society in Dublin had been all but crushed by opposition. However, Charles wrote that 'the little flock stands fast in the storm of persecution',[43] and worked tirelessly to spread the work into the surrounding countryside, where there were a number of embryonic societies that badly needed support and encouragement.

It was not an easy mission, and Charles' account of his ministry in Ireland is a microcosm of his experiences in England. Near Athlone, he and his companions were ambushed and narrowly escaped death. One of his friends was knocked senseless by a rock and Charles himself was attacked by a man wielding a large club. Thankfully, they were rescued by the people of Athlone, who 'expressed great indignation at our treatment'.[44] By the time Charles left in March 1748, he had helped to lay a lasting foundation for the future development of Methodist societies in Ireland. The seven months he spent there, however, took a severe toll on his health, and he arrived back in England emotionally and physically exhausted.

Nursed back to full health by Sally Gwynne and

70. Sun. Night.

This has been a day of trial and pain. I almost despaired of being able to open my mouth or take my leave of this dearest people. Yet at five I went forth to an innumerable multitude, and the Lord astonished me with the power he gave me. Never have I been more drawn out in prayer and preaching. For two hours I spake with a trumpet voice, and the hearts of all were bowed before the Lord, who gave testimony to His Word. My pain and weakness is all gone. I have forced my way through the weeping flock, to finish this. The Lord Jesus give you a share of the innumerable blessings but now showered down upon me by His people. I cannot now doubt of my prosperous journey. Faith laughs at Impossibilities.

Source: Frank Baker, *Charles Wesley as Revealed by His Letters*, Epworth Press 1948, p. 50.

her family, Charles was soon ready to take to the road once more. A second, shorter visit to Ireland followed in September 1748 but, as we have seen in the preceding chapter, domestic matters took on an increased importance. As he took his leave of the people of Cork, Charles penned a letter to Sally in which he summarized his work in Ireland, an excerpt from which is given here. [70]

By 8 October he was back in England, although he continued to take a lively interest in his Irish friends. Despite further persecution, particularly in Cork, Methodism grew steadily. John was to visit Ireland on more than twenty occasions in all, but Charles' brief ministry there had been of almost equal importance. Shortly after his return to England, he wrote to a friend that, 'in spite of all opposition, we pick up every day more lost sheep'.[45]

Charles' Ministry in Bristol

> *Let us join – 'tis God commands –*
> *Let us join our hearts and hands;*
> *Help to gain our calling's hope,*
> *Build we each the other up:*
> *Still forget the things behind,*
> *Follow Christ in heart and mind,*
> *Toward the mark unwearied press,*
> *Seize the crown of righteousness.*

In September 1749, as we saw in the preceding chapter, Charles took up residence at 4 Charles Street in Bristol. Although he continued to itinerate – and, very early on, bent over backwards in trying to show his fellow Methodists that married life had not changed him – his trips to the far-flung corners of the country gradually lessened, and by the 1750s he had become more settled in Bristol. Domestic matters became more important: in 1750 Sally had a miscarriage and, shortly afterwards, Charles' sister Hetty died. It is true that Sally accompanied him on a number of his 'tours of duty', but these occasions became fewer. In 1756 Charles undertook a major tour of a number of northern towns, including Manchester,

Bolton, Bradford, Leeds, Sheffield and York, but this was to be the last major venture of this kind. Thereafter his preaching was mainly confined to the southern counties.

There was always a demand for Charles to preach, of course, and at times both he and (surprisingly, and rather unfairly) John were criticized for neglecting parts of the country which they had formerly visited. As the number of Methodist societies grew, so did the need for greater encouragement and oversight and – when one bears in mind John's somewhat autocratic nature – control. But the simple fact was that the brothers could only be in one place at a time, as Charles pointed out to John Bennet in May 1750, when the latter asked him why neither he nor John had been north recently. '*You* know that we have but one body apiece,' he wrote. 'However, be not discouraged. The Lord of the harvest shall in His own time send you more fellow-labourers.'[46]

In truth, the work of the Methodist revival needed more preachers. Yet, as with all radical or reforming movements which are initially characterized by a strong sense of spontaneity, there was a need to regularize procedures and guide the individuals involved. The first Methodist Conference in 1744 had met partly in order 'to regulate our doctrines, discipline and practice',[47] and it was agreed that the itinerant lay preachers should meet with the ordained ministers for guidance and instruction. That this was not entirely successful is shown by John's letter to Charles in September 1750, which included the request:

> I wish you could talk a little with every preacher and every exhorter that comes in your way. Perhaps you may find some who are capable of being taken into the general work.[48]

Behind this letter lay an anxiety on John's part that in some places standards were slipping, and that a general enquiry was needed into existing, as well as new, preachers. In June 1751, for example, Charles and John had to suspend James Wheatley, who had taken it upon himself to leave Bristol against

71. Mon., August 5th.

I went to the room, that I might hear with my own ears one, of whom many strange things had been told me. But such a Preacher have I never heard, and hope I never shall again. It was beyond description. I cannot say he preached false doctrine, or true, or any doctrine at all, but pure, unmixed nonsense. Not one sentence did he utter that could do the least good to any one soul. Now and then a text of Scripture, or a verse quotation, was dragged in by head and shoulders. I could scarce refrain from stopping him. He set my blood a-galloping, and threw me into such a sweat, that I expected the fever to follow. Some begged me to step into the desk, and speak a few words to the poor dissatisfied hearers. I did so, taking no notice of Michael Fenwick.

I talked closely with him . . . and told him plainly he should either labour with his hands, or preach no more. He hardly complied, though he confessed it was his ruin, his having been taken off his business. I answered I would repair the supposed injury, by setting him up again in his shop.

Source: T. Jackson (ed.), *The Journal of The Rev. Charles Wesley, M.A.*, London, John Mason 1849, Vol. II, pp. 77–8.

Charles' advice in order to preach in Yorkshire.[49] It was a painful task, and Charles wrote shortly afterwards:

It put my brother and me upon a resolution of strictly examining into the life and moral behaviour of every preacher in connexion with us; and the office fell upon me.[50]

Charles was determined to carry out the task of 'purging the preachers' with vigour and thoroughness. One such example (on this occasion, of incompetence) which he witnessed in a preacher was at Leeds in August 1751. Charles had been seriously ill, and his temper therefore was somewhat shorter than normal, but his description of Michael Fenwick's preaching leaves the reader in no doubt as to Charles' feelings about the need for tighter discipline throughout the connexion. [71]

This particular extract from Charles' journal[51] reveals both his passion for rectitude and his pastoral concern. It was not that Charles was opposed to the idea of lay people preaching. Rather, his deep respect for the traditions of the Church made him aware of the need to root out incompetence, doctrinal error and moral unworthiness wherever he found it.

Charles kept a detailed record of his activities and frequently wrote to John for advice on sensitive issues. At times they disagreed, Charles being less tolerant in some ways than his brother. In a letter to the Countess of Huntingdon[52] in August 1751, he expressed grave misgivings concerning lay people who had given up their jobs for itinerant preaching and put themselves at severe financial risk. Charles felt that they should return to their trades and only venture on preaching excursions for limited periods of time. He also wrote that 'no one be allowed to preach with us, till my brother and I have heard him with our own ears, and talked fully with him . . .'[53]

72. The second reason which I have for insisting on the labourers keeping themselves (which I cannot mention to my brother lest it should be a reason with him against it) is, namely, [that] it will break his power, their not depending on him for bread, and reduce his authority within due bounds, as well as guard against that rashness and credulity of his, which has kept me in continual awe and bondage for many years. Therefore I shall insist on their working as one point, the single condition, of my acting in concert with him. Because without this I can neither trust them nor him. If he refuses I will give both preachers and society to his sole management, for this ruin shall not be under my hands. If he complies, I hope to take up my cross and bear it more cheerfully than ever I have done heretofore.

Source: Frank Baker, *Charles Wesley as Revealed by His Letters*, Epworth Press 1948, p. 85.

However, Charles' impulsive nature asserted itself over and above his sense of propriety, and towards the end of this letter he gave vent to his deeper fears as to what was happening. The passage in question is sufficiently important to be reproduced here. [72]

The underlying issue was not so much John's 'rashness and credulity', nor even the degree of power which Charles felt that he was acquiring. Charles was deeply concerned that many of the lay preachers had ambitions of becoming ministers, and that there was a consequent danger of a breach forming between the Methodists and the Church of England. This, as we shall see in Chapter 8, was a prospect too terrible for Charles to contemplate, and it helps to explain the extreme terms in which he wrote to the Countess of Huntingdon. When John saw the contents of the letter[54] he was not amused! If too many were prevented from preaching, he feared that the resulting shortage would hamper the overall work. However, the disagreement between the brothers was settled fairly quickly.

Even though he was living a more sedentary life in Bristol, Charles continued to take a lively interest in the growing number of Methodist societies and a steady stream of letters to the preachers flowed from his pen. Gradually – perhaps inevitably – he realized that he was becoming out of step with many of them, and this was an early sign of the future break between Methodism and the Church of England.

At this point we leave Charles' work as a preacher and pastor and turn to his immense contribution, not only to Methodism, but also to the wider Church, as a hymn-writer and poet.

Chronology

1735	30 November	First record of Charles preaching
1738	July	His first visit to Newgate Prison
1739	29 May	Begins field-preaching
1744	25 June	First Methodist Conference
1747	September	His first visit to Ireland
1748	August	Makes his second visit to Ireland
1749	September	Charles and Sally settle in Bristol
1751		'Purging the preachers'
1756	September	His last visit to the north of England
	November	The end of his published journal
1771		The family move to 1 Chesterfield Street, Marylebone

For Discussion

1. Why was Charles so reluctant to preach in the open air? What made him convinced that he should, in fact, do this?

2. How far do you think Charles' preaching would be relevant to our own time? What kind of reception do you think he would receive today?

3. What, in your opinion, makes a good sermon?

4. What place has the giving of testimonies in worship and preaching today?

7
Hymn-Writer and Poet

My heart is full of Christ, and longs
Its glorious matter to declare!
Of him I make my loftier songs,
I cannot from his praise forbear;
My ready tongue makes haste to sing
The glories of my heavenly King.

This chapter can serve as only the briefest of introductions to Charles Wesley as a hymn-writer and poet. In comparison with the relative paucity of material that is available to us from his journal and letters, he has left us an enormous collection of hymns and poetry. Furthermore, compared to the rest of Charles' life and work, there is a wealth of material available concerning his hymn-writing.

Exactly how many hymns and poems Charles wrote has been a matter of long debate. Most scholars estimate the number to be in the region of 9,000, about 4,600 being published in Charles' lifetime and a further 3,100 appearing in print after his death. Hundreds of poems survived in incomplete form and the remainder (about 1,300) were published only quite recently.[1]

A question often asked is, 'What constitutes a hymn?', because it is not always clear where the boundary lies between a hymn and a spiritual poem. Dr Frank Baker cites four criteria which, he suggests, are specific to hymns as opposed to poems. A hymn is *religious* (i.e. it can be used in an act of worship); it is *communal*, in the sense that, even though it may be written from an individual perspective, it can be used by a group or congregation; it is *lyrical* (i.e. it is

intended to be sung); it is *regular* in structure and metre and consists of at least two verses.[2] However, even Dr Baker acknowledges that 'no such definition can be so absolutely satisfactory as to erect a watertight barrier between hymns and poems, and there will still be room for disagreement in its applications'.[3]

Charles himself was not always certain of the distinction. The earliest collection of religious verse (produced by John Wesley in 1737 and 1738 in two volumes) was entitled *A Collection of Psalms and Hymns*. However, when Charles became involved in the production of further editions in the following three years, the name was changed to *Hymns and Sacred Poems*, which contained over fifty pieces that could really have come into either category. As time went on, the distinction became further blurred, and in later collections, such as *Short Hymns on Select Passages of the Holy Scriptures*, Charles included both hymns and poems without making it clear which was which.

In the preface to their most famous hymnbook, *A Collection of Hymns for the Use of the People Called Methodists* (1780), Charles was at pains to explain the spirit in which the hymns were written. In the extract here (which almost certainly he, rather than John, wrote) his comments on the nature and importance of the art of poetry illustrate how difficult it is to separate hymnody from poetry. [73]

In reality, sacred poems can be set to music and become, in effect, hymns. Equally, as many Christians have found, hymns can be used in an individual's private devotions, in which case one could

> **73.** May I be permitted to add a few words with regard to the poetry? Then I will speak to those who are judges thereof, with all freedom and unreserved. To these I may say, without offence: (1). In these hymns there is no doggerel, no botches, nothing put in to patch up the rhyme, no feeble expletives. (2). Here is nothing turgid or bombastic on the one hand, nor low and creeping on the other. (3). Here are no *cant* expressions, no words without meaning. Those who impute this to us know not what they say. We talk common sense (whether they understand it or not) both in verse and prose, and use no word but in a fixed and determinate sense. (4). Here are (allow me to say) both the purity, the strength, and the elegance of the English language – and at the same time the utmost simplicity and plainness, suited to every capacity. Lastly, I desire men of taste to judge – these are the only competent judges – whether there is not in some of the following verses that true spirit of poetry, such as cannot be acquired by art and labour, but must be the gift of nature. By labour a man may become a tolerable imitator of Spenser, Shakespeare, or Milton, and may heap together pretty compound epithets, as 'pale-eyed', 'meek-eyed', and the like. But unless he is born a poet he will never attain the genuine *spirit of poetry*.
>
> *Source*: *A Collection of Hymns for the Use of the People Called Methodists*, 1780 edition, pp. 74–5.

argue that they become poetry. The Wesley brothers, of course, knew this very well, which is why, elsewhere in the same preface to *A Collection of Hymns for the Use of the People Called Methodists*, they wrote that it was 'in effect, a little body of experimental and practical divinity'.[4]

The Structure of Charles' Hymns

> *Jesus, the First and Last,*
> *On thee my soul is cast:*
> *Thou didst thy work begin*
> *By blotting out my sin;*
> *Thou wilt the root remove,*
> *And perfect me in love.*

> *Yet when the work is done,*
> *The work is but begun:*
> *Partaker of thy grace,*
> *I long to see thy face;*
> *The first I prove below,*
> *The last I die to know.*

As a young man Charles Wesley had been trained in logic, and he found it natural to give his hymns an ordered structure. The fact that, when we sing his hymns in worship, the orderliness and intricacy of their structure often go unnoticed, is an indication of the effortless way in which Charles constructed them. The hymn which begins this particular section is a perfect example of Charles' gift for encapsulating the essence of the process of salvation within just two verses.

Consider also the hymn 'What shall I do my God to love' (*Hymns and Psalms*, 46),[5] which is frequently sung and generally considered to be well-known. [74] In the original poem that was first published in 1749, there were ten verses written in a deeply penitential mood, which came before those which compose the present hymn. Two verses were subsequently omitted by the committees which compiled the *Methodist Hymn Book* of 1933 and *Hymns and Psalms* which appeared fifty years later. In this hymn we have a beautifully crafted exposition of the love of God, based on the prayer found in Ephesians 3.18–19:

[I pray] that you may have the power to comprehend, with all the saints, what is the breadth and length and height and depth, and to know the love of Christ that surpasses knowledge, so that you may be filled with all the fullness of God. (RSV)

A brief analysis of each verse will show how the structure of the hymn follows a logical progression of thought:
- Verse 1. This sets out the author's purpose, and the next five verses deal with each 'dimension' in turn.

74.

What shall I do my God to love,
  My loving God to praise?
The length, and breadth, and height to prove,
  And depth of sovereign grace?

Thy sovereign grace to all extends,
  Immense and unconfined;
From age to age it never ends;
  It reaches all mankind.

Throughout the world its breadth is known,
  Wide as infinity;
So wide it never passed by one,
  Or it had passed by me.

My trespass was grown up to heaven;
  But, far above the skies,
In Christ abundantly forgiven,
  I see thy mercies rise.

The depth of all-redeeming love
  What angel tongue can tell?
O may I to the utmost prove
  The gift unspeakable!

Deeper than hell, it plucked me thence;
  Deeper than inbred sin,
Jesus's love my heart shall cleanse
  When Jesus enters in.

Come quickly, gracious Lord, and take
  Possession of thine own;
My longing heart vouchsafe to make
  Thine everlasting throne.

Assert thy claim, maintain thy right,
  Come quickly from above;
And sink me to perfection's height,
  The depth of humble love.

Source: *A Collection of Hymns for the Use of the People Called Methodists*, 1780 edition. The two verses in italics were omitted from *The Methodist Hymn Book* and *Hymns and Psalms*.

- Verse 2 – 'length'. Wesley uses the phrase 'sovereign grace' to link the first line of the second verse to the last line of the preceding one. The 'length' of God's grace is seen in its timelessness – 'from age to age' – which, therefore, includes *all* people. The observant will notice that Charles Wesley changes the order that is in Ephesians, and begins with 'length' rather than 'breadth'.

- Verse 3 – 'breadth'. The connection between the verses is maintained with the phrase 'throughout the world' following on immediately from the word 'mankind' of the previous stanza. The humility that characterized so much of Charles Wesley's writings is even evident in this hymn of adoration, but the last two lines – 'So wide it never passed by one, or it had passed by me' – are significant more for the way they emphasize Charles' Arminian convictions.

- Verse 4 – 'height'. Although Charles does not use the word 'height' in this verse, the sense, nonetheless, is there. We are given a graphic picture of his sins being literally piled up 'to heaven', yet above all is God's mercy which is higher still.

- Verses 5 and 6 – 'depth'. As the hymn stands in its modern version (without verse 6), the author's treatment of 'depth' seems to lose a little of its force. However, when the missing verse is re-inserted, the full impact of 'depth' becomes readily apparent. The grace of God reaches to the very depths that human sin can descend.

- Verses 7 and 8 complete the picture of God's all-encompassing love, and the last verse of the original ends with a typically Wesleyan paradox. The height of perfection *is* the depth of humble love! The question posed at the beginning of the hymn can only be answered by recourse to the grace of God – his free love which can only be truly appropriated by the humble, penitent sinner.

We can also see Charles Wesley's careful structuring techniques on a smaller scale. Even within individual verses we can find balance and symmetry. For example, in the hymn 'Jesus, lover of my soul' (*Hymns and Psalms*, 528), we have the following, in verse 3:

Just and holy is thy name,
    I am all unrighteousness;
False and full of sin I am,
    Thou art full of truth and grace.

Students of literature will immediately recognize the device known as chiasmus,[6] where lines 1 and 4 enclose lines 2 and 3 in the pattern 'A–B–B–A' to enhance the impact of the words, which contrast the sinner's frailty with the perfection of God.

On a smaller scale still is the following example:

Let *earth* (A) and *heaven* (B) agree,
Angels (B) and *men* (A) be joined.
       (*Hymns and Psalms*, 226)[7]

This was a technique which Charles employed so much that it often goes unnoticed when sung in worship. In one of his most famous hymns, 'O for a thousand tongues to sing' (*Hymns and Psalms*, 744) the seventh verse is beautifully crafted:

See all your sins on Jesus laid: (A)
    The Lamb of God was slain; (B)
His soul was once an offering made (B)
    For every soul of man. (A)

It makes an interesting exercise to look at a range of Charles' hymns and to examine such instances of his craftsmanship. These devices were there for a purpose, to instruct and clarify, but always to increase the effectiveness of the message he was proclaiming. They were, in Frank Baker's words, 'integrated artistic structures, not random heaps of building blocks, no matter how decorative'.[8]

Charles' Use of Scripture

Come, divine interpreter,
    Bring us eyes thy book to read,
Ears the mystic words to hear,
    Words which did from thee proceed,

Words that endless bliss impart
Kept in an obedient heart.

Charles read extensively and was well versed in the Classics, so it was natural for him to draw upon these sources in his poetry and hymn-writing. We have already seen how easily he slipped into Latin or Greek in his correspondence, particularly when he was writing in confidence to John and wished to keep his comments hidden from prying eyes.[9] It should therefore come as no surprise that Charles used a great number of words derived from Latin (and, to a lesser extent, Greek) which have become almost incomprehensible to modern readers.

The same is true, alas, for Charles' scriptural allusions, which dwarf all the other kinds of references and quotations that are to be found in his hymns. 'And can it be' (*Hymns and Psalms*, 216) so popular with revivalists, contains no fewer than eleven references to passages from the New Testament alone. Charles literally plundered the Bible for images, and a recent scholar has shrewdly observed that 'Methodist admirers of the Wesleys have sometimes taken solace in the notion that if one day the Bible should disappear, its text could nearly be completely reconstructed based on the Wesleyan deposit of hymns alone.'[10]

Sometimes Charles would base a whole hymn upon a passage of Scripture. For example, 'My heart is full of Christ, and longs its glorious matter to declare' (*Hymns and Psalms*, 799), is certainly not a paraphrase – that is quite obvious from the very first line of the first verse – but is heavily based upon Psalm 45. Originally twenty-one stanzas in all, only the first four verses appear in *Hymns and Psalms*, although the fifth verse is reproduced in the accompanying extract [75] because it epitomizes the message that underlies so many of Charles' sermons. In its shortened form the hymn is an admirable example of the way Charles was able to take the essence of a psalm and transform it into a hymn of praise to Christ.

75.

My heart is full of Christ, and longs
    Its glorious matter to declare!
Of him I make my loftier songs,
    I cannot from his praise forbear;
My ready tongue makes haste to sing
The glories of my God and King.

Fairer than all the earth-born race,
    Perfect in comeliness thou art;
Replenished are thy lips with grace,
    And full of love thy tender heart:
God ever blest! We bow the knee,
And own all fullness dwells in thee.

Gird on thy thigh the Spirit's sword,
    And take to thee thy power divine;
Stir up thy strength, almighty Lord,
    All power and majesty are thine:
Assert thy worship and renown;
O all-redeeming God, come down!

Come, and maintain thy righteous cause,
    And let thy glorious toil succeed;
Dispread the victory of thy cross,
    Ride on, and prosper in thy deed;
Through earth triumphantly ride on,
And reign in every heart alone.

Still let the word of truth prevail,
    The gospel of thy general grace,
Of mercy mild that ne'er shall fail,
    Of everlasting righteousness,
Into the faithful soul brought in,
To root out all the seeds of sin.

Source: *A Collection of Psalms and Hymns*, 1743
edition. The verse in italics was omitted from *The
Methodist Hymn Book* and *Hymns and Psalms*.

Watts, because he is dominated by the notion of paraphrasing, puts Scripture very often into his own words; it is not always to the advantage of Scripture. Wesley does little paraphrasing. He puts his own notions into scriptural language, and it is always to their advantage. Each is scriptural; they are equally scriptural, but in different ways, and the literary luck is with Wesley.[11]

The individual, of course, has to come to his or her own conclusion, but a further example of the way Charles Wesley used Scripture as a basis for getting his central message across can be found in the way he Christianized the most famous psalm of all – Psalm 23 – in his hymn 'Jesus, the good Shepherd is' (*Hymns and Psalms*, 263). It is reproduced here [76], because it makes for an interesting comparison with the more frequently sung 'The Lord's my Shepherd' and 'The King of love my Shepherd is' (70 and 69 in *Hymns and Psalms* respectively). Notice how, in the second line of the first verse, Wesley makes it clear that Christ's death is the key to life in all its fullness.

Perhaps the best known hymn in which Charles adapted a section of Scripture is his 'Come, O thou Traveller unknown' (*Hymns and Psalms*, 434), which appeared in print in 1742 with the title 'Wrestling Jacob'. Too long to be reproduced here, it nonetheless deserves more than a passing mention. The hymn was based on Genesis 32.24–32, the story of Jacob's encounter with God at Peniel, but contains dozens of allusions to passages from both Old and New Testaments. Originally consisting of fourteen stanzas, it has been considered sufficiently important to have been retained almost in its entirety: twelve verses appear in *Hymns and Psalms*, though whether all of them are sung by today's congregations is a moot point! However, it should be pointed out that Charles did not originally envisage that the hymn would be sung in worship and wrote it as a lyrical poem. It was probably intended to be read in private devotions or at class and band meetings.

Almost certainly 'Come, O thou Traveller unknown' was inspired by Charles' own experience at Pentecost in May 1738, since it seems to match his

Comparisons are often drawn between Charles Wesley and Isaac Watts, who also placed heavy reliance upon Scripture for his raw material. In his study of the hymns of these two authors, Bernard Manning makes the following interesting comment:

intense struggle to find spiritual peace of mind so accurately. It is clear that not all of his hymns which were written in the first person singular referred to him personally; so, for example, in the children's hymn 'Gentle Jesus, meek and mild' Charles was not actually speaking of *himself* in the line 'Suffer me to come to thee'. Even so, one cannot but conclude that it was true in this case. Certainly, the passage from Genesis on which the hymn is based was one of Charles' favourite themes in his preaching.

What we have, in effect, are two parallel stories. Jacob is on a journey which is both real and metaphysical and, in a night of turmoil, encounters an 'angel' and receives a blessing. Charles – the 'I' in the hymn – also went through a night of 'wrestling' on 20–21 May 1738 and, with the dawn, he too found himself blessed by God. The opening stanza can apply equally well both to Jacob and to Charles, but the line 'Look on thy hands, and read it there' in the second verse suggests that the 'traveller unknown' is, in fact, Christ. By the third verse – 'Art thou the man that died for me?' – it is clear that the 'name' which the author longs to know is that of Christ his Saviour.

The penitential tone of the early verses changes to a note of triumph and, by the seventh verse, the identity of the 'unknown' is revealed in all its fullness: ''Tis Love! 'Tis Love! Thou diedst for me!', and 'Pure, universal love thou art'. Finally, the repetition of the statement 'Thy nature and thy name is Love' at the end of each of the final six verses reinforces the tremendous sense of release which comes with the assurance of pardon and restoration. It is, indeed, one of Charles Wesley's finest compositions, and Isaac Watts is said to have commented, 'That single poem, *Wrestling Jacob*, is worth all the verses which I have ever written.'

Incidentally, Charles Wesley was not afraid to adapt secular poetry if it suited his purpose. His great hymn, 'Love divine, all loves excelling', for example, is thought to have been inspired by Purcell's song 'Fairest isle, all isles excelling'. It has even been suggested that there are just as many allusions in Charles' hymns to Milton's *Paradise Lost* as there are to the Bible, though since the former itself draws so heavily upon Scripture, it is difficult to know what exactly this proves!

76.

Jesus the good Shepherd is,
   Jesus died the sheep to save;
He is mine and I am his,
   All I want in him I have:
Life, and health, and rest, and food,
All the plenitude of God.

Jesus loves and guards his own;
   Me in verdant pastures feeds,
Makes me quietly lie down,
   By the streams of comfort leads:
Following him where'er he goes,
Silent joy my heart o'erflows.

He in sickness makes me whole,
   Guides into the paths of peace;
He revives my fainting soul,
   Stablishes in righteousness;
Who for me vouchsafed to die,
Loves me still – I know not why.

Love divine shall still embrace,
   Love shall keep me to the end;
Surely all my happy days
   I shall in thy temple spend,
Till I to thy house remove,
Thy eternal house above!

Source: *Hymns and Psalms*, Methodist Publishing House 1983, 263.

Theology

'Tis Love! 'Tis Love! Thou diedst for me!
   I hear thy whisper in my heart;
The morning breaks, the shadows flee,
   Pure, universal love thou art;
To me, to all, thy mercies move:
Thy nature and thy name is Love.

77.

THE CONTENTS.

PART I.

Containing Introductory Hymns.

PART II.

PART III.

PART IV.

PART V.

Source: A Collection of Hymns for the Use of the People Called Methodists, 1780 edition.

In this book, as with the author's introductory volume to the series, *The Making of Methodism*, verses of hymns appear at the beginnings of chapters and sections, and it will have become clear to the reader, even before he or she has begun to read this present chapter, that Charles' hymns cover a wide range of theology as well as human emotion. Dr Frank Baker has written that, 'the "sweet singer" of Methodism provided in his robust scriptural song both spiritual education and an inspiring means of giving expression to the richly varying experiences of those pressing along the highway of personal religion.'[12] In view of Charles' prolific output, it is not surprising that there is hardly an aspect of evangelical theology that is not covered by his hymns, and a recent commentator has aptly described him as 'the spiritual librettist of the Methodist revival'.[13]

However, the hymns which John and Charles intended the early Methodists actually to *sing* did not cover the entire theological spectrum. For example, a brief study of the contents of the Methodist hymnbook of 1780, *A Collection of Hymns for the Use of the People Called Methodists*, [77] shows that there were significant omissions. In contrast to *The Methodist Hymn Book* of 1933 and *Hymns and Psalms*, the choice seems extraordinarily narrow. The doctrines of creation, the trinity, incarnation and atonement, to name but a few, are all conspicuous by their absence.

This did not mean that Charles neglected these important themes. The table of contents of the 1780 hymnbook (as, indeed, with its title) shows, rather, that it was meant to be a supplement to other hymnbooks already in existence. Hence the omission of hymns covering the sacraments and the major Christian festivals. Even 'Hark! the herald-angels sing' and 'Christ the Lord is risen today' had to wait for a later edition which had more sections added at the end.[14] Charles actually wrote many fine Christmas and Easter hymns, and John Wesley remarked in a letter to a friend in 1774, 'some of my brother's Christmas hymns are some of the finest compositions in the English tongue'.[15]

J. Ernest Rattenbury, who was one of the greatest authorities on Charles' hymns of the last century, writes that the 1780 hymnbook 'was not meant to be comprehensive; it was designed for a separate society which [John] Wesley hoped would continue as such, but would at the same time retain its Church connections'.[16] The original version of 1780 was, in truth, a hymnbook for a revival movement, and the table of contents was put together to represent the pilgrimage of what John Wesley called in the preface 'a real Christian'. Its twentieth-century successors, by contrast, were intended for a *church*, rather than a collection of societies. The next extract, part of the preface to the 1780 hymnbook, clearly shows the underlying reasons as to why it took the form it did. [78]

It could be argued that the term 'speculative' (John's word, not Charles') was not entirely appropriate, because Charles' hymns were essentially practical in nature. They were 'experimental' in the sense that they dealt with religious experience, and often the experience, as we have noted already, came from Charles' own spiritual journey.[17]

The 1780 hymnbook was not actually the final

---

78. Such a Hymn-Book you have now before you. It is not so large as to be either cumbersome or expensive; and it is large enough to contain such a variety of hymns as will not soon be worn threadbare. It is large enough to contain all the important truths of our most holy religion, whether speculative or practical; yea, to illustrate them all, and to prove them both by Scripture and reason; and this is done in a regular order. The hymns are not carelessly jumbled together, but carefully ranged under proper heads, according to the experience of real Christians. So that this book is, in effect, a little body of experimental and practical divinity.

. . . I would commend it to every truly pious reader, as a means of raising or quickening the spirit of devotion; of confirming his faith; of enlivening his hope; and of kindling and increasing his love to God and man.

Source: A Collection of Hymns for the Use of the People Called Methodists, 1780 edition.

collection produced by John and Charles Wesley. In 1785 and 1787 abridged versions of the *Collection* appeared under the title *A Pocket Hymnbook, for the Use of Christians of all Denominations*. However, the 1780 *Collection* was, in effect, the Wesleys' 'Methodist manifesto'. Bernard Manning summed up what many felt about this book when he wrote:

> This little book . . . ranks in Christian literature with the Psalms, the Book of Common Prayer, the Canon of the Mass. In its own way it is perfect, unapproachable, elemental in its perfection. You cannot alter it, except to mar it; it is a work of supreme devotional art by a religious genius.[18]

Whilst he was not a theologian in the sense that Augustine, Aquinas, Luther or even his brother were, it would be unfair to say that Charles' hymns simply reiterated John Wesley's theological ideas. Rattenbury uses an interesting metaphor when he says that Charles 'was not a scientific theologian . . . His hymns are not museum pieces; they are flowers in a flower garden; his doctrines are alive.'[19]

While space prevents a fully comprehensive treatment of the theology of Charles' hymns, there are certain areas which are sufficiently important to warrant brief examination.

The root of Charles' theology lay in what God had done for all humankind[20] in Christ. Both John and Charles Wesley were Arminians, in the sense that they believed the grace of God to be available to *all* people. Therefore, we find Charles giving great emphasis to the universal love of God. His hymns are littered with such phrases as 'the all-atoning Lamb' and 'all-redeeming Lord', and it would be an interesting statistical exercise to count how many times he used the word 'all' in his hymns. The reason for this emphasis upon the universal nature of God's grace lies partly in the pains which Charles and his brother took to counter the Calvinist doctrine of predestination which George Whitefield and others were preaching at the time. As a contemporary scholar has observed: 'The constant emphasis on God's will for universal salvation originates, in no small measure,

by way of negative designs. It is meant to refute . . . a particularistic understanding of salvation as embraced by the Calvinist followers of George Whitefield.'[21]

To give but one noteworthy example, the word 'all' appears no less than fifteen times in the hymn 'Father, whose everlasting love' (*Hymns and Psalms*, 520), and at least once in every single verse. It is reproduced here in its earliest and fullest form. [79] Moreover, the abundance of inclusive terms, 'unconfined', 'general', 'undistinguishing' and 'universal', points to Charles' firm conviction that salvation was possible for *all* people, and not just for some. The substitution of the word 'nations' for 'Gentiles' in the second line of the last verse would have almost certainly met with the author's approval, for this very reason. Incidentally, the very last line of the hymn has been taken by some to suggest that Charles was a universalist. This is probably to take his Arminian beliefs too far, and the word 'shall' should be read as being in the subjunctive mood, rather than in the future indicative. That is, he is expressing a wish, a fervent hope, that all will come to faith, not necessarily a belief that all actually *would*.

This can be seen in his fine hymn, 'Come, sinners, to the gospel feast' (*Hymns and Psalms*, 460), based on Luke 14.16–20, the parable of the Great Dinner, and which is often sung at Holy Communion. That the invitation is for all is explicit in the first verse,

> Come, sinners, to the gospel feast,
>   Let every soul be Jesu's guest;
> You need not one be left behind,
>   For God hath bidden all mankind.

The word 'let' in the second line confirms this feeling of hope and expectation. A line in a later verse, 'His love is mighty to compel', might suggest that God's grace is irresistible. However, Charles is simply expressing what could almost be described as astonishment at the thought of anyone refusing the invitation.

Another very important aspect of Charles Wesley's

79.

Father, whose everlasting love
  Thy only Son for sinners gave,
Whose grace to all did freely move,
  And sent Him down a world to save.

Help us Thy mercy to extol,
  Immense, unfathomed, unconfined;
To praise the Lamb who died for all,
  The general Saviour of mankind.

Thy undistinguishing regard
  Was cast on Adam's fallen race;
For all Thou hast in Christ prepared
  Sufficient, sovereign, saving grace.

Jesus hath said, we all shall hope,
  Preventing grace for all is free:
'And I, if I be lifted up,
  I will draw all men unto Me.'

What soul whose drawings never knew?
  With whom hath not Thy Spirit strove?
We all must own that God is true,
  We all may feel that God is love.

Behold the Lamb of God, who takes
  The sins of all the world away!
His pity no exception makes;
  But all that will receive Him, may.

The world he suffered to redeem;
  For all he has the atonement made;
For those who will not come to him
  The ransom of his life was paid.

Why then, thou universal Love,
  Should any of thy grace despair?
To all, to all, thy bowels move,
  But straitened in our own we are.

Arise, O God, maintain Thy cause!
  The fullness of the nations call:
Lift up the standard of Thy cross,
  And all shall own Thou diedst for all.

Source: Hymns and Psalms, Methodist Publishing House 1983, 520. The verses in italics are verses which originally appeared in *A Collection of Hymns on God's Everlasting Love* (1741), and which were subsequently omitted.

theology can be found in his hymns concerning Christian perfection.

In the preface to his *Short Hymns on Select Passages of the Holy Scriptures*, which was published in 1762, Charles was careful to point out that 'several of the hymns are intended to prove and several to guard the doctrine of Christian Perfection'.[22] The word 'doctrine' which he used here was, in fact, a very loose term, because there was no single, clearly delineated body of teaching on the subject. The notion of Christian perfection was a very fluid concept reflecting a wide range of beliefs. Indeed, Charles' views differed somewhat from those of his brother John, as we shall see in the next chapter. It will be sufficient to note at this point that whereas John saw the possibility of it being instantaneous, achievable in this lifetime, and 'limited' by human faculties, Charles viewed perfection as a more gradual process, only coming at the very end of a person's life, when the individual was transformed into nothing less than the image of Christ. In *Hymns and Sacred Poems* (1742), Charles included a hymn (though it appears to be more a poem than a hymn) entitled 'A Funeral Hymn for Mrs Hooper'.[23] The sixth verse clearly shows Charles' views on perfection:

She died in sure and steadfast hope,
  By Jesus wholly sanctified;
Her perfect spirit she gave up,
  And sunk into His arms, and died.

A fuller illustration of the way in which Charles conceived Christian perfection is to be found in a hymn that is still frequently sung on Sundays (though perhaps not so well known outside Methodism), 'God of all power, and truth, and grace' (*Hymns and Psalms*, 726), a shortened version of which forms the next extract. [80] Originally twenty-eight verses, it was another of Charles' early hymns and was entitled 'Pleading the Promise of Sanctification'. The title itself is revealing, because Charles never conceived of perfection as a gift from God for which the believer should give thanks. He wrote no hymns

80.

> God of all power, and truth, and grace,
>   Which shall from age to age endure,
> Whose word, when heaven and earth shall pass,
>   Remains and stands for ever sure.
>
> That I thy mercy may proclaim,
>   That all mankind thy truth may see,
> Hallow thy great and glorious name,
>   And perfect holiness in me.
>
> Thy sanctifying Spirit pour
>   To quench my thirst and make me clean;
> Now, Father, let the gracious shower
>   Descend, and make me pure from sin.
>
> Give me a new, a perfect heart,
>   From doubt, and fear, and sorrow free;
> The mind which was in Christ impart,
>   And let my spirit cleave to thee.
>
> O that I now, from sin released,
>   Thy word may to the utmost prove,
> Enter into the promised rest,
>   The Canaan of thy perfect love!
>
> Now let me gain perfection's height,
>   Now let me into nothing fall,
> Be less than nothing in thy sight,
>   And feel that Christ is all in all.

Source: *Hymns and Psalms*, Methodist Publishing House 1983, 726.

which express the latter idea. Rather, perfection was given as the believer entered 'the promised rest', for which Charles used the evocative image of 'the Canaan of thy perfect love'. This can be seen in the way in which the hymn develops into a plea for perfection that, by God's grace, would be granted in the future.

What then, was necessary for the attainment of 'perfection's height'? Charles insisted that the creation of a new heart in the Christian was a precondition for the life of perfect love in paradise, and this idea is to be found in many of his hymns. So, for example, we find him writing in his hymn 'O for a heart to praise my God' (*Hymns and Psalms*, 536), the verse:

> A heart in every thought renewed,
>   And full of love divine;
> Perfect, and right, and pure, and good,
>   A copy, Lord, of thine!

In his own search for 'full redemption' and perfect love Charles was mindful of the spiritual struggle through which he himself had gone, and which was a part of every Christian's continuing journey of faith, including his own. Thus, alongside the heights of elation at what God had done for him, were the depths of sorrow at his own unworthiness. The contrast can be seen in the last verse of 'God of all power, and truth, and grace' and clearly shows the essential paradox of the human condition. A further example can be found in the final verse of the hymn 'What shall I do my God to love' (Extract 74). Rattenbury was of the opinion that 'Charles overstated suffering as a necessity of the imitation of Christ',[24] and a reading of Charles' hymns supports this conclusion.

As a result, many of Charles' hymns have been criticized for displaying what some (perhaps unkindly) have called his 'worm theology'. In this respect we may not find all his language appealing today. Lines such as

> If so poor a worm as I,
>   May to Thy great glory live . . .

and

> If now thou talkest by the way
>   With such an abject worm as me . . .

may seem very strange to us now. Our credulity may be stretched even further by

> That only name to sinners given,
>   Which lifts poor dying worms to heaven.[25]

The word 'worm', of course, appears in several psalms but Charles used the term on many occasions in his hymns because of his intense belief in the unworthiness of the individual. Moreover, he was not afraid to write about sin and death – and joy and heaven, too. He was a man of his time who expressed himself strongly. 'Whether we are attracted or repelled by Charles Wesley's heightened spiritual temperature,' writes Frank Baker, 'one thing cannot be questioned – his utter sincerity.'[26] If in today's somewhat lower spiritual temperature we find his words over-emotional, we should recall that they were simply a reflection of his intense desire to see salvation obtained by all.

If space permitted, we could explore further aspects of Charles Wesley's theology as revealed in his hymns. So far we have confined ourselves to just two: the universal nature of God's love and will that all should experience salvation, and the nature of Christian perfection which, through his hymns, was one of Charles' main contributions to the development of evangelical theology.

However, there is one area which merits brief discussion: that of the sacrament of Holy Communion, or the Eucharist, on which Charles wrote many hymns.[27]

In his other major work on Charles Wesley's hymns, *The Eucharistic Hymns of John and Charles Wesley*, J. Ernest Rattenbury points out that one of Charles' motives was to encourage the revival of the Church of England, as well as a revival of the spiritual life of the country as a whole. It should not come as a surprise, therefore, to find that the brothers' *Hymns on the Lord's Supper*[28] ran to no fewer than nine editions in their lifetime. Both the Wesleys urged their followers 'constantly to attend on all the ordinances of God; in particular . . . to be at Church and at the Lord's Table every week . . .'[29] An indication of the importance which Charles attached to the Eucharist can be seen in the number of short hymns, often consisting of only two verses, which he wrote. These were intended to be sung during these services, and since eighteenth-century liturgies were invariably much longer than those of today, there was considerable scope for their use.

One such hymn is 'Come, Holy Ghost, thine influence shed' (*Hymns and Psalms*, 602), which is reproduced here in its entirety. [81] It is a beautifully succinct and poetic form of epiclesis – a Greek word meaning 'invocation' – which is the prayer for the consecration of the elements during the communion service. It did not appear in *A Collection of Hymns for the Use of the People Called Methodists* but was included in the supplement of 1796. At first glance the hymn seems to be promoting a very high view of the Eucharist, but Charles was careful not to suggest that the Holy Spirit was being invoked to change the bread and wine into the body and blood of Christ *literally*. The phrase 'fit channels' made it clear that the reality of Christ's presence was to be felt in his love being received by faith into believers' hearts.

Charles shared his brother's view that it was a *converting*, as well as a *confirming* ordinance, and John encouraged him to publish them so that their use might become more widespread. Indeed, the early years of the Methodist Revival saw a marked increase in the number of people taking communion in those parishes where Methodist influence was most strong. Consider one of Charles' lesser known hymns on the Eucharist. [82] In all probability the brothers collaborated in its writing.

81.

Come, Holy Ghost, thine influence shed,
  And realize the sign;
Thy life infuse into the bread,
  Thy power into the wine.

Effectual let thy tokens prove
  And made, by heavenly art,
Fit channels to convey thy love
  To every faithful heart.

Source: *Hymns and Psalms*, Methodist Publishing House 1983, 602.

82.

> Jesu, at whose supreme command
>   We now approach to God,
> Before us in thy vesture stand,
>   Thy vesture dipped in blood!
> Obedient to thy gracious word,
>   We break the hallowed bread,
> Commemorate thee, our dying Lord,
>   And trust on thee to feed.
>
> Now, Saviour, now thyself reveal,
>   And make thy nature known;
> Affix thy blessed Spirit's seal,
>   And stamp us for thine own:
> The tokens of thy dying love
>   O let us all receive;
> And feel the quickening Spirit move,
>   And sensibly believe!
>
> The cup of blessing, blessed by thee,
>   Let it thy blood impart;
> The bread thy mystic body be,
>   And cheer each languid heart.
> Thy grace which sure salvation brings
>   Let us herewith receive;
> Satiate the hungry with good things,
>   The hidden manna give.
>
> The living bread, sent down from heaven,
>   In us vouchsafe to be;
> Thy flesh for all the world is given,
>   And all may live by thee.
> Now, Lord, on us thy flesh bestow,
>   And let us drink thy blood,
> Till all our souls are filled below
>   With all the life of God.

Source: *A Collection of Hymns for the Use of the People Called Methodists*, 1780 edition, 901.

The second and third verses show quite clearly how John and Charles saw communion as both an agent of conversion and a means whereby the faith of established believers could be strengthened.

John or Charles?

It is quite clear that Charles wrote many more hymns than his elder brother John. It is also a well-established fact that it was John, rather than Charles, who selected, arranged and edited the hymns that formed the various collections that appeared as *Hymns and Sacred Poems* from 1739 onwards, and in *A Collection of Hymns for the Use of the People Called Methodists* which was published in 1780.

It is true, of course, that John amended parts of his brother's hymns where he considered Charles' language unsuitable or too emotive. In 1749 John wrote, 'My brother printed two volumes of "hymns and sacred poems". As I did not see these before they were published, there were some things in them I did not approve of.'[30] Nonetheless, he had enormous respect for Charles' gifts. So, for example, we find that in 1760 John Wesley wrote a letter to John Berridge, the vicar of Everton, who had himself published a collection of hymns earlier that year, and complained of the way that Berridge had altered many of Charles' hymns. In the accompanying brief extract from this letter, in which 'Mr. B.' is Mr Berridge, John expresses his objections in no uncertain terms. [83]

A problem arises, however, when we consider the question of authorship. For example, there are many instances where phrases and couplets which appear in one brother's hymns are duplicated in those which were (apparently) written by the other.

83. London, April 18, 1760.

. . . After we had been once singing an hymn at Everton, I was just going to say, 'I wish Mr. Whitefield would not try to mend my brother's hymns. He cannot do it. How vilely he has murdered that hymn, weakening the sense as well as marring the poetry!' But how was I afterwards surprised to hear it was not Mr. Whitefield, but Mr. B.! In very deed it is not easy to mend his hymns any more than to imitate them.

Source: John Wesley, *Letters*, Vol. IV, p. 93.

Frank Baker gives a noteworthy example in the rhyming lines 'No condemnation now I dread . . . Alive in thee, my living head . . .', which appeared in a hymn that John translated from the German and also in Charles' 'And can it be that I should gain' (*Hymns and Psalms*, 216), and which he feels is unlikely to be coincidental.[31] It has been very difficult for scholars such as Dr Baker to decide whether these are examples of copying, or simply the result of one brother suggesting an amendment to the other during a conversation.

Although John and Charles agreed not to append their names to individual pieces in *Hymns and Sacred Poems*, by 1748 they no longer followed this practice. By then both brothers had published two collections under their own names.[32]

There are clues. Virtually all the hymns that were translated from German – and to a lesser extent French and Spanish sources – were written by John. Moreover, the language which John used in his hymns tended to be more formal and academic than that used by Charles, and Frank Baker points out that 'wherever unduly amorous terminology is applied to God in a hymn supposedly written by John, it should arouse immediate suspicion'.[33] John was, by nature, more restrained than his younger brother, and so his hymns lack the sentimentality which creeps into many of Charles' compositions. For example, John considered Charles' hymn 'Jesus, lover of my soul' to come into this category, and he was almost certainly responsible for its omission from *A Collection of Hymns for the Use of the People Called Methodists* until the 1797 edition, which appeared after Charles' death. There can be no doubting, therefore, that where a hymn contains the heights of exuberance and the depths of despair and longing, then it almost certainly was penned by Charles.

For a fuller examination the reader can do no better than consult Frank Baker's introduction, to which references have already been made, and from there to look at the works of such scholars as Bernard Manning, Henry Bett, Oliver Beckerlegge and others that are cited in the bibliography.

Charles' Poetry

> Not unto me, O Lord,
> Not unto me, the praise,
> If I with power have spoke Thy word
> And testified Thy grace.
> Thou didst the power bestow,
> Thou didst Thy servant find,
> And raise, and send me forth to show
> Thy love to all mankind.[34]

In this final section we turn to Charles the poet although, as we observed at the beginning of the chapter, it is not easy to put his hymns and poetry into separate, neat categories. Understandably, Charles' rather haphazard approach to categorizing his verse should have led to the widespread view that he was a hymn-writer rather than a poet. In fact, he wrote more poems than William Wordsworth and Robert Browning put together. It is worth noting that S. T. Kimbrough and Oliver Beckerlegge classify as poems many pieces which others have previously regarded as hymns. In his foreword to the first volume of *The Unpublished Poetry of Charles Wesley*, Kimbrough writes: 'The myth that Charles Wesley wrote about 6,500 hymns should once and for all be laid to rest. While he wrote hundreds of hymns, indeed a few thousand, his work extends far beyond the realm of lyrical lines specifically intended to be set to music and sung in Christian worship.'[35]

Another misunderstanding which has arisen is that Charles only really started writing poetry after May 1738, when the resolution of his spiritual crisis saw him compose 'Where shall my wondering soul begin'. Actually, Charles was probably writing poetry before he was eight years of age, although unfortunately very few of these poems have survived. Readers will recall that Charles' father Samuel was a poet of some ability, if lacking in flair, and his eldest brother Samuel had undoubted poetic gifts, as did their sister Hetty. However, Susanna Wesley's influence more than equalled that of any single individual and we should not underestimate the impact which the recitation of psalms in the Epworth rectory kitchen had upon the young Charles. Thus his earliest years were spent in an environment which helped his literary talents develop quickly, and Frank Baker's extensive studies of Charles' writings – over more than sixty years – led him to the conclusion that by 1738 Charles was already 'a matured poet'.[36] Dr Baker adds, by way of emphasis, that 'Charles Wesley's art of versification was quite consciously an *art*, and a carefully practised art, long before he was fired with religious inspiration.'[37]

While at Oxford, he spent a great deal of time writing poetry based on the classics, a love of which he had acquired in his Westminster schooldays. Henry Moore, one of John Wesley's earliest biographers and a close friend of the Wesley family, gives us a fascinating picture of Charles' method of working. In the brief extract here from his *Life of the Rev. John Wesley* he describes Charles both as a youth and as an old man. [84] It is an endearing little vignette, clearly written with great affection, and demonstrates that Charles' organizational skills did not always match his gift for poetic inspiration!

It is also a reminder that Charles' literary output spanned almost his entire life. Even just a few days before he died, he dictated a poem to his wife:

> In age and feebleness extreme,
> Who shall a helpless worm redeem?
> Jesus, my only hope thou art,
> Strength of my failing flesh and heart.
> O could I catch a smile from thee
> And drop into eternity![38]

Some of Charles' poems had no overtly religious theme but, as the years went on, it was inevitable that virtually all his poetry should have a spiritual emphasis. So, for example, a poem entitled 'At Sending a Son to School' (almost certainly written for Charles Jr) began with the lines:

> Jesus, to Thee my child I bring,
> His guardian, counseller, and guide . . .[39]

84.

When at the University, in early youth, his brother (as he informed me) was alarmed whenever [Charles] entered his study. *Aut insanity homo, aut versus facit.*[1] Full of the muse, and being short-sighted, he would sometimes walk right against his brother's table, and, perhaps, overthrow it. If the 'fine phrenzy' was not quite so high, he would decompose the books and papers in the study, ask some questions without always waiting for a reply, repeat some poetry that just then struck him, and at length leave his brother . . .

When he was nearly fourscore, he retained something of this eccentricity. He rode every day (clothed for winter even in summer) a little horse, grey with age. When he mounted, if a subject struck him, he proceeded to expand, and put it in order. He would write . . . with his pencil, in shorthand. Not infrequently he would come to our house in the City-road, and, having left the pony in the *garden* in front, he would enter, crying out, 'Pen and ink! Pen and ink!'

[1] [Moore's footnote translates:] 'The man is mad, or making verses'.

Source: Henry Moore, *Life of the Rev. John Wesley*, London 1824–5, Vol. II, pp. 366–7.

And when his younger son Samuel contracted smallpox in 1753, a poem written on that occasion commenced:

> Jesus, with human eyes
> Regard my misery;
> My Isaac on the altar lies,
> And gasps for life to Thee![40]

One particular poem which had a secular theme was 'Derdham Downs', which is reproduced here because it is relatively untypical of the verse that Charles mostly wrote. [85] Derdham Downs is just outside Bristol, where Charles and his family lived, and the reference to 'the mountains of Wales' in the third verse is to Sally's original home. It is a playful piece

85.

DERDHAM DOWNS

1. Alack & alack!
    The Clouds are so black
    And my Coat is so flimsy & thin,
    If we farther ride on,
    The rain will come down
    And wet little Sam to the skin.

2. But to clear up the doubt
    The Sun is broke out,
    And says, We may do as we will:
    So before the next shower
    Or'e the Downs let us scour
    Or gallop away to the Hill.

3. Gallop on my grey Nag,
    As fleet as a Stag,
    Or a Ship with her rudders & sails;
    Or (Mamma to affright)
    As skittish & light
    As a Goat – on the mountains of Wales.

4. How rapid the course
    Of my swift-flying Horse!
    I have got the Poetical Beast,
    And on Pegasus I
    Leap over the sky
    Or leap over the Severn at least!

Source: S. T. Kimbrough and Oliver A. Beckerlegge, *The Unpublished Poetry of Charles Wesley*, 3 Vols., Abingdon Press 1988–, Vol. I, p. 283.

intended for his children, especially for Samuel Jr (the 'little Sam' in verse 1) and is a good illustration of Charles' gentle sense of humour.

It could be argued that 'Derdham Downs' is quite unexceptional as a poem, and it may well be true that part of the reason why Charles has been underrated as a poet is because so much of his unexceptional verse – and some of it was – has survived.

Let his brother John have the last word. On 15 December 1788, nine months after Charles' death, he wrote, 'This week I dedicated to the reading over my brother's works . . . Some are bad; some mean; some most excellently good: they give the true sense of Scripture, always in good English, generally in good verse; many of them are equal to most, if not to any, he ever wrote . . .' Then, a week later: 'Lastly, I desire men of taste to judge – these are the only competent judges – whether there is not in some of the following verses the true spirit of poetry, such as cannot be acquired by art and labour, but must be the gift of nature.'[41]

For Discussion

1. What, would you say, constitutes a 'good hymn'?

2. Which of Charles Wesley's hymns is your favourite, and why?

3. What place do you think hymns such as those written by Charles have in today's society with its more secular emphasis?

8

Brothers in Arms

Captain of Israel's host, and Guide
Of all who seek the land above,
Beneath thy shadow we abide,
The cloud of thy protecting love;
Our strength, thy grace; our rule, thy word;
Our end, the glory of the Lord.

By thy unerring Spirit led,
We shall not in the desert stray;
We shall not full direction need,
Nor miss our providential way;
As far from danger as from fear,
While love, almighty love, is near.

In this chapter we shall examine the distinctive part Charles Wesley played in the growth of Methodism in the second half of the eighteenth century, and trace the way in which his relationship with John developed and changed perceptibly, if not radically, as he grew older.

John remained forever the itinerant. Charles adopted a more settled life, first in Bristol and then, from 1771, at 1 Chesterfield Street (off Maryle-bone Road). However, although the Wesleys were acknowledged as the two most important figures in Methodism, their later years saw them diverge on a number of issues, in particular over the break with the Church of England – an issue which gradually came to dominate everything else.

The problem with many surveys of Methodist history in the past has been that Charles' role, apart from writing hymns, has been simplified into a sub-sidiary one which was seen to be 'marred' by his disagreement with his brother over theological questions such as perfection, their attitude towards lay preachers, ordinations and separation with the established church.

In her book *A Tale of Two Brothers*, Mabel Brailsford described John and Charles' partnership as 'an almost ideal instance of the interplay of complementary forces' but, typically of her generation of writers, went too far in adding, 'Charles' genius was derivative, and took its colour from the associate with whom he was most in sympathy at the moment'.[1] From a reading of such (dated) studies, one is forced to conclude that until comparatively recently, little recognition has been given to Charles for his own unique contribution to the development of Methodism as a whole.[2]

Theological Issues

O let me commend my Saviour to you,
I set to my seal that Jesus is true:
Ye all may find favour who comes at his call;
O come to my Saviour! His grace is for all.

Charles and John Wesley's theology was experiential, scriptural and personal in character. If John must take the primary role in his capacity as the leader of the Methodist movement, Charles deserves to be recognized as more than simply a 'conveyor of doctrine'[3] as there were relatively few points of conflict between the brothers. A brief look at three areas of theology will illustrate how Charles could hold – and defend – an independent line of thought: 'stillness', predestination and perfection.

Both the Wesleys distanced themselves from 'stillness', one of the more extreme aspects of Moravian teaching.[4] As we have seen in earlier chapters, Charles and John had been greatly influenced by the Moravians in the 1730s. At that stage in their lives they had needed to become more fully aware of their utter dependence upon God. In all probability Charles had more sympathy than John for the Moravian approach to faith, though their influence upon him lessened over the years. However, neither brother could countenance the passive style of religious life – 'Quietism', or 'stillness', as it was sometimes termed – which many Moravians advocated. In the preface to the 1739 edition of *Hymns and Sacred Poems*, probably written by John, though the thoughts expressed also belonged to Charles, the Wesleys made it clear why they felt that Quietist mysticism went contrary to the Gospel. [86]

In April 1740 Charles was in London and seemed to find evidence of stillness everywhere he went, especially in the bands,[5] many of which had become infected with what he referred to as a 'snare'. In his journal Charles castigates those who believe that they are, '*to be still*; that is, not to search the Scriptures, not to pray, not to communicate, not to do good . . .', describing them as 'lazy and proud', and ones with whom 'I can see no middle point wherein we can meet'.[6] Apart from being theologically erroneous, Charles was concerned that stillness could eventually result in Methodists leaving the Church of England. Very cleverly, he used the Moravians' own terminology to argue that to 'be still and know that I am God' was very different from their quiescence and introspection. The stillness which Charles advocated was a response made by the individual in God's presence to his grace and goodness, and which could perhaps be best experienced at the sacrament. It is not surprising, therefore, to find that many of Charles' eucharistic hymns should be directed against the Moravian doctrine of stillness. One such example, written at the time of this con-

---

86. So widely distant is the manner of building up souls in Christ taught by St. Paul, from that taught by the Mystics! . . . For the religion these authors would edify us in is a solitary religion. If thou wilt be perfect, say they, 'trouble not thyself about outward works. It is better to work virtues in the will. He hath attained the true resignation, who hath estranged himself from all outward works, that God may work inwardly in him, without any turning to outward things . . .'

Directly opposite to this is the Gospel of Christ. Solitary religion is not found there. 'Holy solitaries' is a phrase no more consistent with the Gospel than holy adulterers. The Gospel of Christ knows of no religion but social; no holiness but social holiness. Faith working by love is the length and breadth and depth and height of Christian perfection. This commandment we have from Christ, that he who loves God, loves his neighbour also . . .

Source: G. Osborn (ed.), *Poetical Works of John and Charles Wesley*, London 1868–72, Introduction to Vol. I., p. xix; also found in the Preface to *Hymns and Sacred Poems*, 1739.

---

troversy, was a fierce rebuttal and very different in character from the hymns that are generally sung at communion. [87]

A second theological dispute in which Charles was at one with his brother concerned the doctrine of predestination,[7] to which both were adamantly opposed. Ultimately it was for the same reason that they clashed with the Moravians: that the doctrines of both 'stillness' and predestination were at variance with the second commandment: love for neighbour. Susanna Wesley had often expressed her disquiet at the effect of George Whitefield's preaching on the subject, and in one of her last letters to Charles had written in no uncertain terms of her distaste of the doctrine:

I am fully persuaded that if Whit[efield] could live more years than he will live, he will never do so much good as he has done harm since his return to England. God forgive him. Your brother hath

87.

And shall I let Him go?
If now I do not *feel*,
The streams of living water flow,
Shall I forsake the well?

Because He hides His face,
Shall I no longer stay,
But leave the channels of His grace,
And cast the means away?

Get thee behind me, fiend,
On others try thy skill,
Here let thy hellish whispers end,
To thee I say, *Be still!*

Jesus hath spoke the word,
His will my reason is;
Do this in memory of thy Lord,
Jesus hath said, *Do this!*

Source: *Hymns on the Lord's Supper* (1745), Hymn LXXXVI.

made a noble defence against the enemies; has given them no quarter indeed! But continues daily to serve the Predestinarians as Samuel did Agag – he hews them to pieces before the Lord . . .[8]

Both the brothers were in complete agreement with their mother's sentiments, and Charles was as firm in his attitude as John. The previous October he had preached at the funeral of William Seward, who had been an avowed Calvinist. Charles used the occasion, perhaps rather clumsily, to speak 'with unfeigned concern of our dear departed brother; and with just abhorrence of those unhappy bigots, whose headlong zeal had robbed us of him'.[9] On 16 March 1741 he wrote to John, saying that George Whitefield's 'fair words are not to be trusted to; for his actions show most unfriendly'.[10] The following day, his worst fears were realized, and he added,

G. W. [George Whitefield] came into the desk, while I was showing the believer's privilege, i.e.

power over sin. After speaking something, I desired him to preach. He did – predestination, perseverance, and the necessity of sinning. Afterwards I mildly expostulated with him asking if he would commend me for preaching the opposite doctrines in his Orphan-house . . .[11]

It was typical of Charles that, despite Whitefield's crass insensitivity (and discourtesy, for he was Charles' guest), he should remonstrate with his old friend 'mildly', but hundreds of his hymns were to deal hammer-blows to the notion.[12] If it was true that 'the arms of love' did not, in fact, 'all mankind embrace',[13] then in Charles' eyes the whole concept of holiness would be negated. Predestination struck at the very heart of his belief in the importance of sanctification – the gradual formation of the image of Christ – in the individual. Charles felt that the terrible danger in Whitefield's Calvinistic teaching was that it could mislead foolish and gullible people into thinking that, because they were now one of the 'elect' and destined for heaven, it did not matter what they did. In June of the same year Charles came across a shocking example of the kind of behaviour which he dreaded. [88] The 'other Gospel' referred to in the excerpt is predestination.

In this respect, Charles and John were in total agreement: God's boundless love and universal grace included *all* people. The predestination debate continued throughout the 1740s, though it was still

88. Mon., June 8th. A woman spoke to me of her husband. He was under strong convictions, while he attended the word; but the first time he heard the *other Gospel*, came home *elect*, and, in proof of it, *beat his wife*. His seriousness was at an end. His work was done. God doth not behold iniquity in Jacob; therefore his iniquity and cruelty towards her abound. He uses her worse than a Turk, (his predestination brother,) and tells her, if he killed her, he could not be damned.

Source: T. Jackson (ed.), *The Journal of The Rev. Charles Wesley, M.A.*, London, John Mason 1849, Vol. I, p. 280.

smouldering in the early years of the next decade. In 1752 John wrote a curious letter to Charles from Ireland, parts of which are reproduced here. [89] He began by taking Charles to task concerning the bands, since he had heard from the Irish preachers that Charles had been too easy-going in the guidance he had given them.[14] John then proceeded to question whether or not his younger brother had misled the preachers with regard to predestination. Charles had not, but the fact that John wrote in this vein suggests that he did not assume that Charles' views would automatically mirror his own.

Whilst John and Charles seemed to be of the same

---

89. Athlone, August 8, 1752.

DEAR BROTHER, – I almost wonder that I hear not one word from you since the trial at Gloucester . . . Does every one forget me as soon as we have the sea between us?

Some of our preachers here have . . . openly affirmed that you agree with Mr. Whitefield, touching Perseverance at least, if not Predestination too. Is it not highly expedient that you should write explicitly and strongly on this head likewise?

Perhaps the occasion of this latter affirmation was that both you and I have often granted an absolute, unconditional election of some, together with a conditional election of all men. I did incline to this scheme for many years; but of late I have doubted it more and more: (1) because all the texts which I used to think supported it, I now think prove either more or less – either absolute reprobation and election, or neither; (2) because I find this opinion serves all the ill purposes of absolute predestination, particularly that of supporting infallible perseverance. Talk with any that holds it, and so you will find.

I hope my sister feels herself in a good hand, and that you can trust Him with her and all things. We join in love.

Source: John Wesley, *Letters*, Vol. III, pp. 95–6.

---

mind over the controversies concerning 'stillness' and predestination, the same could not be said to be true over the issue of Christian perfection. We have already seen, in the previous chapter, the degree of importance which Charles gave to the subject[15] and there is a clear connection between this and the two areas discussed above. Quietists could not see the need for the process of sanctification, whereas those who considered themselves predestined to be saved had little interest in the concept of perfection.

John Wesley believed that an individual Christian could indeed reach a state of perfection, though he was careful to qualify this. He never said that a person could attain a state of 'sinless perfection' in the sense of being free from sin in its absolute sense. It could not be perfection in knowledge or complete freedom from human mistakes, infirmities or temptation – 'involuntary sins'. He saw Christian perfection in terms of perfect conformity to God's will and fellowship with him. In one of his most famous sermons he stated that 'indeed, it is only another term for holiness . . .' and added,

> It remains, then, that Christians are saved in this world from all sin, from all unrighteousness; that they are now in such a sense perfect, as not to commit sin, and to be freed from evil thoughts and evil tempers.[16]

Despite the way in which John qualified his statements, Charles felt that there were inherent dangers in what his brother taught. His reasons originated in the same line of thinking which led him to oppose stillness and predestination. He agreed with John that the concept of perfection grew out of the commandment to 'love the Lord thy God with all thy heart, and with all thy soul, and with all thy mind, and thy neighbour as thyself' (Mark 12.30). However, whereas John believed that perfection (as he understood it) could be attained in this life and be instantaneous, Charles had grave doubts. He saw perfection as being part of a more gradual process of sanctification and was deeply suspicious of anyone who claimed to have achieved it in this life.

An incident in May 1741 helped to confirm Charles in his view. He visited a dying woman, Mrs Hooper, who 'expressed, while able to speak, her fullness of confidence and love; her desire to be with Christ'. Charles was so moved by the purity of her faith that he wrote in his journal: 'This is that holiness, or absolute resignation, or Christian perfection!'[17] His definition of perfection, therefore, was perhaps even more exacting than John's, and he remained firm in his views.

Even as late as 1766 the two brothers could not entirely agree and in July of that year John wrote to Charles complaining, 'when you and I [talked] together, you *seemed* at least to be of the same mind with me, and now you are all off the hooks again!'[18] The difference of opinion continued to be evident in the following year, as is shown in a letter which John wrote to Charles. [90]

The fact that John felt he needed to spell out his

---

91.   Norton, Near Stockton, June 14, 1768.

DEAR BROTHER, – I rejoice to hear from various persons so good an account of the work of God in London. You did not come thither without the Lord; and you find your labour is not in vain . . .

But what shall we do? I think it is high time that you and I at least should come to a point. Shall we go on in asserting perfection against all the world? Or shall we quietly let it drop? We really must do one or the other; and, I apprehend, the sooner the better. What shall we jointly and explicitly maintain (and recommend to all our preachers) concerning the nature, the time (now or by-and-by), and the manner of it (instantaneous or not)? I am weary of intestine war, of preachers quoting one of us against the other . . .

Source: John Wesley, *Letters*, Vol. V, p. 93.

---

position in such plain terms is an indication of the seriousness with which he viewed their differences. Three weeks later he was again writing to Charles, saying, 'unless we come to an explanation, we shall inevitably contradict each other', and concluding: 'Is there or is there not any instantaneous sanctification between justification and death? I say, yes; you (*often seem to*) say, No.'[19] These details may seem fairly trivial to us now, but we should remember that in the religious climate of the mid-eighteenth century, neither brother could afford to say things in public which plainly contradicted the other. The early Methodist preachers, as well as their followers, looked to Charles as well as John for leadership and guidance, and this was clearly in the latter's mind when he wrote yet again to Charles in the following year. [91]

---

90.   London, January 27, 1767.

DEAR BROTHER, –
. . . I was thinking on Christian Perfection, with regard to the thing, the manner, and the time.
1. By perfection I mean the humble, gentle, patient love of God and man ruling all the tempers, words, and actions, the whole heart by the whole life.
   Do we agree or differ here? If we differ, wherein?
2. As to the manner. I believe this perfection is always wrought in the soul by faith, by a simple act of faith, consequently in an instant. But I believe in a gradual work both preceding and following that instant.
   Do we agree or differ here?
3. As to the time. I believe this instant generally is the instant of death, the moment before the soul leaves the body. But I believe it may be ten, twenty, or forty years before death.
   Do we agree or differ here?
If it be possible, let you and I come to a good understanding, both for our own sakes and for the sake of the people.

Source: John Wesley, *Letters*, Vol. V, pp. 38–9.

Brothers in Arms

Joined in one spirit to our Head,
Where he appoints we go;
And still in Jesu's footsteps tread,
And show his praise below.

In studying Charles' relationship with John it is important to realize that we are dealing with an association which lasted many decades, in which both brothers developed and changed their views on a whole range of subjects. Richard Heitzenrater tells the amusing story of a professor who gave a talk on John Wesley to a youthful audience. After he had finished speaking, one of the youngsters asked, 'How old was Wesley?' The professor replied, after a moment's thought, 'Well, you see, he was different ages at different times'.[20] We should, therefore, be wary of making over-simplified generalizations and assuming that the brothers either always agreed or disagreed in the same way over the same issues. Frank Baker sums up their relationship accurately when he writes, 'the two brothers were indeed different people, yet very close'.[21] It is an obvious point, but one which needs to be made: that Charles was always 'close' to John, even though at times he disagreed with him quite sharply.

What makes consideration of Charles' point of view a little more difficult from the mid-1750s onwards is that his journal peters out in 1756, roughly at a time when his relationship with John was becoming more strained. Consequently, there is less evidence at our disposal which can give us a detailed insight into Charles' own feelings and we have to rely mainly on his correspondence with his brother, which amounts to over a hundred letters from the early 1750s until Charles' death. Most of the letters are from John to Charles, since those of the latter which have survived, alas, are few and far between.

By the 1750s Charles was acting almost in a 'free-lance' capacity, and did not always think to consult John as to his movements. Although this was probably due more to his lack of organization and a more relaxed approach to planning his itinerancy than any wish to upset his brother, the latter was quick to reproach Charles. On 20 October 1753 John complained,

Either act really in connexion with me, or never pretend to it . . . I mean take counsel with me once or twice a year as to the places where you will labour . . . At present you are so far from this that I do not even know when and where you intend to go; so far are you from following any advice of mine – nay, even from asking it.[22]

John's temper was not helped by the fact that he was quite ill at this time but, as the accompanying extract from a letter he wrote ten days later shows, there was more at stake than Charles' apparent unwillingness to consult with him. [92] When Charles received this letter he added a cryptic note of his own in the margin, 'Brother, Oct. 31, 1753. Trying to bring me under his yoke'[23] – an illustration, perhaps, of the natural rivalry that often exists between any brothers whose fortunes are closely intertwined.

John's illness was so acute that he even rose from his bed to compose his own epitaph.[24] One cannot help but conclude that, in his weakened state, John

---

92. London, October 31, 1753.

DEAR BROTHER, – How can I say, 'I do not know your intentions, when you had told me you intended to winter in Bristol'? I answer: (1) I heard of your intending to be at Bristol before ever I heard it from you. (2) Did you consult with me in this? Was my approbation ever inquired after in the matter? Or any other of the travelling preachers? or stewards? (3) Had you previously consulted with me (which you did not) in this one point, yet one swallow makes no summer.

O brother, *pretend* no longer to the thing that is not. You do not, will not act in concert with me. Not since I was married only (the putting it on that is a mere finesse), but for ten years last past and upwards you have no more acted in connexion with me than Mr. Whitefield has done. I would to God you would begin to do it now; or else talk no more *as if* you did . . .

Why do you omit giving the sacrament in Kingswood? What is reading prayers at Bristol in comparison of this? I am sure, in making this vehement alteration, you never consulted with me.

Source: John Wesley, *Letters*, Vol. III, pp. 113–14.

felt particularly vulnerable and simply missed his brother's company. Even though Charles was forty-five at the time, he was clearly being treated like a younger brother! However, particularly since the Grace Murray episode, it is possible to discern a burgeoning self-confidence in Charles in his relationship with John.

The poignant reference in this letter to John's marriage underlines the fact that their relationship had indeed been severely strained over this issue, though never to the point where John rescinded the decision he had made in 1746, naming Charles as his legal successor. The wounds did take time to heal, however. The summer of 1750 had seen the arrival of John Bennet and Grace Murray's first child, and when Charles heard that Bennet was thinking of arranging a meeting between Grace and his brother – quite what the reason was, we can only guess – he was aghast. Charles wrote immediately to Bennet, saying, 'If you regard me as your real friend (and I know you do), follow my Christian advice, and never let them [i.e. John and Grace] meet till they meet among the sheep on the right hand.'[25] Despite Charles' friendship with Bennet, the latter finally broke with the Wesleys and became an independent minister.[26]

As the years passed, Charles and John continued to disagree at times but the two brothers never reached the point where they either ceased to communicate or lost their love for one another. The letters which John wrote to Charles while on his travels often have poignant references to their partnership and the essential beliefs which they shared in common. In February 1766, conscious of the need for Methodists to see that their founders were united in heart and mind, John urged Charles to recognize that, 'we must, we must, you and I at least, be all devoted to God!' and therefore, as 'chief conductors of *such a work* . . . strengthen each others hands . . .'[27] In the summer of the same year, while on a northern tour, John wrote again in the same vein. [93] There were times when John simply missed his brother's company.

There were also some problems at City Road.

93.　　　　　　　　　　　Whitehaven, June 27, 1766.
DEAR BROTHER, – I think you and I have abundantly too little intercourse with each other. Are we not *old acquaintances*? Have we not known each other for half a century? and are we not jointly engaged in such a work as probably no two other men upon earth are? Why, then, do we keep at such a distance? It is a mere device of Satan. But surely we ought not at this time of day to be ignorant of his devices. Let us therefore make the full use of the little time that remains. *We* at least should *think aloud* and use to the uttermost the light and grace on each bestowed. We should help each other . . .

Source: John Wesley, *Letters*, Vol. V, p. 15. |

Charles was in the habit of preaching there twice a Sunday, which made it difficult – if not impossible – for the preachers in the circuit to occupy the pulpit except on very rare occasions. Some of the preachers complained, saying that Charles had never embraced the idea of lay preachers in the enthusiastic way that his brother had. Thinking, perhaps, that John would be unsympathetic, Charles wrote to his brother justifying his position but happily there was no serious disagreement, although in truth the matter gradually resolved itself as Charles' less than robust health began to deteriorate with the onset of old age.

However, nothing could hide the fact that the relationship of Methodism to the Church of England – the single most important issue over which John and Charles Wesley disagreed – was a problem that would only grow in intensity, and it is to this that we now turn. To do so we need to turn the clock back a little to the 1740s.

Separation from the Church of England

Christ, from whom all blessings flow,
Perfecting the saints below,
Hear us, who thy nature share,
Who thy mystic body are.

Love, like death, has all destroyed,
Rendered all distinctions void;
Names, and sects, and parties fall:
Thou, O Christ, art all in all.

Charles Wesley, from his childhood, had been immersed in the Anglican tradition. His upbringing at Epworth, his days at Westminster School with its close proximity to Westminster Abbey, his time at Oxford – all these exerted a lasting influence upon him. The emphasis he placed in his preaching after 1738 upon the doctrine of justification by faith alone, 'my favourite subject', as he once noted,[28] had its roots in the basic precepts of the Church of England as contained in the Thirty-Nine Articles.[29] Whereas his brother John had a deep-seated reverence for the Church of England, Charles' commitment to the Church went beyond respect, and his emotional attachment was one of love and devotion. This helps to explain why his defence of the Church was more passionate than John's and why, ultimately, he was to disagree so strongly with his brother when the question of Methodism's separation reached crisis proportions in the 1780s.

It was clear that, from the earliest days of the Methodist Revival, relations with the Church of England would pose a serious question. In 1744, even before the very first Methodist Conference had assembled, Charles was alive to the possibilities of a serious breach. In a year which saw the kingdom threatened by war (with France) and rebellion (by the Jacobites[30]) John had written a loyal address to King George II on 5 March.[31] He had felt the need to do this in view of the accusations levelled at Methodists that they were Jacobite supporters, and because on one occasion Charles himself was actually brought before a magistrate on the charge of being a Jacobite sympathizer, because he had mentioned 'God's absent ones' in his prayers at public worship! Charles, nonetheless, had misgivings, and when he saw his brother's letter, wrote to John the very next day expressing his fears. [94]

In 1747 the Conference had examined possible causes of friction and had come to the conclusion –

94. Tues., March 6th. I wrote to my brother: 'My objection to your address in the name of the Methodists is, that it would constitute us a sect; at least it would *seem to allow* that we are a body distinct from the national Church; whereas we are only a sound part of that Church. Guard against this; and in the name of the Lord address tomorrow.'

Source: T. Jackson (ed.), *The Journal of The Rev. Charles Wesley, M.A.*, London, John Mason 1849, Vol. I, pp. 354–5.

guided, of course, by John Wesley – that in fact they were *not* 'guilty of making such a schism' and were being careful to abide by the rules of the Church of England.[32] One of the earliest causes of tension at that time was the way in which John and Charles were being apparently 'thrust out of the Church', a charge which was answered by pointing to the fact that it was the bishops, not the local ministers, who were responsible for this.

The 'purging of the preachers' in 1750–51 had, as we have seen, alerted Charles to the danger of Methodists being seen as schismatic, and in March 1752 he produced a statement of intent with regard to Methodism and the Church of England:

We, whose names are underwritten . . . are absolutely determined, by the grace of God, (1) to abide in closest union with each other, and . . . (2) never to leave the communion of the Church of England, without the consent of all whose names are subjoined.[33]

After Charles had signed the document John added his name and four local preachers added their own signatures. But it was Charles' name that appeared at the top. To Charles' dismay, relatively few Methodist preachers signed the declaration in the years following its publication.

Further tensions appeared almost immediately, this time concerning the administration of Holy Communion, another area in which Charles and John did not exactly see eye to eye. In 1754 the matter came to a head when Charles Perronet, the son of the Wesleys' old friend Vincent Perronet, administered the sacrament despite having no licence to do so. Charles felt that John's acquiescence with Perronet's action would have dire consequences, as is clear from the entry he made in his shorthand diary. [95]

95.

Oct. 17. Charles Perronet gave the Sacrament to the preachers Walsh and Deaves, and then to twelve at sister Garder's . . .

Oct. 19. I was with my brother, who said nothing of Perronet except 'We have in effect ordained already.' He urged me to sign the preachers' certificates; was inclined to lay on hands, and to let the preachers administer . . .

October 24. Was with my brother. He is wavering: but willing to wait before he ordains or separates.

Source: Frank Baker, *Charles Wesley as Revealed by His Letters*, Epworth Press 1948, p. 92.

Almost in despair Charles wrote to his old friend the Revd Walter Sellon, one of the masters at Kingswood School, pleading with him to dissuade John from doing anything that might precipitate separation from the Church of England. By the early part of 1755 Sellon's remonstrations with John seemed to have been successful, and Charles could relax a little:

He has spoken as strongly of late in behalf of the Church of England as I could ever wish; and everywhere declares he never intends to leave her.[34]

However, John wrote a frank letter to Charles in June 1755, saying, 'I dare not in conscience spend my time in externals' and, referring to the Church of England, 'I neither set it up nor pull it down. But let you and I build up the City of God.'[35] Two weeks later he was again writing to Charles pointing out, 'ordination and separation are not the same thing', and adding, 'if so, we have separated already'. In the same letter he added, quite forcibly, 'Your gross bigotry lies here – in putting a man on a level with an adulterer because he differs from you as to Church government.'[36] Frank words indeed!

The Conference of 1755 tackled the issue of separation, and Charles reported to his wife Sally that 'all agreed not to separate. So the wound is healed – slightly.'[37] Undoubtedly, Charles was worried by his brother's shifts in attitude, and published an open letter entitled *An Epistle to the Reverend Mr. John Wesley, by Charles Wesley, Presbyter of the Church of England*, which was widely circulated and, indeed, read out aloud by Charles to large numbers of people. Interestingly, it was written in verse and was a stout defence of his position as a loyal member of the Church of England. The following couplet, at which John must have squirmed, is sufficient to illustrate its general tone:

Was it our aim disciples to collect,
To raise a party, or to found a sect?[38]

A little later, Charles confessed to a friend (the Revd Samuel Walker) with remarkable candour, 'I should have broken off from the Methodists and my brother in 1752', adding that the probability of separation 'has made me tremble for years past'.[39]

The year 1756 – from Charles' point of view – was a good one. The Conference ended on a happy note, its members unanimously resolving to remain faithful to the Church of England. In the autumn, help came from an unexpected quarter. While at Manchester Charles heard that George Whitefield had been urging Methodists to stay loyal to the Church. [96] His reaction to Whitefield's support is an indication of how deep was the two men's friendship, despite their patent theological differences.

In the years that followed, however, Charles felt increasingly uneasy with some of the ways in which he perceived Methodism to be developing. Its growth as a movement, albeit within the Church of England, inevitably created problems which we can think of in terms of 'centre' and 'circumference'. As Methodism spread further and further throughout the country, inescapable tensions grew between the Conference of preachers at the centre – largely con-

96.

Mon., Oct. 25th. Here [in Manchester] I rejoiced to
hear of the great good Mr. Whitefield has done in our
Societies. He preached as universally as my brother . . .
He beat down the separating spirit, highly commended
the prayers and services of our Church, charged our
people to meet their bands and classes constantly, and
never to leave the Methodists, or God would leave
them. In a word: he did his utmost to strengthen our
hands, and deserves the thanks of all the churches, for
his abundant labour of love.

Source: T. Jackson (ed.), *The Journal of The Rev.*
Charles Wesley, M.A., London, John Mason 1849,
Vol. II, pp. 133–4.

trolled by John Wesley – and the scattered societies
and their members at the grass roots.

Why did Charles Wesley not leave Methodism?

From a study of his correspondence, it becomes
obvious that he felt he could do more to control the
dissidents from within the movement than from outside it, even though his struggle to do so both pained
and wearied him. Charles also felt torn between
loyalty to his brother, who seemed to change his
stance from one year to the next, and loyalty to the
established church. Finally, in his more optimistic
moments, he entertained the rather tenuous hope
that Methodism would be able to continue as a kind
of 'ginger group' within Anglicanism. In a letter to
Sally in 1760, a year which saw a fresh crisis over the
administration of Holy Communion by unlicensed
(lay) preachers and yet another clash between the
Wesley brothers, Charles gave what was perhaps
the clearest summary of his position. [97]

In 1766, John urged Methodists not to absent
themselves from Anglican worship, the preachers *not*
to end Methodist services with the Lord's Supper,
and for the services to be held at a different time from
the Anglican ones. However, despite the Conference
passing resolutions of loyalty periodically, Charles
remained unhappy and fearful. In spite of his cease-
less efforts to keep Methodism within the Church of
England in the 1760s and 1770s, he began to suspect

that he was fighting a losing battle. In 1773, he expressed the hope that Methodism, along with the
Moravians, would 'die together' and their organ-
izations and – above all – spiritual energy, would
be subsumed by the Church of England. It was not
to be.

In April 1777, when the foundation stone of New
Chapel in City Road was laid, John Wesley denied
any break with the Church of England. However,
it was a place of worship with provision for a communion area, together with a burial ground. One
cannot help feeling that many of those who were
present on that occasion were aware of the inevitable
trend and drew their own conclusions. By 1780 some
of the preachers were beginning to put pressure on
John to be ordained by *him*, rather than by a bishop.
When John asked Charles if he would come to the
Conference, Charles declined, saying that he would
be able neither to influence proceedings, nor to control his temper!

The year 1784 saw the long-awaited crisis finally
break. Three events hastened the separation which
for so long Charles had feared. Since they have been
described more fully elsewhere,[40] we need only
sketch in the main details here.

The first was the signing of the Deed of Declaration in February, which constituted the Methodist
Conference – the 'Legal Hundred', as it was termed –
as John Wesley's successor and therefore guaranteed

97. My chief concern upon earth, I said, was the pros-
perity of the Church of England; my next, that of the
Methodists; my third, that of the preachers; that if their
interests should ever come in competition, I would
give up the preachers for the good of the whole body of
the Church of England: that nothing could ever force
me to leave the Methodists but their leaving the
Church. In that case they would suffer me to be cast
off, an old faithful servant, worn out by serving them
. . . My business was to pacify and keep them within
bounds.

Source: Frank Baker, *Charles Wesley as Revealed by*
His Letters, Epworth Press 1948, pp. 102–3.

its continued existence as an independent body. The second event was the decision by John to ordain preachers to serve in America, where the first Methodist Society had been formed in 1766, which was a contravention of Anglican Church order and in direct opposition to the Bishop of London.[41] Charles, needless to say, was not informed, almost certainly because John knew that he would have raised the strongest of objections. When he heard the news (two months later!) he wrote to a friend, 'I am thunderstruck' – and no wonder. To ordain Richard Whatcoat and Thomas Vesey was certainly irregular, but the ordination of Thomas Coke was altogether different. Coke was already an ordained minister and his new title 'superintendent' suggested the office of bishop.[42] Thirdly, John Wesley's revision of the Book of Common Prayer, which was published under the title *The Sunday Service of the Methodists in North America, with other occasional services*, helped exacerbate worsening relations with the Church of England because, although the book was intended to be used in America, it was but a small step to allow it to be used by British Methodists in their preaching houses – which in fact it was, in 1788.

These three factors, the Deed of Declaration, the ordinations for America and the revision of the Prayer Book, simply accelerated a process which, by the 1780s, had become virtually inevitable. An example of the way in which Charles responded to his brother's decision to ordain can be found in some verses which he wrote at the time. [98] They were never published, but they show that Charles had not lost his sense of humour, even though it was particularly mordant in this instance. The 'C_____' referred to is Thomas Coke.

Charles' reaction to these developments was, as we would expect, a mixture of sadness, disappointment and anger. When, a little later, he heard that John had ordained three preachers to minister in Scotland, he confided to Sally, 'To turn seventy thousand Church of England people, Dissenters! . . . Surely I am in a dream! Is it possible that J. W. should be turned Presbyterian?'[43] One can under-

---

98.

Wesley himself and friends betrays,
  By his good sense forsook,
When suddenly his hands he lays
  On the hot head of C_____.

But we alas should spare the weak,
  His weak Co-equals *We*,
Nor blame a hoary Schismatic
  A Saint of Eighty-three!

So easily are Bishops made
  By man's or woman's whim?
W_____ his hands on C_____ hath laid,
  But who laid hands on Him?

Hands on himself he laid, and *took*
  An Apostolic Chair:
And then ordain'd his Creature C_____
  His Heir and Successor.

Episcopalians, now no more
  With Presbyterians fight,
But give your needless Contest o're,
  'Whose Ordination's right?'

It matters not, if Both are One,
  Or different in degrees,
For lo! ye see contain'd in John
  The whole Presbytery!

Source: Rupert Davies, A. Raymond George and Gordon Rupp (eds), *A History of the Methodist Church in Great Britain*, Vol. IV, Epworth Press 1988, p. 200.

---

stand his dismay. Ordaining preachers for America was bad enough, but who could prevent the three in question from ministering in England? In Charles' eyes, ordination was indeed tantamount to separation. In April 1785 he wrote a long, mournful letter to Vincent Perronet, part of which is reprinted in the accompanying extract. [99]

Charles remembered his eldest brother Samuel's warnings so many years before: that the course which he and John had embarked upon after May

1738 would endanger the unity of the Church. Samuel's prophesy was now being fulfilled, and in August Charles wrote to John in impassioned words. The letter is a good illustration of the strength of his feelings. [100] The *Reasons* to which Charles refers in the first sentence was John Wesley's *Reasons Against Separation from the Church of England* which appeared in 1758.

---

99. I never lost my dread of separation, or ceased to guard our Society against it. I frequently told them, 'I am your servant, as long as you remain members of the Church of England, but no longer. Should you ever forsake her, you renounce me.' Some of our lay-preachers very early discovered an inclination to separate, which induced my brother to publish *Reasons Against a Separation*. As often as it appeared, we beat down the schismatical spirit. If any one did leave the Church, at the same time he left our Society. For 50 years we kept the sheep in the fold, & having fulfilled the number of our days, only wanted to depart in peace.

After our having continued friends for above 70 years & fellow-labourers for above 50 years, can anything but death part us?

I can scarcely yet believe that in his 82nd year, my brother, my old intimate friend & companion, should have assumed the episcopal character, ordained elders, consecrated a bishop, & sent him to ordain the lay preachers in America. I was then in Bristol at his elbow, yet he never gave me the least hint of his intention. How was he surprised into so rash an action? He certainly persuaded himself that it was right . . .

Thus our partnership dissolved, but not our friendship. I have taken him for better for worse till death us do part – or rather re-unite us in love inseparable. I have lived on earth a little too long, who have lived to see this evil day . . .

Source: Rupert Davies, A. Raymond George and Gordon Rupp (eds), *A History of the Methodist Church in Great Britain*, Vol. IV, Epworth Press 1988, p. 205.

---

100.   Bristol, August 14, 1785.

Dear Brother, – I have been reading over again & again your *Reasons Against a Separation*, and entreat you, in the name of God, and for Christ's sake, to read them again yourself, with previous prayer, and stop, and proceed no farther, till you receive an answer to your inquiry, 'Lord, what wouldest *Thou* have me to do?' . . .

Near 30 years . . . I was your natural ally, and your faithful friend . . . But when once you began ordaining in America, I knew (and you knew), that your Preachers here would never rest till you ordained them . . .

Alas! what trouble are you preparing for yourself, as well as for me, and for your oldest, truest, best friends! Before you have quite broken down the bridge, *stop, and consider!* If your sons have no regard for you, have some regard for yourself. *Go to your grave in peace*: at least, suffer me to go first, before this ruin is under your hand . . . Let us not leave an indelible blot on our memory; but let us leave behind us the name and character of *honest men*.

                           Your faithful friend.

Source: John R. Tyson (ed.), *Charles Wesley: A Reader*, Oxford University Press 1989, p. 433.

A month later, John wrote back to Charles, 'I see no use of you and me disputing together; for neither of us is likely to convince the other. You say I separate from the Church; I say I do not.'[44] The following year, writing from Manchester, he tried to appease his brother by saying, 'I love the Church as sincerely as I ever did; and I tell our Societies everywhere, "The Methodists will not leave the Church, at least while I live."'[45] Charles was not to be mollified. In public he might be guarded in his criticism of John, blaming Coke and the other preachers for the troubles and making the excuse that his brother was by now a very old man, but privately he could not rid himself of an overwhelming feeling of gloom and despondency.

It was, perhaps, fortunate that Charles did not live to witness the further, crucial step of a preacher being ordained to serve in England, which took place in August 1788, just four months after Charles' death. Coke, and others who wished to make a clean break with the Church, saw the death of Charles Wesley as the removal of a major obstacle. For his part, John Wesley might continue to protest his loyalty to the established church, but could see the impossibility of reversing a process that had begun long before. The Conferences of 1791, at which Coke was elected Secretary, and 1793 continued the steady march towards complete disengagement. Although the 'Plan of Pacification' of 1795 attempted a compromise,[46] in truth, the debate was now virtually over.

In retrospect we can see that, for much of his later life, Charles occupied an unenviable position of being both a reforming Methodist and a conforming Anglican. An innocent victim of divided loyalties, one can only speculate as to what he would have done had he lived longer. Happily, he was never forced to make the ultimate choice.

Chronology

1752		John Bennet's secession from Methodism
1754–55		The crisis over the administration of Holy Communion
1766		The first Methodist society in the New World
1770		Death of George Whitefield
1776		American Declaration of Independence
1777		Foundation stone of New Chapel in City Road laid
1783		End of the war with the American colonies
1784	February	Deed of Declaration
	September	The ordinations for America John Wesley's revision of the Prayer Book
1787		Registration of preaching houses
1788	March	Death of Charles Wesley
1791	February	Death of John Wesley

For Discussion

1. Charles disagreed with John over the issue of Christian perfection. Do you think it is possible for an individual Christian to be in any way 'perfect'?

2. What, in your opinion, were the most significant factors in leading to Methodism's separation from the Church of England?

3. To what extent do you feel the breach to have been inevitable?

4. How can Methodists and Anglicans work towards unity today, and what form might that unity take?

9

Postscript

Finish then thy new creation,
Pure and spotless let us be;
Let us see thy great salvation,
Perfectly restored in thee:
Changed from glory into glory,
Till in heaven we take our place,
Till we cast our crowns before thee,
Lost in wonder, love, and praise!

As he reached his eightieth year, Charles' strength finally began to wane. He still preached, rode his little grey mare, and visited the prisoners at Newgate but it was quite clear that he was slowing down. In 1787, just five months before he died, he went to Bristol, where he and his brother preached and ministered together for what turned out to be the last time.[1] John had never lost his brotherly affection for Charles, as can be seen from the following extract from a letter he wrote from Thirsk on 27 June 1781:

> From several I have lately heard that God has blessed your preaching. See your calling! Cease at once to work and live! Peace be with all your spirits![2]

In early 1788, with Charles' health now evidently in rapid decline, John wrote often, his letters invariably containing words of advice and comfort. On 18 February he urged Charles to, 'go out *every day* or die', then added, 'You certainly need not want anything as long as I live.'[3] Two days later came another brief note containing the injunction, 'O *consent* to be

cured!'[4] On 2 March he was still encouraging Charles to 'go out at least an hour a day . . . Never mind expense: I can make that up.'[5]

John's last letter to Charles, written on 17 March 1788 as he was preparing to journey north, expressed the hope that his brother might recover. However, the tone of the letter, which contained such comments as, 'I know you have the sentence of death in yourself . . .', and ended with the words, 'Be strong in the Lord and in the power of His might. Adieu!'[6] suggest that he realized Charles had little time to live. The simple truth was that Charles' body was worn out and that he was dying of old age.

Charles Wesley died peacefully on 29 March 1788, and his daughter Sarah has left us a moving account of his last days, which were full of thoughts of heaven and an assurance of eternal bliss. With his family gathered round him, the scene was one of joy and peace; Charles' final words being ones of trust in the Saviour he had loved and served all his life. On 4 April Sarah wrote to John Wesley a detailed account of her father's last days, extracts of which are reproduced here. Whilst her words were inevitably coloured by her filial emotions, there is no reason to suppose that she gave other than an accurate picture of what she witnessed. [101]

Dr Whitehead, the family doctor and a close friend of Charles and Sally, visited the former several times during his final illness. In some reflections penned five years after Charles had died, he noted that his friend had always had 'a weak body, and a poor state of health'. He recalled that, in his last days,

101. Dear honoured Uncle, – We were all present when my dear, respected father departed this life. His end was, what he particularly wished it might be, peace!

For some months past he seemed totally detached from earth. He spoke very little, nor wished to hear anything read but the Scriptures . . .

He told my mother, the week before he departed, that no fiend [i.e., doubt] was permitted to approach him; and said to us all, 'I have a *good hope!*'

When asked if he wanted anything, he frequently answered, 'Nothing but Christ!' . . . The 28th my mother asked if he had anything to say to us. Raising his eyes, he said, 'Only thanks! love! blessing!'

The last morning, which was the 29th of March, being unable to speak, my mother entreated him to press her hand, if he knew her; which he feebly did . . . His last words which I could hear were, 'Lord – my heart, – my God!' He then drew his breath short, and the last so gently, that we knew not exactly the moment in which his happy spirit fled.

Source: Thomas Jackson, *The Life of the Rev. Charles Wesley, M.A.*, London, 1841, Vol. II, pp. 442–4.

Charles 'possessed that state of mind, which he had always been pleased to see in others – unaffected humility, and holy resignation to the will of God. He had no transports of joy, but solid hope and unshaken confidence in Christ, which kept his mind in perfect peace.'[7]

On 4 April, while in Macclesfield, John Wesley heard of his brother's death, and wrote an affectionate though somewhat formal letter to Sally, ending it with the words, 'to serve you, or your dear family, in anything that is in my power, will always be a pleasure to, dear sister'.[8] He was never one to show his feelings too openly. However, preaching in Manchester ten days later, John attempted to announce his brother's hymn, 'Come O Thou Traveller Unknown', but when he reached the words

My company before is gone
And I am left alone with Thee

he sat down in the pulpit, broke down in tears, and the service ended quietly.[9]

Rather surprisingly, there was no lengthy obituary to Charles at the Conference of 1788 by his brother. Instead, the following notice was read out:

Mr. Charles Wesley, who, after spending four-score years with much sorrow and pain, quietly retired into Abraham's bosom. He had no disease, but after a gradual decay of some months,
The weary wheels of life stood still at last.
His least praise was, his talent for poetry; although Dr Watts did not scruple to say, that 'that

102. Mr. Wesley was of a warm and lively disposition; of great frankness and integrity, and generous and steady in his friendships. His love of simplicity, and utter abhorrence of hypocrisy, and even of affectation in the professions of religion, made him sometimes appear severe on those who . . . were pert and forward in talking of themselves and others . . .

As a minister, he was familiarly acquainted with every part of divinity [theology]; and his mind was furnished with an uncommon knowledge of the Scriptures. His discourses from the pulpit were not dry and systematic, but flowed from the present views and feelings of his own mind. He had a remarkable talent of expressing the most important truths with simplicity and energy; and his discourses were sometimes truly apostolic, forcing conviction on the hearers in spite of the most determined opposition . . .

. . . the Methodists are greatly indebted to him for his unwearied labours and great usefulness at the first formation of the societies, when every step was attended with difficulty and danger. And being dead he yet speaketh, by his numerous and excellent hymns, written for the use of the societies, which still continue to be the means of daily edification to thousands.

Source: John Whitehead, MD (ed.), *The Life of the Rev. Charles Wesley, M.A.*, London, Stephen Couchman 1793, pp. 209f.[10]

single poem Wrestling Jacob, is worth all the verses which I have ever written'.[11]

The tribute written by Dr Whitehead in 1793 did Charles far greater justice. The excerpt here is from this short biographical sketch. [102]

According to his wishes, Charles was buried in the churchyard of Old Marylebone, near his home, rather than in the plot reserved for him behind the City Road Chapel. In spite of John's intention that they should both be interred at City Road, Charles had no wish to be buried in ground that had not been consecrated.[12] Some thirty years before, he had written in his journal, 'no salvation out of the Church; that is, out of the mystical body of Christ, or the company of faithful people',[13] and his loyalty and love for the Church of England remained to the end.

On his tombstone the following inscription was carved:

> *With poverty of spirit bless'd,*
> *Rest, happy Saint, in Jesus rest;*
> *A Sinner sav'd, through grace forgiv'n,*
> *Redeem'd from earth to reign in heav'n!*
> *Thy labours of unwearied love,*
> *By thee forgot, are crown'd above;*
> *Crown'd, through the mercy of thy Lord,*
> *With a free, full, immense reward!*

In Wesley's Chapel, City Road, a fuller and more fitting tribute to Charles can be seen on his memorial plaque. [103]

In the courtyard outside the New Room in Bristol, a life-size bronze statue of Charles was erected. It shows him with a Bible in his left hand and his right hand characteristically held out in a beckoning gesture. This would have pleased him. If it was true that 'Methodism was born in song', then undoubtedly we have to give Charles first place in the contribution which he made to its hymnody. As a Christian poet he may well have 'Stood Unrivaled', but his greatest gift, perhaps, was to be 'a son of consolation', and the outstretched hand of his statue is a fitting symbol of this, perhaps his most endearing quality.

103.

Charles Wesley's Epitaph

God buries his workmen, but carries on his work.

SACRED TO THE MEMORY
of
THE REV. CHARLES WESLEY, M.A.

Educated at Westminster School,
And Sometime Student at Christ-Church, Oxford.
As a Preacher,
He was eminent for ability, zeal, and usefulness
Being learned without pride,
And pious without ostentation;
To the sincere, diffident Christian,
A Son of Consolation;
But to the vain boaster, the hypocrite, and the profane,
A Son of Thunder.

He was the first who received The Name of Methodist;
And, uniting with his brother, The Rev. John Wesley,
In the plan of Itinerant Preaching,
Endured hardship, persecution, and disgrace,
As a good Soldier of Jesus Christ;
Contributing largely, by the usefulness of his labours,
In these Kingdoms.

As a Christian Poet He Stood Unrivaled;
And his hymns will convey instruction and consolation
To the faithful in Christ Jesus,
As long as the English language shall be understood.

He Was Born the XVIII of December, MDCCVIII,
And Died the XXIX of March, MDCCLXXXVIII,
A firm and pious believer in the doctrines of the Gospel,
And a sincere friend to the Church of England.

Source: The memorial plaque in Wesley's Chapel, City Road, London.

Retrospect

It is noteworthy that, over the centuries, the assessment of Charles Wesley by historians has not altered significantly. Aspects of his life and work have been re-evaluated and his place within the 'Holy Club' has been reassessed, as have his sermons and hymns. Family relationships, particularly with John, have been the subject of relatively recent research. New insights have been gained into the way in which the brothers 'agreed to disagree' over particular theological issues such as Christian perfection, and the major question concerning Methodism's relationship with the Church of England.

However, apart from this inevitable process of reinterpretation, what has not altered is the fundamental way in which historians and biographers have seen Charles *himself*, as a person. There has been a remarkable consistency in their views over the years, perhaps because Charles was so much more open by nature than his brother John. When we compare the evaluation made by his near contemporaries with those of today's scholars, it is possible to reach a coherent synthesis, which says much about Charles' integrity and the genuineness of his character.

Often given to rapid mood-swings, and with a temperament that led him to impulsive acts at times – though just as quick to heal and placate – Charles was as capable of making considered, rational judgements as he was of using pure intuition. He could plumb the depths of despair, yet rise to the heights of ecstasy, and his hymns covered the whole range of human emotions. He could be direct to the point of seeming to be intimidatory, yet the gentleness of his nature showed itself in countless acts of sensitivity. Forever prone to self-doubt, he displayed enormous strength and resilience when it came to his Christian convictions. Throughout his life he never lost either his sense of humour or his capacity for making and sustaining deep friendships. He was always 'brother Charles' but he was very much his own man – and one who made a unique contribution to the work of God and the life of the Church.

Today, a memorial to the Wesley brothers can be seen in Westminster Abbey. It depicts John in the foreground, but with Charles slightly in front. Charles would have approved of that.

> Yet when the work is done,
> The work is but begun:
> Partaker of thy grace,
> I long to see thy face;
> The first I prove below,
> The last I die to know.

Appendix:
The Wesley Family Tree

The Wesley Family Tree

Many of the dates below are uncertain, as is the order in which the children were born after Mehetabel. The details below correspond to those given by Dr Frank Baker in *Methodist History* (April 1988) – earlier tables, for example, give Anne's date of birth as 1702, not 17 May 1701, and Charles as 13 December, rather than 18 December 1707. Only the children born to Charles and Sally are shown of this generation.

Those marked * died in infancy; ? stands for an unknown name, sex or date. Dates indicated 'c.' are uncertain or approximate.

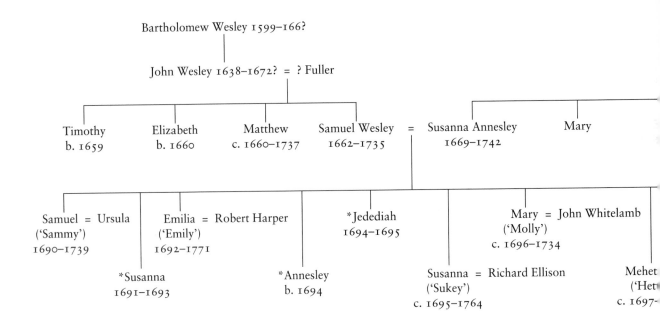

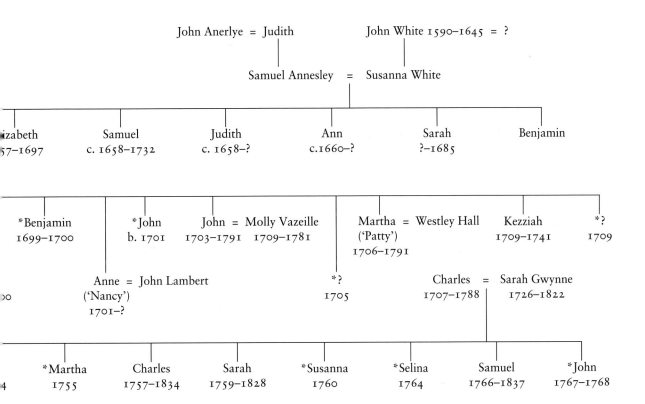

John Anerlye = Judith   John White 1590–1645 = ?

Samuel Annesley = Susanna White

Elizabeth	Samuel	Judith	Ann	Sarah	Benjamin
57–1697	c. 1658–1732	c. 1658–?	c.1660–?	?–1685	

*Benjamin	*John	John = Molly Vazeille	Martha = Westley Hall	Kezziah	*?
1699–1700	b. 1701	1703–1791 1709–1781	('Patty') 1706–1791	1709–1741	1709

Anne = John Lambert   *?   Charles = Sarah Gwynne
('Nancy')   1705   1707–1788   1726–1822
1701–?

*Martha	Charles	Sarah	*Susanna	*Selina	Samuel	*John
1755	1757–1834	1759–1828	1760	1764	1766–1837	1767–1768

Glossary

ANAMNESIS The act of remembrance in Holy Communion, though the word itself means more than simply 'remembering'. Rather, it carries the sense of re-presenting before God what Christ has done in such a way as to make it a reality for those present.

ANGLICAN Usually synonymous with 'Church of England'. The word has also come to mean a church tradition which had its origins in the English Reformation at the time of Henry VIII and Elizabeth. This tradition can be found in churches throughout the world that were founded by the Church of England. However, it was not a term in general use in the eighteenth century.

ANTEPAST A poetic expression, usually found in older hymns, meaning a foretaste or something to whet the appetite.

ANTINOMIANISM Literally 'against the law'. An approach to Christian living which minimized the place of laws and regulations (e.g. the Ten Commandments) and instead stressed the importance of the Spirit's guidance. 'Antinomians' emphasized faith alone over against Christian behaviour or 'works'.

ARMINIAN From Jacob Arminius (1560–1609) who opposed Calvin's teaching concerning predestination. He insisted that all people can be saved, but only by the grace of God. His teaching had a profound influence on the Wesleys.

'ARTICLES' Sometimes used by the Wesleys as shorthand for the 'Thirty-Nine Articles' (q.v.).

ARTISAN A skilled workman, such as a tailor or a weaver.

ASSISTANTS The Wesleys' senior helpers who were ordained ministers. Later they became known as superintendent ministers.

ATONEMENT The reconciliation (literally, 'at-one-ment') between God and humankind, which was achieved by his Son Jesus Christ. Over the centuries different theories have arisen which try to explain how this is possible. Some focus on the sacrificial nature of Christ's death on the cross, some on his victory over evil, and others on the 'moral' force of God's love at work through Christ. No one theory explains this reconciliation completely, but each contributes something to our understanding.

AUGUSTINIAN From St Augustine (354–430), perhaps the most famous of the Early Church Fathers. His best known works were the *Confessions* and *The City of God*. An opponent of Pelagius (see below), his teachings were dominated by his belief that humanity's original sin could only be countered by the grace of God. He should not be confused with St Augustine, the first Archbishop of Canterbury, who lived in the sixth century.

BANDS Similar to 'classes' (q.v.), except that they were smaller and composed of members who were considered to be more advanced in faith.

'BOWELS' In Hebrew culture this was the seat of the emotions – the heart being thought to control the will. Hence the term 'bowels of mercy' to describe a strong feeling of compassion.

CAMBRIDGE PLATONISTS These were an influential group of churchmen who gathered at Cambridge in the latter part of the seventeenth century. They developed a strong link between mysticism and reason, and held that spiritual truths could be understood by a combination of an individual's reason and his or her personal experience of God's indwelling spirit.

CANON The original Greek word meant literally a 'measuring rod', and came to refer to something that was correct or authoritative. It is now a term describing the Bible, which is a collection of those books that were accepted as having sufficient authority to be included. However, it can also be used in an entirely different sense, describing a special title given to an Anglican priest (often, but not necessarily) serving a cathedral.

CANON LAW The collection of rules drawn up by the Church over the centuries which deal with matters of faith, morals and discipline.

THE CAROLINAS The colonial territory in North America named after King Charles which, after the American War of Independence (1775–83), became the states of North and South Carolina.

CATECHISM A system of instructing new Christians in matters of faith and doctrine. It consists of a series of questions and responses concerning basic aspects of belief, the nature of the Church, and so on.

CATHOLIC The universal Church. Often used as an abbreviation for the Roman Catholic Church, although, strictly speaking, this is not correct.

CENTINEL A sentinel or guardsman.

'CHANGE' A term – now archaic – used in the eighteenth century to denote the approach of an individual's death.

CHIASMUS A poetic device in which words or themes are placed in parallel but in reverse order, i.e. following the pattern A–B–B–A, or even A–B–C–C–B–A.

CHURCH Today we think of the word in two senses. 'Church' can mean both the universal institution and also an individual church in a particular location. It can describe a particular building, but more properly, it means the body of people who belong to it. In the eighteenth century 'church' in common speech invariably meant the Church of England.

CHURCH FATHERS The title given to important figures in the early centuries of the Church's history (e.g. Clement of Rome, St Ignatius of Antioch, Tertullian, St Irenaeus and Origen), whose writings shaped its development, particularly in the area of doctrine.

CIRCUIT A group of Methodist churches linked together at local level. Circuits were grouped together in districts, which formed the Methodist Connexion.

CLASSES Small groups of Methodists meeting together for prayer, Bible study and fellowship. In many areas they have been replaced by house groups.

CLASS TICKET Now replaced by an annual ticket as proof of membership and as a reminder of the privileges and duties of being a member of the Methodist Church. It was originally given each quarter to class members as a ticket of entry to meetings.

'CLEAVE' In the eighteenth century it generally meant 'to unite' or 'to adhere to', rather than having today's sense of 'to divide' or 'to split'.

COMMUNICANT A person receiving Holy Communion, i.e. one who 'communicates'.

THE CONFERENCE The central governing body of Methodism which first met in 1744 and which today meets annually in June and/or July. Most of its members are elected representatives – lay people and ordained ministers – from the Districts, though some are ex-officio. It meets in three separate sessions but final authority on most matters lies with the Representative, rather than the Ministerial or Diaconal Sessions.

CONGREGATIONALISTS A Protestant group emerging from the Reformation which believed in the autonomy of the local church. Eventually in England they joined with the Presbyterians (q.v.) to form the United Reformed Church.

CONNEXION The national network of Methodist churches comprising local churches, circuits and districts, linked together in progressively larger units, under the government of the annual Conference.

'CONSIDERABLENESS' An archaic term which simply meant a person's worth or self-esteem.

'CONVINCING' (GRACE) Sometimes written as 'convicting' (grace). The Wesleys used it in connection with repentance, to remind their followers that the grace of God works in the heart of an individual at the earliest stages of coming to faith.

COVENANT SERVICE Usually held early in January, it is a service in which Methodists rededicate themselves to God's service for the coming year.

CURATE Historically, the word means an Anglican clergyman who has care of a parish. In practice a curate is one who assists a vicar or who takes temporary charge of a parish when it is vacant.

DEACON Literally, 'a servant'. In the Methodist Church, a member of the diaconal order is a man or woman who has been set apart for a full-time ministry of service. In the Church of England it denotes the third rank of ordained ministry below that of priest and bishop, a person usually being a deacon for a short period of time prior to ordination as a priest.

DEED OF DECLARATION Approved in February 1784, this made Conference the legally constituted governing body of Methodism.

DEISM/DEISTS Originally this word was used in contrast to Atheism (belief in the existence of no god) and Polytheism (belief in many gods). In the eighteenth century, however, it referred to a group of thinkers in England who applied the principles of the Enlightenment to religion. They believed that there was a divine creator, but that he remained aloof from the world. Deists, therefore, expressed doubts concerning aspects of Christian doctrine that depended upon revelation – e.g. the Trinity, Christ's incarnation, miracles, the authority of the Bible, and the reality of immortality.

DENOMINATION A group of people called by the same name. The term describes a religious organization that is more formally developed than a sect but not yet recognized as an independent church, though nowadays it often has a less specific meaning.

'DESK' Charles Wesley sometimes used the term to denote a lectern in a church, though he more usually preached from the pulpit.

DIOCESE The area governed by a bishop.

DISSENTERS All those eighteenth-century Protestant groups in Britain who were not Anglican and who refused to adhere to the various acts of Parliament which laid down the rules for conformity to the Church of England.

DISSENTING ACADEMY From the late seventeenth century Dissenters set up a number of institutions to enable their children to receive the equivalent of the secondary education provided by church schools which they could not attend.

DISTEMPER A general term denoting any troubled condition of the body or mind.

DISTRICT There are currently thirty-three Districts in the 'home stations' of the Methodist Church, i.e. England, Scotland and Wales, each of which consists of a number of circuits.

DIVINES A loose term referring to scholars, theologians or clerics of recognized stature.

DIVINITY Another word for theology.

DOMESTIC SYSTEM The method of production (for example of woollen cloth) based on small units (usually families) working from home. With the onset of the factory system it went into steady decline, though in some parts of the country it still survives in the form of local cottage industries.

ECUMENISM/ECUMENICAL The term originates from the Greek οικουμενε: (*oikoumene*), meaning 'the whole inhabited world'. It describes the movement, particularly in the twentieth and twenty-first centuries, which seeks understanding and co-operation between churches in a spirit of unity.

'EFFECTUAL' Virtually synonymous with the word 'effective' but having the sense of being successful in producing the desired result.

ELECTION Another word for 'choice'. Specifically it was used in the context of the doctrine of predestination (q.v.) to denote those who, some believed, were chosen or 'elected' to be saved by God.

ELECTUARY Prescribed medicine made into a syrup by, for example, the addition of honey.

'ENTHUSIASM' Used at the time of the Wesleys as a term of abuse for any form of religious extremism. The label 'Enthusiast' therefore indicated that a person was regarded as a fanatic.

EPISCOPACY The office of bishop. The concept of the historic episcopate, in which bishops today are believed to be the successors of Peter and the apostles, has been a major bone of contention between the Church of England and the other Protestant churches.

ESTABLISHED Usually denoting the Church of England which was established by an Act of Parliament. The Church of Scotland, however, is also an established church. Moreover, *all* the churches are controlled by Acts of Parliament.

EUCHARIST Literally, 'thanksgiving'. One of the names given to the sacrament of Holy Communion.

EVANGELICAL A loose term having a number of different meanings. In the nineteenth century it described an informal group within the Church of England who were known for their piety and who laid great stress on the need for personal conversion and the spreading of the gospel. Nowadays it refers to Christians who emphasize the importance of the doctrine of justification, evangelistic outreach and the authority of Scripture.

EVANGELISM The proclamation of the gospel. From the Greek ευαγγελιον (*euangelion*), meaning 'gospel' or 'good news'.

'EXPERIMENTAL' In the eighteenth century it described an approach to faith that was related closely to a person's experience. The present equivalent would be 'experiential', but this loses the sense of testing which the Wesleys believed was necessary.

EXTEMPORE A sermon or prayer given without the help of notes, sometimes impromptu, is said to be delivered 'extempore'.

FLUX A general expression for diarrhoea; the expression 'bloody flux' was commonly used in the eighteenth century as a synonym for dysentery.

FUNDAMENTALISM Fundamentalists believe in the verbal inspiration of Scripture and therefore in its supremacy as the inerrant word of God. Consequently, they insist on the literal interpretation of the Bible.

GENTILE Originally this meant anyone who was not a Jew, but the word came to denote any person who was not a Christian. It is now rarely used.

GRACE From the Greek word χαρις (*charis*) meaning 'charm', gracefulness or graciousness. In Christian theology, it refers to God's free love for humankind, and is always seen in the context of God's initiative in reaching out to sinners. In Charles Wesley's day it could also mean the benefits received from God, particularly at the sacraments.

'GRUMBLETONIAL' A nickname used in the eighteenth century to describe a supporter of the Country as opposed to the Court party after the Glorious Revolution of 1688. Such a person would be seen to represent those who were out of favour and outside the benefits of Court patronage and, therefore, inclined to 'grumble'!

GUINEA An old, pre-decimal coin originally made from gold (which came from Guinea in West Africa), whose value, by the eighteenth century, had been fixed at 21 shillings.

HELPERS Mr Wesley's preachers.

HERRNHUT The centre of the Moravian revival in Saxony.

HOLINESS Literally, the quality of being 'kept apart for religious use', but when used in connection with the individual's life of faith in Charles Wesley's day, it referred to the process of sanctification and purity of heart.

HOMILY Originally, short sermons written by Bishop Thomas Cranmer for those priests who could not write their own. Later it became a general term for a short sermon or meditation, especially on a passage of Scripture.

'HORRIBLE' In the context of Whitefield's preaching concerning the doctrine of limited redemption, the term (first coined by John Calvin) literally meant 'hair-raising', i.e. that which makes the hair stand on end.

INCUMBENT A member of the Anglican clergy who has charge over a parish.

INDEPENDENT A term used until about the end of the eighteenth century for a Congregationalist (q.v.).

'INDIFFERENTLY' Impartially, without any special regard or favour. Today the word has another sense altogether, and implies a lack of any strong feeling about an issue.

INTERCESSIONS Prayers on behalf of others, whereas petitions are normally thought of as being for those who are offering prayer.

ITINERANT The term used to describe ministers who travel around the country, staying in one circuit for a limited period of time. Today a minister is invited for an initial period of five years, whereupon his or her term can be extended.

JUSTIFICATION The word was used by St Paul to express God's forgiveness and 'acquittal' of sinners. It came into theology as a term for part of the process of salvation, and has been interpreted in various ways. John and Charles Wesley equated it with the idea of 'acceptance' and 'pardon', and used it to describe the change in the relationship between a person and God, in which God took the first step.

LAITY Another term for lay people, in contrast to the ordained clergy.

LATITUDINARIANISM An attitude common in the eighteenth century which emphasized the virtues of practical religion at the expense of doctrine. 'Latitudinarians' believed that doctrines did not matter so much as living a moral life in accordance with the gospel. They allowed, therefore, a certain amount of 'latitude' in the interpretation of Scripture and Christian doctrines.

LEADERS' MEETING The forerunner of the Church Council in Methodism, i.e. the governing body of the local church.

'LEGAL HUNDRED' The hundred specified members of the Methodist Conference as drawn up by the Deed of Declaration of 1784 (q.v.).

'LIGHTNESS' As used in the eighteenth century it simply meant a tendency towards frivolity.

LITURGY Literally, 'the work (of the people)'. It originally meant either the formal services of the Church contained in the Book of Common Prayer (as opposed to private devotional prayers) or, occasionally, the Eucharist itself. Nowadays the term can denote any formal order of worship.

LIVING Another name for a parish, since the priest depended upon its income for his livelihood.

LOCAL PREACHER A lay person who preaches and leads worship, mainly in his or her own local area. In the Wesleys' day, some of the lay preachers were itinerant.

LOCAL PREACHERS' MEETING The quarterly meeting of all local preachers in a particular circuit (which ordained ministers also attend), in which business is dealt with and matters of faith are shared. In modern Methodism it is more usually – and more accurately – known simply as the 'Preachers' Meeting', since the ordained presbyters, who are also members of the meeting, will themselves have been local preachers at some stage.

'LOG-HOUSE CONVERTS' A slang phrase referring to those colonists who (hypocritically) attended services with the aim of currying favour with the authorities.

LOVE-FEAST A service in which bread is broken and water drunk from a common cup. Methodist love-feasts included hymn-singing, testimonies and prayers.

MANSE The Methodist equivalent of a vicarage, i.e. the house which, owned by the circuit, is the home of the minister and his or her family.

MASS The celebration of Holy Communion or Eucharist in Roman Catholic churches, though it is possible to hold a Mass without communion for the congregation.

'MECHANIC' Nothing to do with car maintenance! In the eighteenth century it was generally a term of contempt, referring to a person, usually of limited education, who was engaged in manual labour.

MINUTES OF CONFERENCE The Methodist 'year book' in which the main decisions of the previous Conference are recorded and which contains details of the Methodist Church, addresses of ministers and so on.

MORAVIANS Originally known as the Church of the Brethren, founded in fifteenth-century Bohemia, in what is now the Czech Republic. A Protestant group closely linked to Lutheranism, they experienced a revival under Count Nicholas von Zinzendorf in the 1720s at Herrnhut in Germany and were probably best known for their piety.

MYSTICISM This has been a widespread approach to religion in general, not just Christianity. Mystics believe that it is possible to know God in this present life through personal religious experience, the highest state of which is sometimes described as a 'mystic marriage' with God. Christian mystics have laid great stress upon prayer, humility and charity as the outward sign of their spirituality. In seventeenth-century England the chief exponents of mysticism were to be found in the group known as the Cambridge Platonists (q.v.).

'NEW BIRTH' The beginning of the individual's new life in Christ. Whereas justification marks a *relative* change in us because God treats us as though we were righteous and so restores our relationship with him, the 'New Birth' sees the beginnings of a *real* change in the life of a believer.

NONCONFORMIST A general term referring to Protestant denominations not belonging to the established church. It was first used to denote those groups refusing to conform to the Uniformity Acts (q.v.).

NON-JURORS The name given to members of the Church of England who refused to take the oaths of allegiance and supremacy to William and Mary on the grounds that they would be perjuring themselves, in that they still regarded their previous oaths to James II as being valid.

OPEN TABLE The term used to describe the Methodist policy of allowing 'all who love the Lord Jesus Christ' to participate in Holy Communion, irrespective of whether they are members of the Methodist Church.

'OPINIONS' Religious views distinguishing various denominations. John and Charles Wesley used the term to mean the attitudes which they considered to be over and above the basic minimum necessary for a genuine faith in Christ.

ORDINANCE Literally, 'that which has been ordained' (by God). The Wesleys described the means of grace – prayer, reading the Bible, and receiving Holy Communion – as 'ordinances', since they felt that observing them was a matter of obedience.

'ORDINARY' In the context in which Charles was writing, the term referred to the chaplain who attended prisoners condemned to death.

PATRONAGE The right exercised by a person to appoint someone to a particular office. In the eighteenth century members of royalty, the aristocracy or powerful politicians and churchmen could, as 'patrons', exercise influence in this way. Many church offices were 'in the gift' of an individual. Often a wealthy land-owner was able to control local elections because the majority of voters were his tenants. This possibility only finally disappeared when the secret ballot was introduced.

PELAGIAN From Pelagius, an English theologian and teacher who lived in the late fourth and early fifth centuries. He asserted that, because God had given men and women free will, they could choose whether or not to accept salvation. His greatest opponent was St Augustine, and his teachings were generally condemned by the Church because it was felt Pelagius was encouraging salvation by works.

PERFECTION A very fluid concept reflecting a wide range of beliefs, though it was never used to mean that an individual could be flawless. The Wesleys saw it in terms of perfect conformity with God's will and fellowship with him, though they differed as to how and when it could be attained.

PETITIONS Prayers of supplication, usually for those offering prayer.

'PICKTHANKS' A term, now archaic, which was used to describe an obsequious person – often someone who would try to curry favour by spreading gossip. Literally, one who 'picks thanks'.

PIETISM A movement that began in sixteenth-century Germany which sought to reinvigorate (Protestant) spiritual life by encouraging the practice of prayer, Bible study and contemplation. The Wesleys translated some the Pietists' hymns from the German.

THE 'PLAN' The Circuit Preaching Plan gives details of all the services held each quarter in a circuit, and the names of the preachers planned to conduct worship in each of the churches. When a local preacher becomes fully accredited, he or she is sometimes said to have 'come on full plan'.

PREACHERS Originally the word referred to those men appointed by John Wesley who could either be ordained ministers (of the Church of England) or laymen. In the nineteenth century 'the preachers' more often than not meant the ordained Methodist ministers. In modern times the term applies equally to ordained and lay men and women.

PREDESTINATION The doctrine which teaches that God knows, and has decreed, who will be saved. It was developed by St Augustine (354–430), the key biblical passage being Romans 8.29. In the Reformation era the doctrine came to be associated with Luther's and (especially) Calvin's teachings, though the latter laid great stress on the importance of assurance and human responsibility. The elect – those predestined to be saved – are, therefore, to strive to live holy lives rather than passively to accept the privilege of salvation. The theory of 'double predestination' is the doctrine taken to its logical extreme, i.e. that if some only are saved, then, inevitably, some must be preordained to damnation. It should be pointed out that Christians who accept the doctrine do so because they believe that *all* of sinful humanity deserves damnation, and that it is a sign of God's infinite love and mercy that at least some are saved.

PRESBYTERIANS Protestant groups arising from the Reformation who organized the government of their churches through a system of presbyters and elders, though patterns vary widely. Their doctrines are usually Calvinist in emphasis. In 1972 English Presbyterians joined with the Congregationalists to form the United Reformed Church.

PREVENIENT GRACE 'Prevenient' literally means 'going before'. Put in simple terms it is the capacity, possessed to a greater or lesser extent by every individual, for responding to the love of God. The Wesleys denied that anyone was devoid of the grace of God – which John sometimes referred to as 'natural conscience' – though they felt that many people stifled it as they grew into adulthood. 'No man sins because he has not grace,' wrote John Wesley, 'but because he does not use the grace which he hath.'

PREVENTING (GRACE) Another word for prevenient (grace).

PROTESTANT Those churches adhering to the principles of the Reformation of the sixteenth century. Although it can denote any non-Catholic church, some Anglicans prefer not to think of themselves as Protestants – rather, as Catholics who are not at present in communion with the Church of Rome.

PUBLICANS In New Testament times it meant 'tax collectors' but, used poetically (as in Charles Wesley's hymn, 'Where shall my wondering soul begin') it had a more general sense, standing for any dishonest persons.

PULPIT The raised platform, usually enclosed, used by preachers when leading worship. The name comes from the Latin *pulpitum*, which literally means 'scaffold'. This will be of special significance to preachers who are 'on trial'.

PURITANS A blanket term describing the more extreme English Protestants who were dissatisfied with the Reformation settlement under Elizabeth. They laid great emphasis upon the authority of Scripture, preaching and Sunday observance, and attacked elaborate forms of worship and anything that resembled 'Popery'.

QUAKER Another term for a member of the Society of Friends, founded by George Fox in the mid-seventeenth century. The group's main characteristics include free, non-liturgical worship, the absence of any ordained ministry, and an emphasis upon the inward spiritual life. In the latter part of the eighteenth century many Quakers came under the influence of Quietism.

'QUICK' Literally, 'alive'. In the eighteenth century, 'to quicken' meant to 'enliven'.

QUIETISM A passive kind of spirituality which played down the part of human activity and responsibility. At best it was a tranquil resting in God; at worst it denied the value of social action and even, in its extreme form, the importance of corporate worship.

'QUIRE' An old spelling of the word 'choir'.

RATIONALISM In the eighteenth century, it meant an appeal to the use of the mind in matters of faith. Rationalists in the Wesleys' day held that certain things could be known about God by reason alone. Some went as far as claiming that reason could prove the existence of God.

RECTOR In the Church of England, the incumbent who receives the tithes from the parish, as opposed to a vicar (q.v.), who does not. Today, neither in fact receives tithes!

RECTORY The house in which a rector lives. Virtually synonymous with 'vicarage'.

REFORMATION The great religious revolution of the sixteenth century that began with Martin Luther in Germany, though some would say it began earlier. Criticism of the Roman Catholic Church in general and the Papacy in particular led to both movements of reform and schism within the Church as a whole.

REFORMERS A loose term describing the leaders of the Reformation, such as Luther, Calvin and Zwingli.

REGENERATION The process whereby the image of Christ is formed in an individual. In other words, spiritual rebirth. Many high-churchmen in the eighteenth century believed that infants were 'regenerated' spiritually at their baptism.

RUBRIC Statements of rules or instructions (originally written in red ink) concerning religious procedures, specifically concerning liturgy and worship.

SACERDOTAL Although it can simply mean 'priestly', the word is often used in a pejorative sense to describe an excessive priestly influence over people or situations.

SACRAMENTALIST A Christian who lays great stress on the observance of the sacraments, especially Holy Communion.

SANCTIFICATION The continuing of God's work in the heart of a Christian, following justification (q.v.). As a process of growth in holiness, it marked a *real* change in an individual's character and life.

SECT Although the word can be used in a variety of senses, in the context of religion it means a subdivision of a denomination. Usually, the term describes a group which is looser and less formally organized than a denomination (q.v.).

SEE Another term for a diocese (q.v.). The word comes from the Latin *sedes*, meaning 'seat', of the bishop.

'SENSIBLE' In the eighteenth century it did not mean 'wise' or 'practical' as it does in today's usage. Rather, it referred to the senses, i.e. human perception. See, for example, the line from Charles Wesley's hymn: 'and sensibly believe' (Document 82, verse 2).

'SINGULARITY' As used by Charles Wesley's contemporaries it could not only mean 'individuality', but also have the pejorative sense of 'peculiarity'.

SOCIETY The basic Methodist 'unit'. When the early Methodists met together, they avoided using the term 'church' in order not to give the impression that they were competing with the local parish church.

SPECULATIVE When used in the eighteenth century by the Wesleys and others in connection with theology, it meant 'theoretical', 'based upon reflection', and did not have the sense of 'guesswork' that it does today.

STANDING ORDERS The numbered rules and regulations of the Methodist Church to be found in *CPD* (*The Constitutional Practice and Discipline of the Methodist Church*). Amendments to these have to be approved by Conference.

STANDING VOTE The method of voting in the Methodist Church when important decisions need to be made, for example when Conference approves candidates for ordination.

'STATIONS' Circuits and other appointments to which ministers are assigned by the Conference. They can be home and overseas.

STEWARDS In the Methodist Church today, Church stewards are lay people elected to be responsible, with the minister, for the life of the local church. Circuit stewards oversee the welfare of the ministers and churches in a circuit. The term can also apply to lay people who perform certain duties relating to the celebration of Holy Communion (Communion stewards), the welcoming of people into church on Sundays (door stewards), or the care of church buildings (property stewards).

'STILLNESS' Often used in a similar sense to 'Quietism' (q.v.). It was one of the main features of Moravian piety, and arose from an over-literal interpretation of the text 'Be still and know that I am God' (Psalm 46.10). Those who advocated 'stillness' maintained that corporate acts of prayer and worship – even Bible study – were unnecessary until a Christian was completely purified. Otherwise they might be seen as attempts to gain God's favour.

'STRAITENED' An old word meaning 'constrained', or being compelled to act in a certain way.

STUDENTSHIP An endowment for a student at a college.

SUPEREROGATIONISTS Another nickname given to members of the Holy Club, because they were accused of trying to outdo their fellow Oxonians in good works.

SUPERINTENDENTS Superintendent ministers, formerly known as 'assistants', are senior ministers placed in charge of a circuit.

SUPERNUMERARY An ordained minister who has reached the age of retirement.

SYNOD The meeting, at District level, of ministers and lay people in the Methodist Church. It can also refer to any important church gathering, such as the General Synod of the Church of England.

'TABERNACLE' The tabernacle was the tent carried by the Israelites in the wilderness and used as a movable shrine. Charles Wesley used the word as a metaphor for the most important area of an individual's life, i.e. where a person's priorities lay.

'TEMPORALS' From 'temporal', relating to the secular world, as opposed to spiritual matters. In the eighteenth century the word was used to describe belongings, or financial resources.

THIRTY-NINE ARTICLES The statements of doctrine set out by the Church of England which defined what was acceptable as orthodox, as opposed to the teachings of Roman Catholicism on the one hand and Protestant positions (for example, Puritanism) on the other. They first appeared in 1563.

TRADUCED 'Translated'.

TOLERATION ACT Introduced in Britain in 1689, granting freedom of worship to dissenters under carefully laid down conditions.

'UNDISTINGUISHING' The same as 'indifferent' (q.v.).

UNIFORMITY ACTS Along with a whole series of other Acts of Parliament in the seventeenth century, their aim was to ensure the loyalty of the clergy to the Church of England. They did this by defining what was acceptable. The last one in 1662 required all clergy to declare their public adherence to the Book of Common Prayer and make a declaration of loyalty to the King. It has been estimated that nearly 2,000 dissenting clergy were forced to give up their livings.

UNITARIAN A person who rejects the doctrine of the Trinity and who denies the divinity of Jesus Christ. Some Unitarians maintain that Christ *became* divine at his resurrection.

USHER In the eighteenth century it was a term referring to a senior pupil in a public school who became an assistant teacher. Nowadays it has quite a different meaning.

VICAR In the Church of England, an incumbent of a parish where the tithes are allocated to some other person or institution, for example, the local monastery. A vicar performs the same duties as a rector (q.v.).

VOUCHSAFE The word could either mean to 'guarantee', or, more usually in the eighteenth century, to 'graciously allow'.

WATCH-NIGHT A nocturnal vigil involving prayers and hymn-singing. In the Methodist Church today it often takes place on New Year's Eve, though this was not always the case.

Suggestions for Further Reading

This list is not intended to be exhaustive. Rather, it is a personal selection of books which you may wish to consult for more detailed study. If you have not done any reading or study for some time, you may wish to consult Appendix 3 of *The Making of Methodism*, entitled 'A Guide to Reading and Study'.

Lists of books which relate to associated topics can be found in the bibliographies of the other volumes in the *Exploring Methodism* series and, in particular, in the final volume of *A History of the Methodist Church in Great Britain*. The shorter books which are more suitable for general reading have been marked with an asterisk.

Those of you with access to the internet will have a veritable treasury of information at your disposal. Starting with the Methodist Church in Britain's own web-site (*www.methodist.org.uk*), and then following the appropriate links, will quickly put you on the right track. Another approach is to use your favourite search-engine and look up references to Charles Wesley. The full text of his journal, for example, can be accessed in this way.

Note. Those wishing to pursue further study of Charles Wesley will find the *Proceedings of the Wesley Historical Society* of great value, particularly the bibliography which the society publishes annually. The Charles Wesley Society, which was founded as recently as 1990, has produced a whole range of informative articles on Charles which are too numerous to list here.

General introductions to the historical background

The eighteenth century

Clark, J. C. D., *English Society, 1660–1832*, Cambridge University Press 2000.
  A completely revised edition of a detailed and scholarly work.
Cook, C., and Stevenson J., *The Longman Handbook of Modern British History, 1714–2001*, Longman 2001. *

A compact and accessible reference work which is intended for the general reader as well as the serious student.

Langford, Paul, *Eighteenth Century Britain: A Very Short Introduction*, Oxford University Press 2000. *

Part of the Oxford Illustrated History of Britain series. A good starting-point.

Langford, Paul, *The Eighteenth Century, 1688–1815*, Oxford University Press 2002.

Takes a thematic approach, giving due weight to social and religious developments.

Lee, Christopher, et al., *This Sceptred Isle*, Vol. 6: *The First British Empire, 1702–1760*, Audio CD, BBC Audio (Spoken Word) 1998.*

Lee, Christopher, et al., *This Sceptred Isle*, Vol. 7: *The Age of Revolutions, 1760–1792*, Audio CD, BBC Audio (Spoken Word) 1998.*

Part of the Radio 4 series telling the history of Britain from the Roman invasion to the death of Queen Victoria. Easy to listen to and extremely helpful for those with little background knowledge of the eighteenth century.

Marshall, Dorothy, *Eighteenth Century England*, Longman 1962.

In the Longman History of England series, which contains detailed, solid works by reputable authors. They are becoming a little dated, but are more readable than the relevant volumes in the Oxford History of England series which pre-date them.

Plumb, J. H., *England in the Eighteenth Century*, Penguin 1950*; *The First Four Georges*, Fontana 1966.*

Dated, but they make excellent introductions. Both have been regularly reprinted.

Porter, Roy, *English Society in the Eighteenth Century*, Penguin 1982.*

A detailed, but very 'user-friendly' survey of the social scene.

Sharpe, J. A., *Early Modern England*, Arnold 1997. Covers the period 1550 to 1760, with an emphasis on social developments.

Surveys of church history

Bainton, Ronald, *The Penguin History of Christianity*, Vol. II, Penguin 1967.*

Covers a huge sweep of history, but the later chapters provide helpful background material.

Comby, J., and MacCulloch, D., *How to Read Church History*, Vol II: *From the Reformation to the Present Day*, SCM Press 1986.

Blends historical narrative with a clear presentation of selected primary sources.

Cragg, Gerald R., *The Church and the Age of Reason 1648–1789*, Penguin 1960.

The fourth volume in the *Pelican History of the Church* series. A little dated now, but still useful for general reference.

Hole, Robert, *Pulpits, Politics and Public Order in England, 1760–1832*, Cambridge University Press 2002.
Detailed and informative, the author covers the theological principles of all the major denominations.

Hylson-Smith, K., *The Churches in England from Elizabeth I to Elizabeth II*, Vol. II: *1689–1833*, SCM Press 1997.
A modern, scholarly survey.

MacCulloch, D., *Groundwork of Christian History*, Epworth Press 1987.*
Admirable, but has less material on the modern period.

Methodism

Methodism in the eighteenth century

Baker, Frank, *A Charge to Keep*, Epworth Press 1947.*
A classic short survey of the Wesleys and early Methodism. It is beautifully written and, if seen in a second-hand bookshop, should be purchased immediately!

Baker, Frank, *John Wesley and the Church of England*, 2nd edn, Epworth Press 2000.
A masterly study which has been thoroughly revised since it first appeared in 1970.

Bates, Jim, *The Methodist Church*, Pergamon 1977.*
A brief, but informative introduction which is suitable for the newcomer.

Cooney, Dudley Levistone, *The Methodist in Ireland: A Short History*, Columba Press 2001.
A recent survey which, in its early chapters, gives a clear (and honest) appraisal of the early work undertaken in Ireland by John and Charles Wesley.

Davies, Rupert E., *Methodism*, 2nd revd edn, Epworth Press 1985.*
Still one of the best short accounts.

Davies, Rupert E., George, A. Raymond, and Rupp, E. Gordon, (eds), *A History of the Methodist Church in Great Britain*, 4 Vols, Epworth Press 1965–88.
Undoubtedly the best source for the reader looking for further material. The chapters consist of essays written by different authors on a wide range of topics, from general surveys to quite specialized themes. The final volume is a collection of edited documents and a bibliography that should satisfy the most ardent student of Methodism.

Heitzenrater, Richard P., *Wesley and the People Called Methodists*, Abingdon Press 1995.
A learned work that contains the results of much of the author's research.

Heitzenrater, Richard P., *Mirror and Memory: Reflections on Early Methodism*, Abingdon Press 1989.
A scholarly, but eminently readable series of essays.

Townsend, W. J., Workman, H. B., and Eayrs, G., (eds), *A New History of Methodism*, 2 Vols, Hodder & Stoughton 1909.
  The original standard history, and suitable for more detailed study. It is rather anecdotal, but still very useful.

Tabraham, Barrie W., *The Making of Methodism*, Epworth Press 1995.*
  The opening volume to this series, in which the discussion of ideas is set within a historical framework.

Turner, John Munsey, *Conflict and Reconciliation*, Epworth Press 1985.
  A series of detailed, well-researched essays on Methodism over the past two hundred and fifty years, with particular emphasis on Methodism's relationship with other churches.

Vickers, J. (ed.), *A Dictionary of Methodism in Great Britain and Ireland*, Epworth Press 2000.
  An indispensable work for general reference. Every student of Methodism should endeavour to acquire a copy!

Yrigoyen, Charles, and Warrick, Susan Eltscher, *Historical Dictionary of Methodism*, Scarecrow Press 1996.
  Of particular interest to American Methodists.

Theology and Ideas

Davies, Rupert E., *What Methodists Believe*, 2nd edn, Epworth Press 1988.*
  A short guide to the essential teachings of the Methodist Church.

Langford, Thomas A., *Methodist Theology*, Epworth Press 1998.*
  A very useful introduction to the distinctive theological emphases of Methodism by an American scholar. The third volume in the *Exploring Methodism* series.

Outler, Albert C. (ed.), *John Wesley*, Oxford University Press 1964.
  In the *Library of Protestant Thought* series. This is a collection of Wesley's writings together with a great deal of discussion and analysis.

Piette, Maximin, *John Wesley in the Evolution of Protestantism*, London 1937.
  An old, but valuable study concentrating mainly on ideas.

Rattenbury, J. E., *The Conversion of the Wesleys*, Epworth Press 1938.
  Concerned less with Charles, but useful as a starting-point for those wishing to examine the events of May 1738 and their origin in greater detail.

Schmidt, Martin, *John Wesley: A Theological Biography*, 2 Vols, Epworth Press 1962–73.
  Although, strictly speaking, this is a biography of John Wesley, it contains a great deal of scholarly analysis of ideas, and is worth consulting.

Townsend, Michael, *Our Tradition of Faith*, Epworth Press 1980.*
  A short, thought-provoking study.

The Wesleys

The writings of John and Charles Wesley

Note. Abingdon Press have been steadily producing a multi-volume series entitled *The Works of John Wesley*. These are relatively expensive, but contain a huge amount of detail, and most readers will probably need to order them from their local libraries.

Curnock, Nehemiah (ed.), *The Journal of the Rev. John Wesley*, 8 Vols, Epworth Press 1938. This has been reprinted at regular intervals and is also available in a one-volume abridged version.

Heitzenrater, Richard P. (ed.), *Sermons and Hymns of John Wesley*, Abingdon Press 1999.
  This is not a book but a CD-ROM. It contains Volumes I, II, III, IV and VII of *The Works of John Wesley* and extensive notes by such noted scholars as Frank Baker, Richard Heitzenrater and Albert Outler. Readers who have computers with Microsoft Windows 95 or higher, at least 16MB of RAM, 12MB of space on their hard disks (and a CD-ROM drive, of course!), will find this a magnificent resource. They will also save a great deal of money compared with purchasing the books themselves!

Holway, James, *Sermons on Several Occasions*, Methodist Publishing House 1986.*
  Provides a paraphrase which makes John Wesley's sermons much easier to read, though purists might object!

Jackson, Thomas (ed.), *The Works of John Wesley*, 14 Vols, Conference Office 1872.
  The standard work of reference, but gradually being supplanted by the series being produced by Abingdon Press. The original has now been reprinted in the USA by Baker Book House, Grand Rapids, Michigan (1978).

Jackson, Thomas (ed.), *The Journal of the Rev. Charles Wesley, M.A.*, 2 Vols, London 1849; Baker Book House, Grand Rapids, Michigan 1980.
  Volume II contains selections of Charles' correspondence and poetry. It was out of print for over a hundred years, but copies of the original still appear from time to time in second-hand bookshops.

Newport, Kenneth G. C. (ed.), *The Sermons of Charles Wesley*, Oxford University Press 2001.
  A major work, recently published, which makes available all of Charles' sermon material for the first time. It places Charles' preaching in the context of early Methodism and the eighteenth century generally, and includes detailed analysis of Charles' style and the sources he used. It is quite costly, so keen students will need to obtain library copies.

Telford, John (ed.), *The Journal of Charles Wesley, M.A.*, London 1909.
  Covers the early years only, i.e. from 1736 to 1739.

Telford, John (ed.), *The Letters of the Rev. John Wesley*, 8 Vols, Epworth Press 1931.
  Ditto remarks as for Thomas Jackson (ed.), *The Works of John Wesley* (above).
Wesley, John, *A Plain Account of Christian Perfection*, Epworth Press 1990.
  This and other examples of John's writings have been reprinted from time to time, particularly in the USA.

John Wesley

Biographies of John Wesley are plentiful. Books listed below are some of the more recent studies which are more readily available. For a fuller list, consult the fourth volume of Davies et al., *A History of the Methodist Church in Great Britain* (above).

Ayling, S. E., *John Wesley*, Collins 1979.
  Written by a secular historian and which claims, therefore, to be more objective than biographies written by Methodists!
Collins, Kenneth J., *A Real Christian: The Life of John Wesley*, Abingdon Press 1999.
Edwards, Maldwyn, *The Astonishing Youth*, Epworth Press 1959.*
  A very readable introduction.
Heitzenrater, Richard P., *The Elusive Mr. Wesley*, 2 Vols, Abingdon Press 1984.
  The first volume contains a wide selection of John Wesley's own writings; the second reveals Wesley through the eyes of his contemporaries and biographers.
Pollock, John, *John Wesley*, Lion 1989.*
  A popular introduction which makes use of recent research by Heitzenrater and others.
Rack, Henry D., *Reasonable Enthusiast: John Wesley and the Rise of Methodism*, Epworth Press 1989.
  One of the most recent biographies of John Wesley. It has since been revised (2002) and is a major, detailed work.
Tuttle, Robert G., Jr, *John Wesley: His Life and Theology*, Zondervan 1978.*
  Takes an unusual approach in that part of the narrative is written in the first person from Wesley's own point of view.

The Wesley family

Edwards, Maldwyn, *Family Circle*, Epworth 1949.*
Edwards, Maldwyn, *The Astonishing Youth*, Epworth 1959.*
Edwards, Maldwyn, *Sons to Samuel*, Epworth 1961.*
  All eminently readable, yet based on sound research.
Greetham, M. and P., *Samuel Wesley*, Foundery Press 1990.*
Greetham, M., *Susanna Wesley*, Foundery Press 1988.*

Longworth, Allan, *Samuel Wesley Junior*, Foundery Press 1991.*
  All form part of the *Mini Wesley* series and are excellent short studies.
McMullen, M., *Hearts Aflame: Prayers of Susanna, John and Charles Wesley*,
  SPCK 1995.*
  A carefully constructed anthology for private devotion.
Maser, Frederick E., *The Wesley Sisters*, Foundery Press 1990.*
  Another in the *Mini Wesley* series.
Maser, Frederick E., *Seven Sisters in Search of Love*, Academy Books, Rutland,
  Vermont 1988.
  Brings a more critical eye to the study of the Wesley family.
Newton, John A., *Susanna Wesley and the Puritan Tradition in Methodism*,
  Epworth Press 1968.
  One of the best treatments of Susanna Wesley to have been written.
Pellowe, Susan, *A Wesley Family Book of Days*, River Street Press, Illinois
  1994.*
  Readily available in the UK. A delightful selection of writings and notes for
  each day of the year.
Quiller-Couch, Arthur, *Hetty Wesley*, London: Dent & Sons 1931.*
  Old, but books on Hetty Wesley are few and far between.
Wallace, Charles, Jr, *Susanna Wesley: The Complete Writings*, Oxford Univer-
  sity Press 1997.
  The only book which contains the whole of Susanna's correspondence and
  writings – a rich resource.

Charles Wesley

Biographies and general studies

Baker, Frank, *Charles Wesley as Revealed by his Letters*, Epworth Press 1948.*
  Long out of print, but combines readability with scholarly analysis based on
  original sources.
Brailesford, Mabel R., *A Tale of Two Brothers*, London 1954.
  A rather dated, uncritical but clear narrative of the lives of John and Charles.
Capon, John, *John and Charles Wesley, the Preacher and the Poet*, Hodder &
  Stoughton 1988.*
  A popular but accurate treatment of the two brothers.
Dallimore, A., *A Heart Set Free: The Life of Charles Wesley*, Evangelical Press
  1988.
  Written from a particular theological point of view.
Gill, Frederick C., *Charles Wesley, the First Methodist*, Lutterworth Press 1964.
  A well-written (if rather uncritical) biography that is now somewhat dated and
  suffers from the fact that no references to the sources used are provided.
Kimbrough, S. T., Jr (ed.), *Charles Wesley: Poet and Theologian*, Abingdon Press
  1992.

A series of scholarly essays by various authors which embody the results of recent research.

Telford, John, *The Life of the Rev. Charles Wesley, M.A., sometime student of Christ Church, Oxford*, London: Hodder & Stoughton 1886.
An old, but scholarly work.

Tyson, John R. (ed.), *Charles Wesley: A Reader*, Oxford University Press 1989.
A 'must have' for any serious student of Charles Wesley: a wide range of source material linked by clear narrative and supplemented by informed comment.

Vickers, John A., *Charles Wesley*, Foundery Press 1990.*
The third title in a series of short, very readable studies on the Wesleys and various aspects of Methodism, and a very useful brief introduction to Charles.

Wiseman, Frederick Luke, *Charles Wesley, Evangelist and Poet*, Epworth Press 1933.
An older biography that is worth consulting, though it has a simplistic approach and contains no index, references or notes to help the reader.

Young, Norman, *Charles Wesley: A Tribute*, Melbourne, Uniting Church Historical Society, Victoria 1988.*
A brief, but informative monologue.

Hymns and poetry

Baker, Frank, *Charles Wesley's Verse: An Introduction*, Epworth Press 1964.*
Perhaps the best short treatment.

Baker, Frank (ed.), *The Representative Verse of Charles Wesley*, Abingdon Press 1962.
A more detailed study by this acknowledged expert.

Baker, Frank (ed.), *Hymns for the Nativity of Our Lord*, The Charles Wesley Society, Madison, New Jersey 1991.*
Part of a series of facsimile reprints, with a very helpful introduction.

Beckerlegge, Oliver (ed.), *Hymns for Our Lord's Resurrection*, The Charles Wesley Society, Madison, New Jersey 1992.*
Ditto remarks for the above.

Berger, Teresa, *Theology in Hymns? A Study of the Relationship of Doxology and Theology According to 'A Collection of Hymns for the Use of the People Called Methodists'*, translated by T. E. Kimbrough Jr, Kingswood Books, Abingdon Press 1995.
One of the most important studies of Charles' hymns since the writings of J. E. Rattenbury appeared in the 1940s.

Bett, Henry, *The Hymns of Methodism and their Literary Relations*, 3rd edn, Epworth Press 1945.
An older study, but worth looking at.

Dudley-Smith, Timothy, *A Flame of Love: A Personal Choice of Charles Wesley's Verse*, SPCK 1987.*
Suitable for private devotions.

Flew, R. Newton, *The Hymns of Charles Wesley: A Study of their Structure*, Epworth Press 1953.*
Dated, but a beautifully concise analysis.

Gregory, A. S., *Praises with Understanding*, Epworth Press 1938.

Hart, E., Hobbs, G., and Webb, P. (eds), *All Loves Excelling*, Methodist Publishing House 1997.*
Hymns and poems of Charles Wesley which are compiled into a series of daily meditations for personal use.

Hildebrandt, Franz, and Beckerlegge, Oliver A., with the assistance of Dale, James, *A Collection of Hymns for the Use of the People Called Methodists*, The Works of John Wesley, Vol. 7, Oxford University Press 1983.

Kimbrough, S. T., Jr, and Beckerlegge, Oliver A., *The Unpublished Poetry of Charles Wesley*, 3 vols, Kingswood Books, Abingdon Press 1988–92.
An indispensable resource.

Lawson, John, *A Thousand Tongues: The Wesley Hymns as a Guide to Scriptural Teaching*, Paternoster 1987.
A fairly recent treatment which students of hymnody will find very helpful.

Manning, Bernard L., *The Hymns of Wesley and Watts*, Epworth Press 1942.*
A minor classic.

Rattenbury, J. E., *The Evangelical Doctrines of Charles Wesley's Hymns*, Epworth Press 1941.
A detailed, scholarly examination which is essential reading for those wishing to study Charles Wesley's hymns.

Rattenbury, J. E., *The Eucharistic Hymns of John and Charles Wesley*, Epworth Press 1948.
This, and the above, are classic works and both have now been reprinted – but not by Epworth, though they are obtainable in the UK.

Watson, J. R., *The English Hymn*, Clarendon Press 1997.

Wiseman, Frederick Luke, *Charles Wesley, and his Hymns*, Epworth Press 1933.*
An off-print from Townsend, W. J., Workman, H. B., and Eayrs, G., (eds), *A New History of Methodism*, 2 Vols, Hodder & Stoughton 1909. A rather dated survey, but useful as a brief introduction.

Notes

Introduction

1. All the verses at the beginning of chapters and chapter-sections are taken from Charles Wesley's hymns. Some are in *Hymns and Psalms*, which appeared in 1983, though they can all be found in the *Methodist Hymnbook* compiled fifty years earlier. Both are published by the Methodist Publishing House. The words are taken from the earliest versions of the hymns.

2. John Vickers, *Charles Wesley*, Foundery Press 1990.

3. A. Dallimore, *A Heart Set Free: The Life of Charles Wesley*, Evangelical Press 1988. The fact that the previous 'standard' biography, Frederick Gill's *Charles Wesley, the First Methodist*, was published by Lutterworth in 1964 is sufficient illustration of the dearth of recent material for the general reader.

4. This commences 9 March 1736, on Charles' arrival in Georgia. There are significant gaps in 1740 and 1741, nothing at all between September 1741 and January 1743, and only fragments for the last two years. His journal comes to an abrupt end on 5 November 1756.

5. This is Kenneth Newport's *The Sermons of Charles Wesley: A Critical Edition with Introduction and Notes*, published in September 2001 by Oxford University Press.

6. This view was suggested by Thomas Jackson in *The Life of the Rev. Charles Wesley, M.A.*, London 1841, p. iii. In the present author's opinion this was not the most likely reason.

7. John Wesley, *Letters*, Vol. VIII, p. 93. This, and all subsequent extracts from John Wesley's letters, are taken from the standard edition of *The Letters of the Rev. John Wesley* edited by John Telford (8 vols), Epworth Press 1931.

8. Charles was persuaded by John to use John Byrom's *Universal English Shorthand*, which is by no means easy to decipher.

9. Dr Maldwyn Edwards, *Sons to Samuel*, Epworth Press 1961, p. 53.

10. Quoted by John Telford (ed.), *The Letters of the Rev. John Wesley*, Epworth Press 1931, Vol. VIII, p. 267.

11. This comparison was made in *The Making of Methodism* (p. 11) and is the author's own assessment. It is, of course, open to challenge!

1. The Early Years

1. It was Dr Frank Baker who was able to establish 18 December 1707 as the correct date of Charles' birth, confirming the entry in the register of Westminster School where Charles was a pupil.

2. The name sometimes appears as 'Westley', owing to the fact that the family had come originally from Westleigh, a tiny village in Devon near the Somerset border.

3. See the Glossary for a brief description of this and other terms no longer in current usage.

4. This was in breach of the Five Mile Act of 1665 – see the Glossary. John was actually imprisoned four times, the longest being a six-month sentence served at the prison in Poole.

5. He was actually nominated for an Irish bishopric in 1694, though his young age may have counted against him on this occasion.

6. Dr Maldwyn Edwards goes into some detail concerning Samuel's financial problems and cites a poignant letter which the rector wrote to Archbishop Sharpe in 1700, in which he confessed that, 'I doubt not but one reason of my being sunk so far is my not understanding worldly affairs . . .' *Family Circle*, Epworth Press 1949, p. 16.

7. The precise number of children is not known for certain. Susanna was Samuel Annesley's second wife and it is generally accepted that she bore him twenty-four children in all. Only six of them were known by name: Elizabeth, Judith, Anne, Sarah, Samuel and, of course, Susanna.

8. Edwards, *Family Circle*, p. 6.

9. Henry Rack, *Reasonable Enthusiast: John Wesley and the Rise of Methodism*, Epworth Press 1989, p. 50.

10. The term 'churched' refers to the practice known as 'The Churching of Women'. It originated from the Jewish rite of purification (Leviticus 12.6) and became a service of thanksgiving which Christian women made after childbirth. It has now been replaced by the blessing at the end of the service of baptism.

11. Charles Wallace Jr (ed.), *Susanna Wesley: The Complete Writings*, Oxford University Press 1997.

12. Ibid., p. 18.

13. Susanna actually gave birth to nineteen children in all, though only ten survived infancy.

14. For example, in his hymn 'Where shall my wondering soul begin?', whose first verse has as its fourth line, 'A brand plucked from the eternal fire' – a reference to Zechariah 3.2.

15. There is a further extract from this on p. 9 of the author's *The Making of Methodism*, Epworth Press 1995. The full text appears in *Family Circle*, pp. 58–62.

16. Charles himself gives the year as 1715 (see Extract 7). However, the actual date of his entry into Westminster School was April 1716.

17. The later paragraphs are particularly interesting in view of Charles' feelings about the way in which early Methodism developed, especially in its relationship with the Church of England.

18. Cited in Frederick C. Gill, *Charles Wesley, the First Methodist*, Lutterworth Press 1964, p. 31.

19. The boys were required to speak only in Latin during formal lessons.

20. In a recent article in the *Proceedings of the Wesley Historical Society*, Vol. 53, Part 4 (February 2002), Henry Rack has shown that, whilst the details of the Irish inheritance were embellished over the years, the essence of the story of Garret Wesley's offer is true. Rack also notes that the connection between the Wesley and Wellesley families was still current in the early part of the nineteenth century, and cites the example of one of the Wellesleys standing for Parliament in 1830 and being 'hopefully smeared by his opponent as a relative of John Wesley' (p. 126).

2. *The Oxford Methodist*

1. Stanley Ayling, *John Wesley*, Collins 1979, p. 44.

2. Quoted by Frank Baker, *Charles Wesley as Revealed by His Letters*, Epworth Press 1948, p. 10. Charles Wesley to Dr Thomas Bradbury Chandler; London, 28 April 1785, *A History of the Methodist Church in Great Britain*, Vol. 4, Epworth Press 1988, pp. 204f. See also Extracts 12 and 17.

3. Baker, *Charles Wesley as Revealed by His Letters*, p. 14.

4. Ibid., p. 18.

5. Maldwyn Edwards' *Family Circle* provides a very readable introduction to Hetty and the other Wesley sisters. Charles' relationship with his sisters is covered in Chapter 5. There is also Frederick Maser's *The Wesley Sisters* in the *Mini Wesley* series published by Foundery Press (see Suggestions for Further Reading).

6. See the Glossary.

7. Little has been written specifically about Samuel. Allan Longworth's short study and Maldwyn Edwards' two excellent books on the Wesley family: *Sons to Samuel* and *Family Circle* are probably the best short studies – see Suggestions for Further Reading.

8. In a letter to his son just before he died, Samuel referred to 'your pity to your mother and me in a very liberal manner, wherein your wife joined with you, when you did not overmuch abound yourselves' (Edwards, *Family Circle*, p. 101).

9. The breakdown in their relationship seems to have begun in 1725, on that occasion taking the form of 'Nutty' attempting to curb Charles' appetite at the dinner table! The reason for this has never been discovered.

10. In the extracts reproduced in boxes, text within brackets marked (. . .) are the author's own words in parenthesis; those marked [. . .] are the *editor's* addition or suggested translation of Latin or Greek text. Charles Wesley was notoriously lax when it came to punctuation and often he omitted words and phrases on the assumption that the reader knew the details to which he was referring. The same is true for people's names, which were frequently shortened to a capital letter.

11. See Chapter 3.
12. See Extract 10.
13. In 1969 he came across the diary of Benjamin Ingham which contained a key for the symbols and hiero-glyphics that John used in his diary, which enabled him to decipher much material relating to the period 1725–35 that had hitherto not been widely available.
14. Richard P. Heitzenrater, *Mirror and Memory: Reflections on Early Methodism*, Abingdon Press 1989, p. 65.
15. By 1730 the name had become sufficiently established for Samuel Wesley Sr to use it in a letter to John, when he referred to himself as its 'grandfather', because he himself had engaged in similar activities in Oxford a generation earlier.
16. Baker, *Charles Wesley as Revealed by His Letters*, p. 13.
17. John Byrom was born in Manchester in 1692 and, after completing his degree at Cambridge, studied medicine in France, becoming a Fellow of the Royal Society in 1723. He spent most of his life in the Manchester area after inheriting the family estate the following year. Prior to this, Byrom taught a method of shorthand – which he himself had devised – in London, and his pupils included Charles and John Wesley. He is perhaps best remembered for writing the hymn 'Christians, awake, salute the happy morn'.
18. Quoted by Frederick C. Gill, *Charles Wesley, the First Methodist*, p. 39.
19. R. Heitzenrater, *Mirror and Memory*, pp. 82f.
20. The Wesleys usually referred to themselves as the 'company', but it is interesting that William Morgan and his younger brother (named Richard, after his father) used the word 'society' – though the 'Holy Club' had little in common with either earlier religious societies of the previous century or the Methodist societies which came later.
21. R. Heitzenrater, *Mirror and Memory*, p. 104.
22. Charles' earlier biographers, such as Thomas Jackson, tend to exonerate him from such seemingly selfish motives.
23. N. Curnock (ed.), *The Journal of the Rev. John Wesley, A.M.*, Standard Edition, Epworth Press 1938, Vol. VIII, p. 265.
24. Samuel died the next month, in fact – on 25 April 1735.
25. See Barrie Tabraham, *The Making of Methodism*, Epworth Press 1995, p. 13 (Extract 12) for the text of John's letter to his father in December 1734.
26. Baker, *Charles Wesley as Revealed by His Letters*, p. 20.
27. The exact date is uncertain – this by Charles' own reckoning!

3. *Georgia*

1. Charles actually began keeping his journal in 1729.
2. Oglethorpe made such an impression upon the younger Samuel that the latter wrote a lengthy poem as a eulogy to the General which had the enormous title, *The prisons Opened: a Poem, occasioned by the Glorious Proceedings of the Committee of the House of Commons, appointed to inquire into the state of the Jails of this kingdom, in the year 1728*, which included the following couplet:
   Yet, Britain, cease thy captives' woes to mourn,
   To break their chains, see Oglethorpe was born!
   A large part of this poem is to be found in T. Jackson (ed.), *The Journal of The Rev. Charles Wesley, M.A.*, London, John Mason 1849, Vol. I, pp. xi–xv.
3. And also Protestants from Salzburg and other parts of Germany, notably Bavaria.
4. See his letter to John Burton dated 10 October 1735 (John Wesley, *Letters*, Vol. I, pp. 188–91), an extract from which is to be found in *The Making of Methodism*, p. 22.
5. Cited in R. P. Heitzenrater, *The Elusive Mr. Wesley*, Abingdon Press 1984, Vol. II, p. 48.
6. Ibid., p. 47.
7. The passengers numbered about 150 but the entire party totalled nearly 700 (including crew), the remainder sailing on a second vessel, the *London Merchant*, which had been chartered at the same time as the *Simmonds* by the Georgia trustees.
8. See the Glossary.
9. For example, see *The Making of Methodism* p. 23, esp. Document 21.
10. For a long time this letter was thought to have been written by John, rather than Charles. It was Frank Baker who correctly identified the author's handwriting on studying the manuscript in 1945. See his article in S. T. Kimbrough (ed.), *Charles Wesley, Poet and Theologian*, Abingdon Press 1992, p. 73.
11. Anne Granville (see Chapter 2, p. 14).
12. T. Jackson (ed.), *The Journal of The Rev. Charles*

Wesley, M.A., London, John Mason 1849, Vol. I, p. 2.

13. Ibid., p. 3.
14. R. P. Heitzenrater, *Mirror and Memory: Reflections on Early Methodism*, Abingdon Press 1989, p. 155.
15. For example, see his journal entries for 21 and 22 June and 9 July 1738: *Journal*, Vol. I, pp. 107, 108 and 109.
16. John Wesley, *Letters*, Vol. I, p. 196.
17. Ibid.
18. See Extract 28, where Charles specifically refers to this.
19. His journal entry for 5 April, 'At one this morning the sandflies forced me to rise, and smoke them out of the hut' is a typical example of the conditions Charles had to endure.
20. See the Glossary.
21. *Journal*, Vol. I, p. 4.
22. Thomas Jackson, *The Life of the Rev. Charles Wesley, M.A.*, London 1841, p. 52.
23. Ibid., p. 53.
24. See Chapter 6 for a more detailed examination of this.
25. *Journal*, Vol. I, p. 14.
26. Ibid., pp. 16–17.
27. Ibid., p. 4.
28. Ibid., p. 6.
29. John Wesley, *Letters*, Vol. I, p. 200.
30. *Journal*, Vol. I, p. 16 – the title of his sermon on 4 April.
31. Ibid.
32. Ibid., pp. 35 and 36.
33. For more detail on John's experiences in Georgia, see *The Making of Methodism* pp. 22–5, and for a much fuller account, the bibliography.
34. Although Charles was patient to a degree with Appee, his journal entries make it clear that he was not deceived by his protestations of innocence. Appee was finally transported.
35. Frank Baker, *Charles Wesley as Revealed by His Letters*, Epworth Press 1948, p. 27.
36. Ibid., p. 28.
37. *Journal*, Vol. I, p. 55.
38. See Chapter 2.
39. Two Cambridge scholars whom Charles had met in Boston.

4. 'Wrestling Jacob'

1. The title of this chapter is taken from the name given to the tune composed by Charles' grandson, Samuel Sebastian Wesley, which is sometimes sung to the hymn, 'Come, O Thou Traveller unknown', (*Methodist Hymn Book*, 339).
2. The reference is, of course, to the rectory fire of 1709.
3. In his journal on 18 December Charles incorrectly refers to the beginning of 'my twenty-seventh year'. See Chapter 1, note 1.
4. T. Jackson (ed.), *The Journal of The Rev. Charles Wesley, M.A.*, London, John Mason 1849, Vol. I, p. 56.
5. Oglethorpe clearly felt the need to defend himself against rumours that the Georgian venture was in a state of collapse.
6. *Journal*, Vol. I, p. 65.
7. Ibid., p. 66.
8. Ibid., pp. 68–9. Charles had agreed to remain as Secretary for the time being, until he had fulfilled his obligations to the Georgia trustees.
9. From a meditation written on the evening of 17 May 1771, entitled 'S. J.' It is believed that the initials stand for 'Son John'. Charles Wallace (ed.), *Susanna Wesley: The Complete Writings*, Oxford University Press 1997, pp. 235 and 249, note 7.
10. *Journal*, Vol. I, p. 68.
11. Ibid., p. 58.
12. Ibid., p. 66.
13. See Thomas Jackson, *The Life of the Rev. Charles Wesley, M.A.*, London 1841, p. 108. Jackson contends that the change more aptly described Charles' 'unconverted' state. The word 'Death', he argued, was more appropriate to 'a real Christian', a phrase which he clearly did not think applied to Charles at this time.
14. See the Glossary for a brief definition of this term.
15. *Journal*, Vol. I, p. 74.
16. Mehetabel, Charles' sister.
17. Ibid., p. 75.
18. Ibid.
19. Ibid., p. 77.
20. Ibid., p. 78.
21. Ibid., p. 79.
22. These activities were not entirely in vain – for example, his journal entry on 4 December 1737, when he described being 'much melted at the sacrament' (*Journal*, p. 80).

23. J. E. Rattenbury, *The Conversion of the Wesleys*, Epworth Press 1938, p. 85.

24. See *The Making of Methodism*, p. 24, Extract 22, for the text of this conversation.

25. *Journal*, Vol. I, p. 66.

26. Jackson, *The Life of the Rev. Charles Wesley, M.A.*, p. 117.

27. It is interesting that the original Greek word 'hypochondria' actually referred to the region of the abdomen below the ribs, which was believed to be the seat of melancholy. In this context, could Charles perhaps have been a true 'hypochondriac', in that his poor health was a physical manifestation of his troubled mind or restless spirit?

28. *Journal*, Vol. I, p. 85.

29. Ibid.

30. Ibid., p. 86.

31. Ibid., p. 87.

32. Martin Luther, *Commentary on Saint Paul's Epistle to The Galatians*, London 1838, p. xxxvi.

33. William Holland was a commercial painter who belonged to one of the growing number of small religious societies that were springing up in London. He became a leading member of the Moravian Church, although he left it in 1747 because his loyalty to the Church of England made it impossible for him to belong to both denominations at the same time.

34. Martin Luther, *Commentary on Saint Paul's Epistle to The Galatians*, p. xxxvii.

35. *Journal*, Vol. I, p. 89.

36. Ibid., p. 90.

37. Charles had met the Musgraves in August of the previous year, when he dined with them at their home in Ludgate. We know little else about her.

38. *Journal*, Vol. I, p. 94.

39. Frank Baker, *Charles Wesley as Revealed by His Letters*, Epworth Press 1948, p. 33.

40. N. Curnock (ed.), *The Journal of the Rev. John Wesley, A.M.*, Standard Edition, Epworth Press 1938, Vol. I, p. 464.

41. Ibid.

42. This is the eighth verse of Charles' hymn, 'Come, O Thou Traveller unknown', as it appeared in the *Methodist Hymn Book*, 339.

43. For a slightly fuller introduction, see the author's *The Making of Methodism*, Epworth Press 1995, pp. 25–30. More detailed accounts can be found by referring to the bibliography in this book p. 122.

44. Ibid., p. 25.

45. N. Curnock, *The Journal of the Rev. John Wesley, A.M.*, p. 442.

46. Some historians have claimed that the reader was William Holland, but this is by no means certain.

47. Dr John Newton, in a sermon preached in Liverpool on 24 May 1988, on the 250th anniversary of the Wesleys' conversions. Quoted in *The Making of Methodism*, p. 29.

48. Henry Rack in his *Reasonable Enthusiast: John Wesley and the Rise of Methodism*, Epworth Press 1989, pp. 145f., uses this term in making a distinction between the two schools of thought.

49. For example, when commenting on Charles' failure in Georgia, Dallimore writes, 'above all, he was not yet converted' (*A Heart Set Free: The Life of Charles Wesley*, Evangelical Press 1988, p. 51). He also uses the term 'conversion' to describe Whitefield becoming a Christian in 1735 (ibid., p. 57), when it is clear that the experiences of the two men were quite different. Martin Schmidt's *John Wesley: A Theological Biography*, Epworth Press 1962–73, likewise emphasizes the dramatic shift from 'law' to 'grace' in Wesley after May 1738.

50. Quoted by J. E. Rattenbury, *The Conversion of the Wesleys*, p. 59.

51. *Journal*, Vol. I, p. 94.

52. Ibid., p. 98.

53. Frank Baker, *Charles Wesley as Revealed by His Letters*, p. 33.

54. Barrie Tabraham, *The Making of Methodism*, p. 29 and note 19.

55. See, p. 40.

56. N. Curnock (ed.), *The Journal of the Rev. John Wesley, A.M.*, Vol. I, p. 422. It is interesting that Rattenbury, despite offering a balanced analysis of John's and Charles' spiritual journey, makes no mention of this entry.

57. Charles Wallace Jr (ed.), *Susanna Wesley: The Complete Writings*, Oxford University Press 1997, p. 174. Only the first part of the letter survives and therefore the signature is missing, but Charles wrote at the top, 'My mother of faith in Xt.'

58. Ibid.

5. Marriage and Family

1. See Chapter 1.
2. See Chapter 4, Extract 42.
3. The refurbishment of the building actually cost nearer £800. It was replaced as the London headquarters of Methodism by the present Wesley's Chapel in City Road in 1778.
4. See the Glossary for a definition of this.
5. Charles Wallace (ed.), *Susanna Wesley: The Complete Writings*, Oxford University Press 1997, p. 190.
6. Although earlier sources suggested the date of Susanna's death to be 23 July, the most accurate recent evidence puts it on Friday 30 July 1742.
7. Arnold Dallimore, *A Heart Set Free: The Life of Charles Wesley*, Evangelical Press 1988, p. 114.
8. T. Jackson (ed.), *The Journal of The Rev. Charles Wesley, M.A.*, London, John Mason 1849, Vol. I, p. 115.
9. See Chapter 2, Extract 9. This is the only reference to her in Charles' writings.
10. *Journal*, Vol. II, p. 68.
11. Ibid., p. 69.
12. Ibid., Vol. I, p. 80. The 'Wright' referred to was William Wright, Hetty's husband.
13. See Chapter 2, Extract 9.
14. *Journal*, Vol. II, p. 306.
15. Her name is often given as 'Kezziah'; in Charles' journal he sometimes refers to her simply as 'Kez'.
16. For a more detailed account of this entanglement, see Dr Maldwyn Edwards, *Family Circle*, Epworth Press 1949, pp. 151–2, and Frederick Maser, *The Wesley Sisters*, Foundery Press 1990, pp. 28–30 and p. 36.
17. *Journal*, Vol. I, p. 83.
18. Ibid., p. 135.
19. Maldwyn Edwards, *Family Circle*, p. 153.
20. Part of a poem written by Charles in a letter he wrote to Sally on 17 September 1748, which was to be later published (in slightly altered form) in *Hymns and Sacred Poems*.
21. *Journal*, Vol. I, p. 455.
22. Frank Baker was able to deduce this. See his *Charles Wesley as Revealed by His Letters*, Epworth Press 1948, p. 55.
23. Ibid., p. 45.
24. In his journal on 11 November 1748, Charles wrote, 'My brother and I having promised each other, (as soon as he came from Georgia,) that we would neither of us marry, or take any step towards it, without the other's knowledge and consent, to-day I fairly and fully communicated every thought of my heart.' *Journal*, Vol. II, p. 44.
25. Ibid., p. 47. Vincent Perronet took a fatherly interest in Charles, and the latter's journal mentions numerous occasions when he took this kindly man into his confidence, referring to him as the 'Archbishop of Methodism'. Perronet was a lifelong supporter of the Wesleys and incorporated many Methodist practices into the running of his parish.
26. Frank Baker, *Charles Wesley as Revealed by His Letters*, p. 62. To Charles' relief, Miss Cart recovered from her disappointment!
27. *Journal*, Vol. II, p. 45.
28. Ibid., p. 51. In this letter, Perronet graciously paid tribute to Sally's character and good sense, and added in support of Charles' suit, 'I could not help rejoicing at what promised so much happiness to the church of God.'
29. Frank Baker, *Charles Wesley as Revealed by His Letters*, p. 65.
30. *Journal*, Vol. II, p. 52. Sally's brother clearly had thought Charles an unsuitable match.
31. Ibid., p. 53. The italics are mine. Charles does not mention the precise location of this conversation, but it was almost certainly at the New Room, which was the home of the Baldwin Street and Nicholas Street societies in Bristol.
32. Ibid.
33. Ibid., p. 56. John's record of the wedding was, to say the least, terse. His journal entry for 8 April 1749 simply reads, 'I married my brother and Sarah Gwynne. It was a solemn day, such as became the dignity of a Christian marriage.' N. Curnock (ed.), *The Journal of the Rev. John Wesley, A.M.*, Standard Edition, Epworth Press 1938, Vol. III, pp. 394–5.
34. Ibid., p. 57.
35. *Journal*, Vol. II, p. 64.
36. Frank Baker, *Charles Wesley as Revealed by His Letters*, p. 106.
37. See the Appendix. John James, the youngest child, also died from smallpox. Both 'Charley' and Samuel caught, but survived, the dreaded disease.
38. John Bennet had a profound influence upon early Methodism, before he broke with the Wesleys on theological grounds in 1752. It was he, for example, who wrote the minutes of the first Methodist

Conference in 1744 and took a major role in the introduction of the Quarterly Meeting. The best recent
account of his contribution to the development of
early Methodism is Simon Valentine's *John Bennet
and the origins of Methodism and the Evangelical
Revival in England*, Scarecrow Press 1997.

39. *The Journal of the Rev. John Wesley, A.M.*, Vol. III,
    p. 431, note 1. The conversation was an extremely
    heated one, since Charles genuinely believed that John
    was about to marry someone who was already be-
    trothed. It is interesting that Charles' journal has a
    (convenient?) gap between 15 September and 22 Octo-
    ber 1749, during which time this affair took place.
40. Ibid., p. 439.
41. Frank Baker, *Charles Wesley as Revealed by His
    Letters*, pp. 73 and 74.
42. *Journal*, Vol. II, p. 62.
43. Ibid., p. 83.
44. *The Journal of the Rev. John Wesley, A.M.*, Vol. V,
    p. 400.

6. Preacher and Pastor

1. The full text of this sermon can be found in John R.
   Tyson (ed.), *Charles Wesley: A Reader*, Oxford
   University Press 1989, pp. 212–20.
2. See Chapter 3, p. 25.
3. According to R. P. Heitzenrater, *Mirror and Memory:
   Reflections on Early Methodism*, Abingdon Press
   1989, pp. 154–5. Heitzenrater has also established
   that Charles used at least one sermon given to him
   by Benjamin Ingham during his stay in Georgia.
4. For example, on 15, 21 and 22 June and on 9 July
   1738. *Journal*, Vol. I, pp. 107, 108 and 117.
5. Frederick C. Gill, *Charles Wesley, the First Methodist*,
   Lutterworth Press 1964, p. 75.
6. See the Glossary for a brief definition of this term.
7. For example, Charles preached this sermon twice in
   Boston on 26 September 1736. See *Journal*, Vol. I,
   p. 45. Charles transcribed it from his brother in
   August 1736, c.f. R. P. Heitzenrater, *Mirror and
   Memory*, p. 161.
8. *Journal*, Vol. I, p. 132.
9. A volume entitled *Sermons by the Late Rev. Charles
   Wesley* was published in 1816, but of the twelve sermons included in the collection, only five are Charles',
   the remainder being written by John. The only other
   sermon Charles published in his lifetime was curiously
   named 'The Cause and Cure of Earthquakes', which
   appeared in print (anonymously) in 1750.
10. Frank Baker, *Charles Wesley as Revealed by His
    Letters*, Epworth Press 1948, p. 38.
11. See the author's *The Making of Methodism*, Epworth
    Press 1995, pp. 42–3 and Extract 38.
12. Ibid.
13. For example, his sermon on 'innocency' was *not*
    well received, to say the least, and interpreted by
    Mrs Hawkins as a direct personal attack. See *Journal*,
    Vol. I, p. 16.
14. *Journal*, Vol. I, p. 143.
15. Ibid., pp. 143–4.
16. Ibid., p. 148.
17. Ibid., p. 151.
18. Piers' early sympathy with Charles had evaporated,
    and in November 1738 he had refused to allow
    Charles to preach in his church, 'through fear of man;
    pretending tenderness to his flock', as Charles wryly
    observed (*Journal*, Vol. I, p. 135).
19. Ibid., p. 154.
20. Ibid.
21. Ibid., p. 156.
22. Ibid., p. 163.
23. Ibid., p. 168.
24. Ibid.
25. Ibid., p. 171.
26. Ibid., p. 187.
27. This was the same Mr Bray with whom Charles took
    up lodging in May 1738.
28. *Journal*, Vol. I, p. 101.
29. Ibid., p. 125.
30. Ibid, p. 27. Skiddoway was an island near Savannah.
    There were about ten prisoners in the guard-room
    and Charles promised them, 'if possible, that they
    should be supplied once a month', though whether he
    succeeded in arranging this is not known.
31. 25p in today's money, though five shillings was more
    than a day's wage in the eighteenth century.
32. *Journal*, Vol. I, p. 120.
33. Quoted by John Telford, *The Life of the Rev. Charles
    Wesley, M.A.*, London 1900, pp. 276–7.
34. It is uncertain as to whether the hymn was actually
    sung at the very first Methodist Conference which met
    in 1744, but since it was published in the collection
    Hymns and Sacred Poems in 1749, it can be assumed
    that it was used from the middle years of the century
    onwards.

35. i.e. 'faith'.

36. *Journal*, Vol. I, p. 416.

37. Ibid., p. 417.

38. Frank Baker, *Charles Wesley as Revealed by His Letters*, p. 35.

39. The coming of turnpikes made travel a great deal easier, but major expansion did not take place until the middle of the century.

40. *Journal*, Vol. I, p. 172.

41. Frank Baker, *Charles Wesley as Revealed by His Letters*, p. 43.

42. For a fuller examination of the origins of the Dublin society, see D. L. Cooney, *The Methodists in Ireland*, Columba Press 2001, pp. 28f.

43. *Journal*, Vol. I, p. 456.

44. *Journal*, Vol. II, p. 4.

45. Frank Baker, *Charles Wesley as Revealed by His Letters*, p. 53.

46. Ibid., p. 79.

47. Taken from the *Agenda* of the First Annual Conference of 1744.

48. Frank Baker, *Charles Wesley as Revealed by His Letters*, p. 80.

49. It was felt that Wheatley's immorality (probably sexual) was bringing Methodism into disrepute. Charles refers to him as 'a gross sinner', guilty of 'some horrible practices'.

50. *Journal*, Vol. II, p. 84.

51. Very little of Charles' journal after 1751 survives. The fragments which exist cover only a few weeks between August 1751 and November 1756. The final entry ends (significantly) with the words, 'by eleven on Saturday morning, November 6th, God brought me safe to my friends in Bristol'.

52. Selina, Countess of Huntingdon, was a friend of Whitefield and the Wesleys. An early supporter of the Methodist revival, she was a remarkably gifted and energetic woman whose diverse interests included philanthropy, missionary ventures, business management and the founding of a theological college. Eventually she formed her own 'connexion', though her volatile personality and erratic leadership meant that it never developed beyond a relatively small ginger group. Her relationship with John and Charles Wesley was subject to wild fluctuations, but at this point in time the brothers were in her favour.

53. Frank Baker, *Charles Wesley as Revealed by His Letters*, p. 84.

54. For some reason the letter went astray and fell into John's hands.

7. Hymn-Writer and Poet

1. George Osborn's collection, *The Poetical Works of John and Charles Wesley*, which appeared between 1868 and 1872, ran to thirteen volumes. This was the most complete source until the remaining 1,300 or so poems appeared for the first time in print in 1988 in *The Unpublished Poetry of Charles Wesley*, edited by S. T. Kimbrough Jr and Oliver A. Beckerlegge.

2. Frank Baker, *Charles Wesley's Verse*, 2nd edn, Epworth Press 1988, pp. 90–1.

3. Ibid. What makes it more difficult is the fact that neither John nor Charles composed music (though Charles' sons did).

4. *A Collection of Hymns for the Use of the People Called Methodists*, 1780 edition. See the Glossary for an explanation of the term 'experimental'.

5. All the hymns reproduced in the boxes in this chapter are to be found in *Hymns and Psalms*, sometimes in abbreviated form. Verses which appear in italics are from older versions of the hymns and in such cases the earliest source is indicated at the foot of the document itself.

6. The name comes from the Greek letter (Chi), which describes the pattern $\begin{smallmatrix} A & & B \\ & \times & \\ B & & A \end{smallmatrix}$

or perhaps more easily seen in the sequence A–B–B–A, or even A–B–C–C–B–A.

7. See also *Hymns and Psalms*, 109, for a similar example using parallel phrasing.

8. Frank Baker, *Charles Wesley's Verse*, p. 67.

9. For example, see Chapter 3, pp. 26f. and Extract 25.

10. Teresa Berger, *Theology in Hymns? A Study of the Relationship of Doxology and Theology According to 'A Collection of Hymns for the Use of the People Called Methodists' (1780)*, Abingdon Press 1995, pp. 100–1.

11. Bernard L. Manning, *The Hymns of Wesley and Watts*, Epworth Press 1942, p. 105.

12. Frank Baker, *Charles Wesley as Revealed by His Letters*, Epworth Press 1948, p. 141.

13. From an unpublished paper by Stuart Davis, which the author was kind enough to let me use.

14. A committee appointed by the Conference of 1874 added a further 469 hymns.

15. John Telford (ed.), *The Letters of the Rev. John Wesley*, 8 Vols, Epworth Press 1931, Vol. VI, pp. 70–1.

16. J. Ernest Rattenbury, *The Evangelical Doctrines of Charles Wesley's Hymns*, Epworth Press 1941, p. 70.

17. See the Glossary for a more detailed explanation of the terms 'speculative' and 'experimental'.

18. Manning, *The Hymns of Wesley and Watts*, p. 14. Perhaps he should have written 'geniuses', rather than 'genius', since Charles surely deserves as much credit as John for its completion.

19. Rattenbury, *The Evangelical Doctrines of Charles Wesley's Hymns*, p. 86.

20. As a creature of his time, Charles, of course, used 'mankind' rather than 'humankind' because the masculine connotation of the former – as, indeed, much of the vocabulary which we now consider to be sexist – would not have occurred to him. Had he lived in the twenty-first century, his concern for inclusivity would doubtless have led him to use more appropriate words.

21. Teresa Berger, *Theology in Hymns?*, p. 114. For a fuller discussion of these theological issues, see the author's *The Making of Methodism*, Epworth Press 1995, ch. 5.

22. Charles had become concerned that some of the Methodist preachers (for example, Thomas Maxfield) were misleading their congregations and suggesting that 'sinless perfection' was actually attainable in this life.

23. Charles visited Mrs Hooper in early May 1741 and wrote movingly in his journal of her last hours and commented on her death-bed, 'That is that holiness, or absolute resignation, or Christian perfection!' (*Journal*, Vol. I, p. 272).

24. Rattenbury, *The Evangelical Doctrines of Charles Wesley's Hymns*, p. 290.

25. *A Collection of Hymns for the Use of the People Called Methodists*, 1780 edition, 430, 113 and 206 respectively.

26. Frank Baker, *Charles Wesley as Revealed by His Letters*, p. 150.

27. For a brief introduction to the importance of the sacrament of Holy Communion for the Wesleys, see the author's *The Making of Methodism*, pp. 54f.

28. This was first published in 1745. Most of the hymns were written by Charles, though John was largely responsible for the editing of the collection.

29. J. Wesley, *Works*, Vol. VIII, pp. 273–4.

30. Ibid., Vol. XI, p. 391.

31. Frank Baker, *Charles Wesley's Verse*, pp. 102–3.

32. No doubt at this time Charles was anxious to impress upon Sally Gwynne's mother that his income would easily exceed the £100 which had been guaranteed by his elder brother John. See pp. 51–2 above.

33. Frank Baker, *Charles Wesley's Verse*, p. 107.

34. This is not one of Charles' hymns, but the first verse of a poem he wrote after preaching in Cornwall. It is quoted here, not for its poetical merits, but because it is yet another example of Charles' humility and conveys his sense of utter dependence upon God.

35. S. T. Kimbrough Jr and Oliver A. Beckerlegge, *The Unpublished Poetry of Charles Wesley*, 3 Vols., Abingdon Press 1988–, Vol. I, pp. 11–12.

36. Frank Baker, *Charles Wesley's Verse*, p. 11.

37. Ibid., p. 13.

38. Quoted in Frank Baker, *Charles Wesley's Verse*, p. 10.

39. S. T. Kimbrough Jr and Oliver A. Beckerlegge, *The Unpublished Poetry of Charles Wesley*, Vol. I, p. 291.

40. Ibid., p. 290.

41. John Wesley, *Journal*, 15 and 23 December 1788.

8. Brothers in Arms

1. Mabel Brailsford, *A Tale of Two Brothers*, Rupert Hart-Davis 1954, p. 130.

2. Richard P. Heitzenrater has attempted to rectify this in a most helpful article entitled 'Charles Wesley and the Methodist Tradition', in S. T. Kimbrough Jr (ed.), *Charles Wesley: Poet and Theologian*, Abingdon Press 1992, pp. 176ff.

3. The phrase is used by Thomas Langford in his chapter 'Charles Wesley as Theologian', in S. T. Kimbrough Jr (ed.), *Charles Wesley: Poet and Theologian*. To be fair to Dr Langford, in this essay and also in his *Methodist Theology* (Epworth Press 1998) he points out how difficult it is to 'credit either one with the chief role in shaping theology in the Methodist tradition' (*Methodist Theology*, p. 16).

4. See the Glossary for a brief explanation of the term.

5. Ditto.

6. *Journal*, Vol. I, p. 223.

7. See the Glossary for a brief explanation of the term. Despite their earlier very close friendship, it was this issue that caused George Whitefield to part company with the Wesleys.

8. Charles Wallace (ed.), *Susanna Wesley: The Complete Writings*, Oxford University Press 1997, pp. 187–90. The reference to Agag is from 1 Samuel 15 and the butchering of the Amalekite king by the prophet Samuel.

9. *Journal*, Vol. I, p. 254.

10. Frank Baker, *Charles Wesley as Revealed by His Letters*, Epworth Press 1948, p. 41. It is fortunate that we have a record of this incident, since there is another gap in Charles' journal from January 1741 to the beginning of April.

11. Ibid.

12. For example, see Extract 79 in the previous chapter.

13. From his hymn, 'Jesus – the name high over all', *Hymns and Psalms*, 264, verse 4.

14. It was significant that the Conference at Limerick in 1852 was the first to be held in Ireland. One can understand, therefore, why John was concerned that the Methodist societies should be conducting their business properly.

15. See pp. 79–81. In the author's *The Making of Methodism*, pp.38–9, there is a fuller discussion of the place it occupied in John Wesley's 'Order of Salvation'.

16. John Wesley, *Sermons*, Vol. III, p. 27.

17. *Journal*, Vol. I, p. 272.

18. John Wesley, *Letters*, Vol. V, p. 19.

19. Ibid., p. 41. The 1760s saw an upsurge in the number of people claiming to have attained a state of perfection, and this helped to highlight the differences between John's and Charles' views of the subject.

20. Richard P. Heitzenrater, *Mirror and Memory: Reflections on Early Methodism*, Abingdon Press 1989, p. 57.

21. S. T. Kimbrough Jr (ed.), *Charles Wesley: Poet and Theologian*, p. 73.

22. John Wesley, *Letters*, Vol. III, p. 112.

23. Ibid., p. 113.

24. This read as follows: 'Here lieth the body of John Wesley, A Brand plucked out of the burning; Who died of a consumption in the 51st year of his age, not leaving, after his debts are paid, Ten Pounds behind him. Praying, God be merciful to me, an unprofitable servant! He ordered, that this, if any, inscription should be placed on his tombstone.' N. Curnock (ed.), *Journal of John Wesley*, Epworth Press 1938, Vol. IV, p. 90.

25. Frank Baker, *Charles Wesley as Revealed by His Letters*, p. 74.

26. For a recent detailed study of the reasons for his secession from Methodism – which were both theological (Bennet's Calvinism) as well as personal – see Simon Ross Valentine, *John Bennet and the Origins of Methodism and the Evangelical Revival in England*, Scarecrow Press 1997, especially pp. 249–61.

27. John Wesley, *Letters*, Vol. IV, p. 322.

28. *Journal*, Vol. I, p. 169. Charles had been preaching on John 3.16 at a village near Bristol.

29. In particular Article XI, which contains the statement that, 'we are justified by Faith only, [which] is a most wholesome doctrine, and very full of comfort, as more largely expressed in the Homily of Justification'. The 'Homilies', especially the one written by Thomas Cranmer in 1547 on justification, were also a very important influence upon Charles.

30. The Jacobites (named for their allegiance to the family of the Roman Catholic King James II who was ousted from the throne in the 'Glorious Revolution' of 1688) were supporters of the 'Young Pretender', commonly referred to as 'Bonnie Prince Charlie', whose attempt at seizing the throne was finally crushed at the Battle of Culloden in 1745. The word 'Jacobite' derives from the Latin 'Jacobus', meaning 'James'.

31. The text of this can be found in John Wesley, *Journal*, Vol. III, pp. 123–4. Entitled 'The Humble Address of the Societies in England and Wales, in derision called Methodists', it affirmed that 'we are a part (however mean) of that Protestant Church established in these kingdoms'. Charles did not so much object to the content of the letter as to the use of the word 'Methodist' in the title. John added a note in his journal, 'upon further consideration, it was judged best to lay it aside'.

32. Minutes of the Fourth Annual Conference, Wednesday 17 June 1747.

33. Luke Tyerman, *The Life and Times of the Rev. John Wesley, M.A., Founder of the Methodists*, London: Hodder & Stoughton 1870–1, Vol. II, p. 138.

34. Frank Baker, *Charles Wesley as Revealed by His Letters*, p. 93.

35. John Wesley, *Letters*, Vol. III, p. 132.

36. Ibid., p. 136.

37. Frank Baker, *Charles Wesley as Revealed by His Letters*, p. 93.

38. Ibid., p. 94.

39. Ibid.

40. For a brief synopsis of the relationship between

Methodism and the Church of England, and in particular the events of 1784, see, for example, the author's *The Making of Methodism*, pp. 48–51. Fuller details can be found in the relevant books listed in the bibliography.

41. John explained his reasons in an open letter written to 'Our Brethren in America' on 10 September 1784, the text of which can be found in *The Making of Methodism*, Extract 45, p. 50.

42. It is somewhat ironic that when American Methodists took episcopacy into their system, John Wesley himself disapproved in no uncertain terms!

43. Frank Baker, *Charles Wesley as Revealed by His Letters*, p. 138.

44. John Wesley, *Letters*, Vol. VII, p. 288.

45. Ibid., p. 324.

46. This allowed Methodist societies to celebrate the sacraments, provided the local trustees were in favour and Conference gave its permission. The 'Plan', in reality, was no more than an acknowledgement of what had already started to happen.

9. Postscript

1. John noted in his journal on 30 September, 'I read prayers, and my brother preached' (*Journal*, Vol. VII, p. 330).

2. John Wesley, *Letters*, Vol. VII, p. 71.

3. John Wesley, *Letters*, Vol. VIII, p. 36.

4. Ibid., p. 39.

5. Ibid., p. 41.

6. Ibid., p. 46.

7. John Whitehead, MD (ed.), *The Life of the Rev. Charles Wesley, M.A.*, London, Stephen Couchman 1793, p. 209.

8. John Wesley, *Letters*, Vol. VIII, p. 51.

9. Luke Tyerman, *The Life and Times of the Rev. John Wesley, M.A., Founder of the Methodists*, London, Hodder & Stoughton 1870–1, Vol. III, pp. 526–7. By this time he would have read his niece's account of her father's death. It is worth noting that John did not cut short his northern visit when he heard the news of his brother's death!

10. Part of John Whitehead's longer biography: *The Life of the Rev. John Wesley, M.A. Some Time Fellow of Lincoln College, Oxford, Collected From His Private Papers, and Printed Works; and Written at the Request of his Executors. To Which is Prefixed Some Account of His Ancestors and Relations; with The Life of the Rev. Charles Wesley, M.A., Collected from his Private Journal, and Never Before Published. The Whole Forming a History of Methodism, in Which the Principles and Economy of the Methodists are Unfolded*. The tribute to Charles, as can be seen from the title, was a relatively short but important preface to the main work.

11. John Wesley, *Works*, Vol. XIII, p. 514.

12. John's disappointment can be seen in comments made in a letter to a friend on 8 April, when he wrote, ''Tis pity but the remains of my brother had been deposited with me. Certainly that *ground* is *holy* as any in England, and it contains a large quantity of "bonny dust"' (*Letters*, Vol. VIII, p. 52).

13. *Journal*, Vol. II, p. 116. Charles was in Rotherham at the time, at a society which was 'on the brink of separation' from the Church of England.

Index

Abbreviations: CW = Charles Wesley, JW = John Wesley